# Open *Sol.* for Business

## A Practical Guide to
## Open Source Software Licensing

by Heather Meeker

ISBN-13: 978-1511617772
ISBN-10: 1511617772

Library of Congress Control Number: 2015906061
CreateSpace Independent Publishing Platform, North Charleston, SC


Editorial production:
Paula L. Fleming and Doug McNair, Fleming Editorial Services
flemingeditorial.com

Cover and page design:
Nat Case, INCase, LLC
incasellc.com

# Table of Contents

# Preface

These days, there is no need to explain what open source software is. What was once considered an odd twist on software licensing is now the bedrock of the software landscape. If you have picked up this book, you probably want to know more about how open source licensing works and how you can use open source software in business in a responsible way that manages your risk. You may be familiar with the "killer apps" of open source: the Linux kernel, the Apache web server, the MySQL database, and PHP scripting—the so-called "LAMP stack"—as well as popular applications like the Firefox web browser or ubiquitous tools like Sendmail. Open source licensing has its own rules and customs and occupies a key position in today's world. It is the backbone of e-commerce and the go-to toolkit of the developing world.

This book is the result of nearly 20 years' work on open source legal issues in the technology business. It is intended to be a practical guide for lawyers and businesspeople who want to understand legal issues surrounding open source software licensing. But this is not a legal treatise; this book is intended to help not only lawyers but also others who want to understand what their lawyers are telling them. Technology lawyers know that technology always leads and the lawmakers and judges follow, trying to normalize the rules for new paradigms and capabilities. But in open source licensing, the disparity between settled law and best practice is extreme. That's because the first promoters of the open source licensing model— like Richard Stallman—were technologists, not lawyers; they had to invent their own rules and couldn't wait for legal culture to catch up. So, reading about statutes and cases can help one understand open source licenses, but to understand how to make practical business decisions about using open source software, one needs to know quite a bit that isn't in the case law reporters.

It is fitting that we are moving into the teens of the 21st century as open source software licensing is hitting its heady and unpredictable adolescence. This decade has seen the first serious enforcement efforts by licensors of open source software, so we are truly at the dawning of a new age. Today, no one in the technology world can deny that open source is here to stay, that there are real legal risks one must manage if one wants to use open source responsibly in a profit-making business, and that anyone who wishes to understand technology licensing has to understand the precepts of open source licensing. Living in the walled garden of proprietary licensing is no longer possible. Open source software is the hardy plant growing through the cracks of that garden.

## Background: UNIX, Linux, and Software Licensing

The introduction of open source software licensing is the most significant development in software licensing since software licensing began. But software licensing itself has not been with us very long, and in truth, open source licensing has been around for longer than most people realize. In fact, open source licensing was the original model for software licensing, and proprietary licensing is the newcomer. To understand how these two models developed together, we need to understand something about the history of computing.

## Once Upon a Time, There Was an Operating System Called UNIX

When most people say "open source," they are referring to a set of software licenses. These licenses set the terms for use of the software by anyone who wants to use it. In this sense, open source is a licensing model. But also, and perhaps more importantly, open source is a model for software development. The difference is crucial because the risks associated with the licensing model and the development model are very different.

The "killer app" of open source is the Linux operating system. Learning why and how Linux was developed is the best way to understand how the licensing model we currently know as "open source" was developed and how the open source model differs from the proprietary model.

Most people working in the technology business today grew up in the age of Windows, so they don't know much about another operating system—UNIX—that played a pivotal role in computing. UNIX was the reason the "free software" model came about.

In the early days of computing, UNIX was the dominant operating system. It was developed by AT&T Bell Laboratories. At the time, AT&T was such a dominant company that, as the result of an antitrust case, it was bound by a US Department of Justice consent decree prohibiting it from engaging in commercial activities outside the field of telephone service.[1] AT&T's best and brightest engineers therefore worked on computer science development via a not-for-profit entity called AT&T Bell Laboratories.

Ken Thompson and Dennis Ritchie were scientists at Bell Labs, and anyone who has studied computer programming knows their names. They were the creators of UNIX, which was the first general-purpose operating system. In the course of writing it, they invented a programming language called C. C was a flexible and powerful programming language that in today's parlance is called a "low-level" language, meaning a language that affords the programmer a high level of control over how the software interacts with hardware. C is still in common use today, though it has undergone many expansions and improvements—most notably C++, which is an object-oriented adaptation of C.

However, the consent decree prohibited AT&T from exploiting UNIX as a commercial product. So, in a rather extraordinary move that would set the wheels of the technology sector in motion, Bell Labs gave UNIX away in source code form under terms that allowed modification and redistribution. As they say, if you love something, set it free—and computer scientists in the 1970s and 1980s loved UNIX.

Then the consent decree was lifted, and AT&T started granting restricted licenses for UNIX under licensing terms that allowed redistribution only in object code format. This resulted in the "forking" of UNIX into many incompatible versions. Those who had previously enjoyed the ability to make and share modifications suddenly could not do so, and a program written for IBM's flavor of UNIX, for instance, would not necessarily run on Sun's UNIX.

The free software movement was a direct reaction to the forking of UNIX, which itself had happened because of a shift to proprietary licensing. There is nothing computer programmers hate more than a lack of interoperability—particularly at a lower layer of the technology stack, like an operating system—and some of them set out to prevent this from ever happening again.

It's important to understand that, at the time, "proprietary" licensing was not the ubiquitous practice it is today. In the 1980s, I worked on what were then called minicomputers: the PDP, DEC, Wang VS, and Quantel. Like most applications programmers of the time, I wrote custom business applications. I remember walking into an Egghead Software store one day, seeing accounting software one could buy off the shelf, and scarcely being able to believe it was possible. (A sales clerk had to talk me down, assuring me that if I bought a program for my Macintosh, it really would run on that computer.) I had been a programmer for years

---

[1] "Modification of Final Judgment," August 24, 1982, filed in case 82-0192, *United States of America v. Western Electric Company, Incorporated, and American Telephone and Telegraph Company*, U.S. District Court for the District of Columbia, **web.archive.org/web/20060827191354/members.cox. net/hwilkerson/documents/AT&T_Consent_Decree.pdf**.

by then, and the notion of standardized software was foreign to me. Software came in one of two ways—loaded on the computer you bought from the vendor or written by a custom software developer called a systems integrator or OEM. And software was always delivered in source code form. Why? Before the micro-computer (or IBM PC), there was simply not enough standardization to support or require a binary-only software distribution model. Companies almost always bought their hardware and software from the same vendor, in a bundle. People doing technical support needed to use source code, and technical support was particular to the machine, operating system, and environment. (In fact, in about 1985, I met my first technical support representative and was amused by the con-cept because up until that time, as a programmer, I was the person doing technical support.) So why would anyone separate source code and binaries? It just wasn't sensible in the world where I had been working. But I was about to witness a sea change, and the entire computing world was about to transform. Several years lat-er, microcomputers were the norm, and binary software was standard. It was like all the bespoke tailors had gone out of business overnight and in their place had left rows of off-the-rack stores. And if you needed alterations, you had to violate a license to have them done.

## Linux: The "Killer App"

Open source software—and particularly copyleft software licensing—might have remained a legal curiosity had it not been for Linux. Copyleft is a compli-cated licensing model, and the IT industry might never have invested the energy to figure it out, much less grow comfortable with it, if not for the well-deserved popularity of Linux. But if you don't know much about Linux, you are not alone; while most people have frequently used Linux, they may have not understood they were using it. Because Linux began its life as an operating system for computer scientists, it has never had a great user interface. Therefore, many systems use Linux as an operating system core and layer interfaces like Android, Chrome, or even Mac on top of it. But if you don't know about Linux, then you need to learn: to understand open source licensing, it's essential to understand why Linux is so popular and so important.

In the late 1980s, UNIX's popularity was fading. Before the 1980s, most computers were used by large institutions: governments, educational institutions, banks, and other large businesses. The first generation of microcomputers—the Apple II; the TRS-80; and, of course, the DOS Personal Computer—changed all that in a matter of a few years. These machines ran on newer, cheaper processors. Operating systems are particular to processors, and UNIX could not easily be adapted for these platforms.

UNIX had a standard specification—a set of system routines that defined compatibility with a UNIX platform. That standard is now called POSIX. So, various people started seeking a kind of Holy Grail—an operating system that was compatible with POSIX but free of the license limitations propounded by AT&T. One such individual was a computer science professor in the Netherlands who wrote a scholarly project called MINIX. Another was a teenager in Helsinki named Linus Torvalds. Torvalds released the first version of Linux in 1991 and changed the world.

Meanwhile, Richard Stallman, a computer scientist at MIT's artificial intelligence laboratory, started the GNU Project. (GNU is a recursive acronym for "GNU's not UNIX.") The GNU Project sought to create an operating system that would be a free alternative to UNIX. A full operating system requires many elements, and the core of it is the so-called kernel—which runs the computer, manages memory, runs programs, and communicates with peripherals and other hardware. A full operating system also requires development tools like compilers, debuggers, text editors, administrative tools, and a user interface. Torvalds agreed to make his software freely available, and the Linux kernel—improved and adapted from the original version written by Torvalds—became this core of the GNU operating system. That operating system is now usually referred to as Linux.[2]

But Stallman was working in parallel on a licensing paradigm that would prevent privatization of the new, free operating system he was seeking to develop. He called this paradigm "free software," the rules of which were embodied in a license called the GNU General Public License (GPL). This license granted unfettered rights to redistribute software with the condition that source code could not be kept secret. This was the premise of copyleft—using copyright law to compel the sharing of copyrightable works of software.

True to the free software spirit, the Linux kernel has grown, changed, and improved dramatically since it was first developed. Today, it has thousands of contributors, a not-for-profit organization to maintain it, millions of adopters, and billions of users. And it is still free to change, redistribute, and improve. In effect, the open source licensing model forced an entire industry to cooperate, and the result is a robust and scalable system that is maintained by the largest players in IT, as well as by hundreds of volunteers.

But more importantly for our journey into open source licensing, to use Linux, the industry had to use Linux's licensing terms. Therefore, the copyleft paradigm that Stallman pioneered slowly gained traction.

---

[2] Those at the GNU project remind us that it is more properly called the GNU/Linux system, but this kind of "branding" problem is endemic to open source licensing. See Chapter 15: Trademarks.

In about 1996, the GPL began making serious inroads into the technology world. I started practicing in 1995, and soon after, my clients began asking about open source licenses. Most intellectual property lawyers at that time were confused and fearful when presented with questions like "Should I use this software under this license called GPL?" The easy answer was no—that's always the easy answer.

But some lawyers, like me, realized we needed to give a better answer. It was the equivalent of a client asking, "I found this quarter on the ground. Can I use it?" Some lawyers were still saying, "No, you don't know where it's been." But some of us were thinking, "That's 25 cents. Let's think about this some more." So I started trying to understand how to use open source software in a way that was consistent with the objectives of private business.

It was no help that the early free software movement promulgated a rhetoric that was decidedly antibusiness. Their mission was to destroy proprietary software, and most of my clients were proprietary software businesses. But others in the movement were focused on results rather than on doctrine, and some of my clients were early boosters of Linux. So my clients and I started traveling down a new path together, trying to understand whether we could really use free software in private business without destroying either model.

To do that, however, we had to learn a lot about this new licensing model. It was hard going. Advising on GPL is a bit like jumping into intellectual property bizarro-world. There was little law on which to base our analysis, and for lawyers operating in a landscape of billion-dollar malpractice suits, there is no particular reward for dancing out on a limb to find answers. But all around us, the use of open source was burgeoning, and we had to keep up. If you want to spend a career giving safe answers, technology law is probably not the right practice for you.

Twenty years later, I've learned a lot and am still learning—about technology; the law; and, most important, how licensing drives innovation. Whether you think open source is scary, fascinating, crazy, or all of those things, this book is intended to help you navigate the world of open source licensing to advance innovation and drive prosperity.

## Thank You

Many people helped me, directly or indirectly, with the development of the material in this book. In particular, I would like to thank Luis Villa, Alma Chao, Sabir Ibrahim, Maxim Tsotsorin, Aahit Gaba, David Pollak, David Marr, Greta Lichtenbaum, and David Ribner—all of whom helped me directly with the long task of writing and editing. I would also like to thank all the members of the FSFE Legal Network discussion list (especially Matija Suklje and Carlo Piani) and all of those in the open source legal world who participate in free discussion and intellectual inquiry, for joining me on this journey that has few signposts. It is always best to walk new paths with friends.[3]

## Contacting Me

If you are reading this book and need to engage an attorney to help you with open source licensing issues, please feel free to contact me. As a practicing lawyer, I am very easy to find on the Web at my law firm, O'Melveny & Myers, and I maintain my own website at **www.heathermeeker.com**. I also welcome comments and suggestions on this book. Of course, nothing in this book should be considered a statement by my law firm—it only expresses my personal views—and purchasing this book is not intended to create an attorney-client relationship with you, the reader. Finally, the advice in these pages may not apply to the facts of your situation.

If you have purchased a copy of this book and would like information about electronic updates, you are welcome to join my mailing list by sending a message to **hmeeker@heathermeeker.com**.

---

[3] All mistakes should be attributed to me. Only the merits of the book should be attributed to others.

# Part I

# A Foundation

Chapter 1

# The Philosophy of Free and Open Source Software

Most people refer to software like the Linux kernel and the Apache web server as "open source" software. But the progenitors of the open source movement balk at the term *open source*—what they started was the "free software" movement. Those who are new to this subject may find nuances in terminology tedious, but these differences in terminology represent key differences in the philosophies of the participants in this movement. To make informed decisions about using open source software, it is important to understand this divide because it bears directly on how to approach compliance programs, code contributions and releases, risk assessment, and other open source legal decisions.[1]

Richard Stallman, the progenitor of the free software movement, describes his philosophy as one promoting technical and economic freedom. As he put it, "Given a system of software copyright, software development is usually linked with the existence of an owner who controls the software's use. As long as this linkage exists, we are often faced with the choice of proprietary software or none. However, this linkage is not inherent or inevitable; it is a consequence of the specific social/legal policy decision that we are questioning: the decision to have owners."[2] Stallman has called *intellectual property* a "propaganda term," and he generally objects to its use.[3]

Copyleft, therefore, is a system that uses the power of copyright law—which Stallman finds morally objectionable—to cause others to forgo copyright inter-

---

[1] For an interesting and informative explanation of this philosophical divide, as well as a fascinating set of interviews with some of the key technology players from the days of the Internet boom, I recommend the documentary *Revolution O/S*, directed by JTS Moore (Wilmington, DE: Wonderview Productions, 2001), DVD.

[2] "Why Software Should be Free" by Richard M. Stallman, **www.gnu.org/philosophy/ shouldbefree.html**.

[3] "Did You Say 'Intellectual Property'? It's a seductive mirage" by Richard M. Stallman, **www.gnu. org/philosophy/not-ipr.html**. Most lawyers only object to the term being used wrongly, which leaves plenty of fodder for disapproval.

ests. Free software licenses are broad copyright license grants to everyone, conditioned on the requirement to allow sharing and modification of copyrightable works. This is quite different from the broader notion of open source, which includes not only free software but also software licensed under permissive terms.

In the early years of the open source movement, the antibusiness rhetoric of the free software philosophy threatened to discourage open source's adoption, and so a few peacemakers got together to reconcile the interests of the free software advocates and industry. This resulted in the Open Source Initiative (OSI).

Most people approaching open source for the first time think that copyleft requires people to give away software for free. That is understandable, given that the rhetoric of the free software movement tends to be antibusiness and anticapitalist. But that preconception is not exactly right, and the difference between the preconception and the reality of free software licensing is significant—allowing for the existence of successful public companies like Red Hat and MontaVista Software (and, once, VA Linux), not to mention every major consumer electronics manufacturer in existence (because of the Linux and Android platforms).

In fact, the word *free* in "free software" refers to freedom, not price—it is libre, not gratis. As the Free Software Foundation (FSF) says, "Think free speech, not free beer." Free software licenses don't prohibit you from selling copies of the software for money; in fact, that kind of noncommercial restriction is antithetical to open source licensing and, perhaps counterintuitively, more the purview of proprietary vendors like Microsoft and Adobe, who grant low-cost educational licenses with limitations on use. Nevertheless, it is impractical to base a licensing business solely on free software. The technology sector has embraced free software like Linux precisely because it does not need to make money on it. Accordingly, free software is a great model for infrastructure software that everyone uses and a poor one for specialized applications. It's no coincidence that the most popular open source software is the LAMP stack for e-commerce; those who use it are making money selling stuff over the Web, not selling access to the Web. The existence of free infrastructure, with no intellectual property claims to thwart it, promotes prosperity, whereas a complete lack of intellectual property would substantially thwart prosperity. The secret is finding the right balance of public and private goods to advance innovation—and not surprisingly, that is what has happened over the last 20 years as the technology business has embraced free software.

Richard Stallman is the founder of the GNU project and the free software movement. Stallman is the author of the GPL. Stallman believes that programmers should be motivated by the prospect of enhancing their reputation and doing good in the community, rather than by remuneration or profit. In that regard, of course, he differs from most programmers in private business. And if a single person embodies the antithesis of Stallman's free software thesis, it is probably

Linus Torvalds—though many others might claim that role. In 1996, Linus Torvalds wrote the original Linux kernel while he was still a student at the University of Helsinki, and ever since, he has been involved in technological innovation, particularly for the Linux kernel. Today, Torvalds still provides guidance on the direction of the publicly available kernel maintained by the Linux Foundation at **www.kernel.org**. Torvalds is not an advocate for free software ideology so much as an advocate for freely available software. He has occasionally fallen out with those in Stallman's camp, and he is primarily a technologist rather than a political advocate.

In truth, Stallman and Torvalds represent not so much warring ideals as symbiotic ones. The licensing model could not succeed without good software to drive it, and the software could not succeed without a licensing model to enable it.

## The Open Source Development Model

When people talk about open source, they mean two different things: a licensing model and a development model. Most of this book discusses the licensing model, which is embodied in open source software licenses.

The open source development model is actually what creates the value of open source software. The licenses do not, because they are merely vehicles to enable the model. The best way to understand this model is through the analogy made famous by Eric Raymond in his seminal article on open source development, "The Cathedral and the Bazaar."[4] Developing proprietary software is like building a medieval cathedral: a powerful organization (the Church) conceives a project, raises funds, and appoints a master builder, who in turn employs artisans and builders to execute the project. The progress of the project is limited by the sponsor's funds and the ability of the master builder to oversee the project. Open source development is like a bazaar. Anyone can try to sell wares. The marketplace determines what is bought and sold. Development is collaborative, resources are not scarce, and no one person or organization entirely controls the project. If the marketplace demands it, the direction of the project will change, or the project may split into multiple projects.

Many people are confused by the rhetoric of the free software movement when it begins to sound totalitarian: all software must be under GPL, no forking should happen, and so forth. This is quite different from Raymond's vision of a freewheeling market where the substance of development can change to suit the whims of the market. If it seems hard to reconcile these two visions, keep in mind that even in the freest market, there is a natural tendency to standardize. That

---

[4] The online version of Raymond's article has changed over time. The current version is here: www.catb.org/~esr/writings/cathedral-bazaar/cathedral-bazaar/.

means only so much forking—whether of licensing terms or software code—is useful. So even free actors in a market will voluntarily standardize their practices, or else too much effort will be wasted on reconciling incompatibilities. Open source, therefore, is a world in which freedom is paramount but some practices are discouraged—not by fiat but by consensus.

## The Free Software Definition and the Open Source Definition

Given the philosophical differences between the free software purists (like Stallman) and the technological pragmatists (like Torvalds), it should be no surprise that *free software* and *open source software* are defined by their proponents in competing ways.

### The Free Software Definition: The Four Essential Freedoms

0. The freedom to run the program as you wish, for any purpose
1. The freedom to study how the program works and change it so it does your computing as you wish
2. The freedom to redistribute copies so you can help your neighbor
3. The freedom to distribute copies of your modified version to others. By doing this, you can give the whole community a chance to benefit from your changes.[5]

The Open Source Definition, promulgated by OSI, covers both copyleft and permissive software licenses:

1. Free redistribution
2. Source code [must be included]
3. Derived works [must be permitted]
4. Integrity of the author's source code
5. No discrimination against persons or groups
6. No discrimination against fields of endeavor
7. Distribution of license
8. License must not be specific to a product

---

[5] Note that GNU really does number its Four Freedoms from 0 through 3. Items 1 and 3 require access to source code. See **www.gnu.org/philosophy/free-sw.html**.

9. License must not restrict other software

10. License must be technology-neutral[6]

OSI expressly states on its website that the GPL complies with the definition.[7] If that seems surprising, it should not. It anticipates the criticism that item 9 does not fit GPL, because GPL seeks to control software that is added to the work of authorship covered by GPL. Although these two definitions are certainly different, there is little practical consequence to their distinctions. OSI no longer approves all licenses that fit its definition, and FSF only releases licenses it considers suitable to define free software.

OSI once was a key effort to reconcile industry and free software; today, it is probably of marginal relevance—a victim of its own success. OSI was started when the war of words surrounding free software threatened to marginalize that very thing. The purpose of OSI is to "build bridges among different constituencies in the open-source community."[8] It is the organization responsible for certifying software licenses as open source licenses. OSI also stewards the certification trademark Open Source—although the term is probably generic and unenforceable as a trademark.[9] All of the approved open source licenses are posted on the OSI website. In the 1990s, OSI would certify almost any license agreement that fit the open source definition. However, today, OSI approves few new licenses because it wants to discourage "license proliferation"[10] and the creation of "vanity licenses"—though some might observe that many of those licenses previously approved were just that: minor variations on the major licenses that are used for only one or two projects.

---

[6] See **opensource.org/docs/definition.php**. The Debian Social Contract states that the Open Source Definition was based on the Debian definition at **www.debian.org/social_contract/**.

[7] To understand the motivation for this comment and the answer to it, see the in-depth discussion of the GPL compliance in Chapter 8: The GPL 2 Border Dispute.

[8] See **opensource.org**.

[9] Free software advocate Bruce Perens apparently tried unsuccessfully to register the mark. See **en.wikipedia.org/wiki/Open_source_software**. For more on why trademarks become generic, see Chapter 15: Trademarks.

[10] For more on "license proliferation," see Chapter 3: Common Open Source Licenses.

## It's Not a Virus[11]

Open source advocates can be pedantic about terminology, and flame wars about using the right words are regrettably common in the open source world. But eradicating the word *viral* from discussions of open source licensing is long overdue because this word has skewed and limited understanding of open source licensing principles. It is mostly the lawyers who are to blame. When people in the technology business, particularly lawyers, want to describe copyleft licenses, they often use the word *viral*. Unfortunately, the word is not only inflammatory but also inaccurate. For lawyers, being inflammatory is part of the game, but being inaccurate is the worst kind of sin.

There are various choices for the right term: *free software, copyleft, reciprocal, hereditary*. But the best choice is *copyleft*.[12] A copyleft license is one that requires, as a condition of distribution of software binaries, that the distributor make the corresponding source code available under the same licensing terms.[13] A copyleft license sticks to the copyright of the software; no matter how many downstream distributions occur, the license terms stay the same. To a lawyer, this is like an easement on a piece of real estate—an encumbrance that runs with title, no matter how many times the property is sold. Copyleft licenses include GPL, LGPL, MPL, EPL, and a smattering of others. But using the word *viral* to describe this concept is misleading and leads to unnecessary fears. In all the years I have been advising clients in this area of law, the single most significant misconception about copyleft licenses is due, I think, to the use of this word: *viral*.

Combining GPL code with other code in a single program is often referred to as creating a "derivative work." That is because GPL says if there is any GPL code in a given program, all of the code in the program must be made available under GPL. Anything else is a violation of GPL. Companies, with visions of viruses dancing in their heads, worry that if GPL and proprietary code are combined into a single program, the GPL licensing terms will "infect" the proprietary code, and the proprietary code will be automatically relicensed under GPL. The corporate author of the proprietary code then worries that it will be compelled

---

[11] This section is adapted from "Open Source and the Eradication of Viruses," by Heather Meeker, *Open Source Delivers*, March 19, 2013, osdelivers.blackducksoftware.com/2013/03/19/open-source-and-the-eradication-of-viruses/.

[12] The first book I wrote on open source licensing (*The Open Source Alternative: Understanding Risks and Leveraging Opportunities*, Hoboken, NJ: John Wiley & Sons, 2008) tried to normalize the terminology for the different kinds of licenses. To my chagrin, the use of *hereditary* never caught on, so I now refer to licenses like GPL as *copyleft*.

[13] Or, in the case of licenses like AGPL, a lower threshold such as making them available via a network.

by law to provide the source code to its own proprietary code. This is a software company's equivalent of unleashing the big scary monster that hides under the bed. But this is simply not how copyleft works.

In fact, if a company were to combine GPL and proprietary code in a way that violated GPL, the result would be that GPL had been violated—no more, no less. What that means, legally, is that the author of the GPL code might have remedies for violation of GPL, and if the license were terminated as a result, the author would have remedies for others' unlicensed use of the GPL software. Both of these, essentially, are copyright infringement claims. The legal remedies for a copyright infringement claim are damages (money) and injunction (stop using the GPL code).[14]

In fact, there is no legal mechanism for GPL infecting proprietary code and changing its licensing terms. For software to be licensed under a particular set of terms, the author has to take some action that reasonably leads a licensee to conclude that the licensor has chosen to offer the code under those terms. In contrast, combining proprietary and GPL code in a single program in violation of GPL is a license incompatibility—meaning the two sets of terms conflict and cannot be satisfied simultaneously. The better analogy for this kind of licensing incompatibility is that of a software bug rather than a software virus. Just think of the robot on the old TV show *Lost in Space*, flailing its arms and saying, "That does not compute!" and you'll get the idea.

## The Philosophy of "Open"

Regardless of whether you agree with the free software philosophy, at least it is thoughtful and mostly consistent. In the last few decades, a broader notion of openness has developed, capitalizing on the success of open source software. Although these more recent and expansive notions are less rigid than the old-school free software ideology, *open* has also become one of the more overused words in technology journalism. However, it is important to understand how the notion of "open" has changed business practice in the technology industry.

There is no one definition of *open*, and many things claim to be open. But overall, open paradigms seek to involve outside parties rather than exclude them. Open models are also characterized by transparency and a focus on participation based on merit, rather than status. The licensing of intellectual property rights, whether freely or free of charge, is only part of the equation.

To bring this point home, consider the revolutionary nature of the Apple iOS platform for mobile—which, lest we forget, was released in 2007—less than

---

[14] For more detail, see Chapter 5: Conditional Licensing.

10 years ago. This platform was called "open"—but it was not open source software. It was open in the sense that anyone could develop for the platform, using a free set of development tools. Open source advocates would be quick to point out that this was not a truly open technology environment. Developers had to sign a developer agreement, sell only via the App Store, and follow many platform rules. But at the time, Apple's move was dramatic, revolutionary, and open in ways that few people expected.

In 2008, the Android platform was introduced. This platform expanded the notion of openness; it was based on open source software, was provided to many manufacturers, and allowed multiple app stores to compete. Meanwhile, the Linux computer O/S had been growing for quite a while. For many years, Linux did not enjoy penetration beyond the server market and embedded systems; it was notably absent from desktops. It is the closest thing to a truly open platform, but its very openness meant that it was an unattractive basis for a business model. Red Hat went public in 1999, and since then, the market for Linux distros has thinned out. The difficulties inherent in a business model based primarily on service and support mean there is not much room for many players in the market. Yet Red Hat continues to be a thriving business, and the e-commerce economy relies on it almost exclusively.

In the 2010s, it is very popular for industry groups to band together to support open infrastructure initiatives. OpenStack, an open source project that provides Infrastructure as a Service (IAAS), was started in 2010 and has achieved huge popularity. OpenStack is supported by a huge roster of technology players such as Dell, EMC, Oracle, HP, AT&T, Red Hat, IBM, Canonical, Yahoo!, Rackspace, Intel, and Cisco.

The idea that such a constellation of technology companies would cooperate, so quickly and so willingly, on an open source project was unimaginable even 10 years ago. To the extent that there was ever truly a war of ideology between open and closed, open has won. But true to that ideology, the idea of "open" is always changing and expanding, and it doubtless will continue to deliver surprises as it helps shape the future of business.

Chapter 2

# A Tutorial on Computer Software

This chapter is a tutorial for those who are not computer engineers and who want to learn some of the concepts that are useful in understanding open source licensing.

## What Is the "Source" of Open Source?

These days, at least according to the press, everything is open source—textbooks, yoga, seders, plant seeds, databases, and bug farm kits, to name a few. While all these things may be "open," they don't really have any source code. To understand why open source is important, one must first understand what source code is.

Most computer users today use either (a) mobile devices with iOS or Android systems or (b) desktop or laptop computers with Windows operating systems. When you run a program (such as an *app*, or application) on your device or computer, the electronic file that composes the program is called an *executable file*. It is a file like any other on your computer, but it is in a format your computer can execute. On Windows desktop systems, these files have the filename extension *.exe*, for "executable." (On mobile platforms, you won't see the file names at all, but each app is an executable file.)

Computers perform complex operations by breaking the operations into very small steps that the central processor or graphics processor can perform billions of times per second. These operations include moving one to four bytes from one place in memory to another, performing simple arithmetic, and choosing the next step to execute (either by default or based on a test). Each operation is very simple, but by performing many, many operations, the computer can take actions that humans can perceive—like printing a message on a display. The simple instructions that computers understand are in pieces too small for humans to easily understand and organize, so computer scientists have developed languages for writing computer programs that are easier for humans to process. These are what we call programming languages. Each sentence in a programming language translates into many computer instructions.

Humans express programs through *source code*. Computers translate source code into something that can be executed via processes called *compilation* and *interpretation*. For example, most C programs are compiled into binary code that can be directly executed by the CPU. Programs written in Java and Microsoft's C# are translated into an intermediate binary representation called *byte code*, which is subsequently converted into executed binary by a computer program called a *virtual machine*.

Many programming languages, such as C and Java, have source code and executable forms. The source code form is not executable, meaning computers can't run it. The executable form is not readable by humans—it is essentially a bunch of ones and zeroes, sometimes called *object form*.

Source code is the language programmers use to write software. Source code looks like a natural[1] language, more or less. Here's an example:

```
#include <stdio.h>
int main(void)
  {
    int x;
    x=1;
    if (x==1) {printf ("I am the One.\n")};
    return 0;
  }
```

Although this language may look strange to nonprogrammers, some of its parts of speech should be familiar. Computer languages have verbs like *include* or *print*, nouns like *x*, and adjectives like *int* (which stands for integer). Once the programmer has written the code he wants to use, he saves the file as text. He then runs a program called a *compiler*, which processes the source code text file and translates the source code into object code. Once the code is in object form, it can't be modified without going back to the source code. Although theoretically code can be "decompiled," the process is not reliable, and in any case, the decompiled code will not include the commentary that makes the source code more readable. In fact, the truth about decompilation is complex: some languages like Java decompile reliably, whereas others, like C, do not; and decompilers become more accurate and sophisticated every year.

When computers were slower, the time to convert a program from source code to an executable format was measurable and could slow down or interfere

---

[1] A natural language (as opposed to a computer language) is a language that is used by humans; English is an example.

with humans' use of the program. Over the last 20 years, CPUs have gotten much faster. As processing has gotten faster, more and more operations have been moved from the main program into libraries. For example, in the days of the Apple II, each developer who wanted to write code had to move images around the screen. Today, there are many ways to animate images in a browser with a single line of source code.

Because of these advances, code is increasingly distributed in source form. For example, when your browser loads HTML and JavaScript, the browser converts the HTML and JavaScript code into executable code that displays a web page, validates input, and animates the page content. Typical web pages contain more code than could fit in the entire available memory of 20-year-old computers.

To reduce the time to transmit code over the Internet, programmers compress code to make it smaller. While this compressed code may not, technically, be an intermediate form, it looks different from the original source code. Therefore, JavaScript, which executes within a browser (see more below on this), is often changed to delete all white space. In programming, *white space* like blanks and tabs is usually nonfunctional and is only used for readability, so deleting it produces functionally equivalent source code that is just more dense to read. Therefore, the example above could be rewritten thus:

```
#include <stdio.h>
int main(void){int x;x=1;if(x==1){printf("I am the
One.\n")};return 0;}
```

This is the same as the example above but with most of the white space removed. For scripting languages like JavaScript, removing the white space reduces the number of characters in the source code and can therefore speed up the downloading of the code to the user's browser, where it executes. For programmers who are trying to write complex web applications that must be delivered via small pipes (like your mobile device), every bit of speed helps.

## Building, Linking, and Packaging

In reality, most code is far more complex than in our example above. In the real world of programming, our little example would not be very useful. However, small bits of code can be quite useful if they are stitched together properly. For instance, a code snippet that adds numbers or finds a square root can be essential. But a program in the real world might need to use that bit of code over and over, and the programmer only wants to write it once. That is where building and packaging come in.

Of course, few programmers today are keen to write a routine to find square roots because others have already written such routines for them. So, there are techniques for building programs in the real world that allow programmers to reuse existing routines. An existing square root routine has already been tested and therefore is more reliable to use than one written from scratch. These existing code routines are often called *libraries*. Libraries are analogous to legal restatements. Just as a lawyer will refer to a section in a restatement rather than pointing to the underlying precedent, a programmer will use a library routine to perform a well-defined, common operation.

When a programmer builds a program, he first writes the code in source code form and compiles it into object code form. Then he uses a program called a *linker* to link his object with the objects of library routines. If he does this, he does not need the source code for the libraries. A well-written library is usually a *black box* to the programmer, meaning the programmer does not need to know what is inside the box but just what goes in and what comes out—the information required to stitch it all together. This information is called an *interface definition* or sometimes an API (application program interface).[2]

Once the objects are all stitched together, they are called an *executable program*. The executable program has all the pieces it needs to run.

Let us now suppose that the programmer finds a bug in the library routine or maybe just a use case that does not work for the code he has written. For instance, suppose the library selects a date on the Julian calendar (the one used in the United States) but the programmer wants to select a date on the lunar calendar. The library routine will not work for the programmer's purpose, so the programmer will need to access the source code to improve it. This is because compiling is a one-way street—it's not possible to change compiled code. If the programmer wants to make a change to the code, he has to go back to the source code, make the change, recompile the code, and relink the program.

For the lawyers reading this book, think about a redlining program. A redlining program runs in *batch mode*—once the user initiates the program, it runs without user interaction. If you want to change the redline, you go back to the original file, change it, and rerun the batch-redlining program. Computer source code is the same way, and this is why access to source code is so important.

You can't fix bugs without source code. You can't make changes or improvements without source code. All you can do with object code is build it into a larger program, and all you can do with executables is run them.

---

[2] People use the term *API* to mean lots of things, but this usage (respectfully submitted) is the most accurate meaning. Using *API* to mean code libraries is inaccurate but, unfortunately, rather common.

## JavaScript

This language deserves its own section because it is crucial to modern web development and because it causes much confusion among nonprogrammers, for several reasons. First, JavaScript is not Java. Java is a programming language—a compiled one—that is very popular in web deployment. JavaScript, on the other hand, is a scripting language—with no compiled form—that runs programs inside a web browser. Imagine that you are ordering a pair of shoes from an e-commerce seller and filling out the shipping address. The code that checks your input, forces you to complete required fields, and otherwise directs how you interact with the web page is probably JavaScript.

The important things to understand about JavaScript are that, like HTML, JavaScript is delivered to the user's browser in source code form and executes locally on the user's computer. These characteristics make a big difference in open source licensing.

## PERL, Python, PHP, and Other Scripting Languages

There are other popular scripting languages commonly in use, such as PERL, Python, and PHP. A *scripting language* is a high-level language, meaning a small amount of its code can accomplish a lot. It executes in source code format, and it usually runs on top of an *interpreter*, virtual machine, or language engine. To run the script, you need to have the interpreter installed on the user's system. The interpreter knows how to process the script.

## Layers of Computing

Contemporary computer processing happens in many layers. In this respect, computing has changed enormously over the last few decades. Once, a programmer wrote a single program that ran on a single processor. In those days, every bit of functionality took up scarce time and space in the computer's processor. Today, processors are bigger and faster and can handle many programs at once, so computing has become more modular.

A computer system today, such as the one on your desktop, usually looks like Figure 2.1.

The operating system is the "traffic cop" of the computer. It tells which programs to run, keeps track of which ones are running, assigns priority to them, and mediates between the programs and the real world (such as keyboards, screens, and printers).

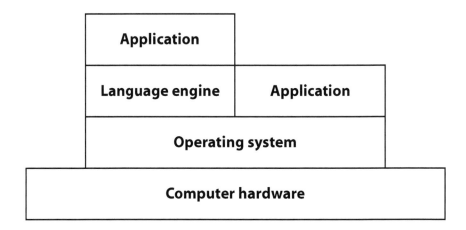

**Figure 2.1** Computer system architecture

Some aspects of open source software licensing depend on how these elements interact. Let's take a more granular look at Figure 2.2. How these elements communicate can be important. For example, you can see that only the operating system "talks" to the hardware. This is a common approach because the means of communication—what hardware pathways communicate with what hardware—may vary from one physical computer to another. Therefore, the operating system must be engineered to work on a particular hardware platform. However, let us suppose that the developer of Application 2 does not want to write a different version of his application for every computer. Instead, he wants to write as few versions as possible while still reaching a large computing audience. He accomplishes this by using a concept called *abstraction*, which is central to modern computing. If the designer of the operating system (such as Windows, Linux, or iOS) provides a specification or API for using that system, then the developer only has to write the program once for that platform. To do this, the operating system vendor uses a set of standard system calls—or an API for that operating system. For example, that API might include an API for showing graphics on a display screen, sending a file to a printer, or getting input from a keyboard. If the programmer follows the syntax and rules for that API, his program will run on any operating system using that API.

This method of creating layers of abstraction promotes not only standardization but also security. An application programmer should not be able to do just any old thing—such as overwrite memory used by other programs or send instructions to the display to draw figures that won't fit there. Limiting the scope and permissions under which programmers operate is sometimes called *encapsulation*. It defines what it means for a program to be compatible with a particular operating system, and it sets limitations on what the program can do without causing technical problems.

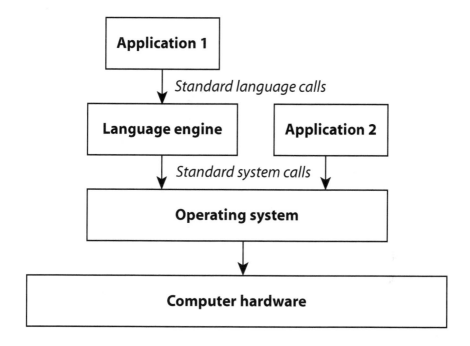

**Figure 2.2** Interaction of the elements of a computer system

It's important to understand that these layers are fundamentally arbitrary—they can be set or changed by the operating system provider. But unless they are used by everyone, standardization will fail. So in fact, APIs for standard computing platforms like operating systems are slow to change. For example, Linux APIs derive from UNIX APIs that were developed in the 1970s at Bell Labs, Android runs on Linux, and iOS runs on a different UNIX derivative called BSD—but the APIs available to Linux, Android, and iOS developers are substantially similar and have evolved from a common root that is decades old.

You probably noticed that the figure above contains an application that runs on top of a language platform instead of directly on the operating system. This provides a further layer of abstraction that does two things. First, if the API for the language is consistent across many operating systems, then this provides even more standardization. The mantra for the Java language, for instance, is "Write once, run anywhere." Java is a very popular language platform, and you are probably using it without knowing it because it's on most desktop and laptop computers and runs many web-based programs. When we get to the details of complying with copyleft licenses like GPL, these concepts will be crucial. To understand modern computing, one needs to think in terms of horizontal layers. Each layer has its own means of abstraction. In fact, sometimes there is an additional layer to consider, as shown in Figure 2.3.

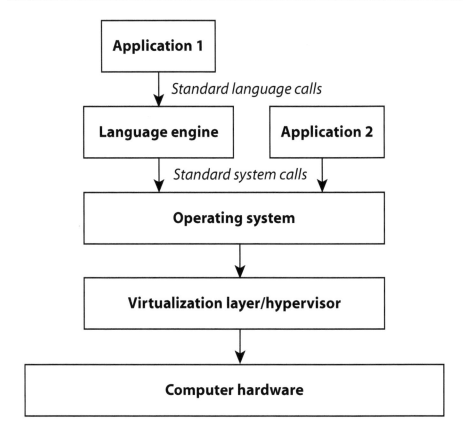

**Figure 2.3** Interaction of the elements of a computer system, with virtualization layer

The virtualization layer allows a user to run programs written for one operating system on a computer that uses another operating system. In fact, this picture can get quite complicated, with multiple operating systems on one computer. But the main thing to understand is that with abstraction, very complex and standardized computing is possible.

### What Is an Operating System?

When we are dealing with open source software, Linux is often the operating system component in Figure 2.3. As mentioned previously, an operating system is like the traffic cop of the computer—on a multitasking system like most general-purpose computers today, it juggles the running of multiple programs and the allocation of hardware resources, making sure each has its own memory space, initiating and terminating programs, and swapping between tasks by picking up the threads of processing where they last left off. The operating system also interfaces with computer hardware, such as keyboards, displays, printers, and modems.

The part of the operating system that does all this is always running while the computer is on. In Linux systems, it is called the *operating system kernel.* This is to distinguish it from other elements of an operating system distribution, or *distro.* To use an operating system kernel on a computer, you also need other programs: the *bootstrap* (the low-level program that launches the operating system kernel when you turn the computer on), compilers and linkers (to create executables for that particular operating system, from source code), and a user interface. Over time, the number of Linux distros has condensed. Today, the most important ones are Fedora (Red Hat) Linux, Ubuntu Linux, and Debian. There are also other specialized distros for embedded systems, real-time applications, or other specific purposes.

For the Linux operating system, these system tools consist mostly of the GNU project of the Free Software Foundation. The FSF is therefore very particular about referring to the operation system as "GNU/Linux"—though most people simply refer to it as Linux.

When a programmer writes an application program, he only wants to write it once. The operating system helps with this by abstracting the information necessary to run a program on a given physical computer. In other words, if you want to write a program for Windows, iOS, or Linux, there is a set of protocols that tell you how to display something to the user on a screen, accept keyboard entries, print documents, access the modem, and so forth. This set of protocols is called the *specification* for the operating system. Often, this abstraction is accomplished by libraries of software called *standard system libraries.* For instance, if you want to write a file to a disk for a Linux system in the C++ programming language, you would invoke a standard library to do that. The specification tells you what information you need to pass to the standard library and how to invoke the standard library. In Linux, the standard libraries are sometimes referred to as *SYSCALL*—code that is stored in a library of that name and that enables standard system calls. In other words, if you write a program that uses SYSCALL, you have written a program that works with Linux. The specification, or *standard interface,* for an operating system defines what that operating system is.

As you read in the introduction, Linux began as a reimplementation of UNIX. There is a standardized specification for UNIX called *POSIX* (Portable Operating System Interface[3]), maintained by IEEE's Portable Application Standards Committee. About 80% of Linux SYSCALL functions are identical to corresponding functions in POSIX. So, although LINUX started as an implementation of UNIX, it has grown beyond that phase. There are standard functions

---

[3] The *X* is an addition that follows the custom of naming "flavors," or versions, of UNIX with an acronym that ends in *X.*

in LINUX that do not exist in UNIX. The important element to understand here is that many of the standard system calls predate LINUX by quite a bit and therefore predate GPL.

## What Is an Application?

*Applications* are the computer programs you are most familiar with—email programs, word processors, drawing programs, mobile apps, and so forth. They are programs that interact directly with users. In a certain abstract sense, there is no difference between an operating system, a language engine, and an application. They are all programs, they are all written in source code, and they all run on your computer. The difference is how they interact with each other.

The processing of an application takes place within a portion of computer memory called *application space* or *user space*. Remember that *memory* is the area in your computer's processor where a program is running—memory is not a disk or USB drive (which is *storage*). Your computer segregates its memory into different *name spaces*, or areas. Remember that the operating system is like a traffic cop, telling applications where to run and with what priority. The application program has an inherently limited set of functions available to it, meaning it can only do what the operating system allows it to do.

So, what constitutes an application and what constitutes application space are arbitrary in a large sense but well defined for a particular operating system platform. The separation between operating system space and application space can break down for smaller, embedded systems. But as computing power gets faster and cheaper, more and more systems are implemented in a way that separates the two. This issue is blurred when more and more applications (like Gmail) run in the browser. When an application runs in a browser, is the application the browser (e.g., Chrome or Firefox) or is the application Gmail? This conundrum affects the interpretation of some open source licenses.

Another way to look at the separation between operating system space and application space focuses on security. Suppose you are in a retail business, like a restaurant. When you walk in, you see places to sit and waiters whose job it is to serve food to you. But there is another part of the restaurant, in the back, where food is prepared, and you can't walk into that part unless you have a key. In the kitchen, other things happen—deliveries of groceries, office work like accounting and staff scheduling, and so forth. If the waiter wants to make a food order, he passes a ticket through to the kitchen, via a hole in the wall. No key is required, but only orders are passed through and only food comes out. The designer of the restaurant has determined, arbitrarily, where the dining room ends and the kitchen begins. As a diner, you only have access to the dining area, and in that area, you can only do certain things. You can't see the grocery deliveries or the staff roster, and what's more, you don't need to. You are there to eat dinner.

The kitchen is like an operating system, the dining room is like application space, the diners are like applications, and the waiters are like standard system calls. The grocery deliveries are the hardware, which resides outside the system. Applications can only run in a specific area of the computer's memory; diners are limited to the dining room. Applications can only make requests to the operating system via standard system calls; the diners get their meals via the waiters, who have a prescribed method of submitting them to the operating system. The kitchen staff prepares meals according to the cooks' culinary skills and the diners' orders so that the meals arrive on time given the diner's orders. The operating system interacts with applications, sets the priority of services to them, and determines how the applications' requests will be fulfilled. The operating system interacts with the hardware; the kitchen staff takes grocery deliveries and puts out the trash.

You, as a diner, have limited information about how the restaurant runs. But the average diner doesn't want to know how the restaurant runs; he only wants dinner. The kitchen staff is trying to manage the dining experience and doesn't want diners running through the kitchen, which could be dangerous and distracting to the kitchen staff.

Therefore, an application is a program that has limited access to hardware, which must interact with the operating systems in a prescribed way and which must run within the space allocated by the operating system. As a result, an application is a simpler and more efficient to program.

## Dynamic Linking and Static Linking

It would be possible, in theory, to sit down with a blank page and write a program that consisted of a single source code file. But no one writes software that way. Lawyers should understand this well because they never write complex documents from scratch; instead, they start with a model or example and tailor it to their needs. Some lawyers who find they are making the same changes every time start to create true form documents that can be more efficiently prepared by filling in the information that changes from one situation to the next. If you are not a lawyer, perhaps you have prepared a form letter or a presentation and then started to prepare another one that you thought was similar. You probably used some portions of the original letter or presentation as a model but discarded other portions.

Programmers write their programs in the same way, but they take this approach of systematic reuse to its logical extreme. Doing so is not plagiarism or cheating—it's good coding practice. That is because code is functional; it has to work correctly. Any code that has already been tested properly should be reused—if it is efficient to do that—rather than rewritten. Programmers, like lawyers, use terms of art both in source code and in the human documents that describe the execution of the program. Unifying those terms of art means that more programmers can be added to a team with minimal learning costs.

For example, suppose the programmer wants the user to input his telephone number into a program. Telephone numbers have a set format—in the United States, one example of the format would be 1-617-542-5942, where 1 is the country code, 617 is the area code, 542 is the exchange, and 5942 is the number. There are different formats for different countries and cities. So, the programmer wants to use some code to confirm that the number is in the right format before allowing the user to move on.

Clearly, many people have had to do this simple computing task, but the programmer does not know all the possible valid formats. So it makes sense for the programmer to use an existing library routine to do it. The programmer will send the input from the user (a string of characters typed in on the keyboard) and will expect to receive in return a Boolean value: TRUE for OK, FALSE for not OK. If such a library routine is well written, all the programmer should have to know is what information to send to it and what the returned information means. The working of the routine is a black box to the programmer, as explained above. To extend the restaurant analogy, if you trust that the kitchen is well run, you don't need to know what happens there—you only need to give the input (your order) and receive the the output (your meal).

Now consider that the programmer wants to do many of these tasks. For instance, if the user is filling in a page of information, every field may need to be checked. Programmers use libraries of code for lots of standard and contained computing purposes—parsing user input, sending output to a printer, and doing mathematical calculations, as well as even more complex tasks like sending an email, checking whether the modem is on, or checking for program updates. In none of these cases does the programmer want to reinvent the wheel. The programmer wants to focus on what new things his program should be doing.

Here is an example of the function described above:[4]

```
BOOL ValidatePhone(CString Num)
    {
    BOOL          RtnVal = TRUE;
    if(Num.GetLength() != 11)
    {
```

---

[4] This function comes from Code Project:
www.codeproject.com/Articles/1874/Validating-E-Mails-amp-Phone-Number/.

```
                RtnVal = FALSE;
        }
        else
        {
                int     Pos;
                int     NumChars;

                NumChars = Num.GetLength();
                Num.MakeUpper();
                for(Pos = 0; Pos < NumChars; Pos ++)
                {
                        if(!isdigit(Num[Pos]))
                        {
                                if(!isspace(Num[Pos]))
                                        RtnVal = FALSE;
                        }
                }
        }
        return RtnVal;
        }
```

In this example, the value returned is a *BOOL,* or a Boolean true or false. The input is a string (of characters) called Num. This routine only checks that the number of characters is correct and that all the characters are digits or spaces. The first line of the routine above shows what information needs to be passed to it (a string) and what is returned (a Boolean value). If the programmer knows this routine will accomplish his goal, all he needs to know is this first line. When he wants this routine to execute, he includes a line like this:

```
until ValidatePhone (MyNum). . .{[code to input My-
Num from the user]};
```

This line will execute until the number is valid and the routine returns a true value.

Once the programmer has all the routines he wants to use, and once he has compiled all the routines into object code, then he needs to stitch them together. In other words, when he writes the line above, the computer needs to find the object for the above routine and execute it, then pass the answer back to the program. To do this, the computer needs to know where to find the routine and where to send the answer back to. This process might look like Figure 2.4.

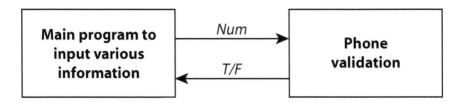

**Figure 2.4** Communication between a program and routine

The entire program will contain both these objects plus information about the entry point from the main program to the phone number routine.

Even assuming the program has efficiently separated routines into modules, there are more decisions to make to create a program that executes efficiently. Programming always involves a tradeoff between memory use and speed. For example, the entire program could exist in one big "binary blob" and would run very quickly, but then it would use a lot of memory.[5] To achieve the right balance of speed and memory, a programmer creates a software *build*.

Consider the diagram in Figure 2.5, which shows the build of a program that uses a date verification routine.

As you can see, the "Linking" option requires less memory. Think of the memory used as the amount of space taken up by the boxes and diamonds. In the Linking option, only one copy of the "Date OK?" routine is used, whereas in the Inline Function option, it appears twice, even though it is identical. But the Linking option will execute more slowly because instead of processing by automatically falling down to the Date OK function, the computer must find the function (represented by the dotted lines above), execute it, and return processing to the main line of processing.

In some languages, like C++, there are different ways to link. Have you ever used a computer and seen the error message "DLL Not Found"? In this case, your computer was instructed to execute a dynamically linked library but could not find it in memory. When a routine is called via *dynamic linking*, the computer must find the routine at execution time, execute it, then flush it from memory and return to the program that called it. The implication is that until the moment the routine runs, it does not need to be present. If, by mistake, the routine is not there and the program never calls it, nothing goes wrong. With *static linking*, by contrast, the routine is always in memory and is part of the same binary file as the routines that call it. That means there cannot be such an error; the routine is by definition resident in memory.

---

[5] Keep in mind that *memory* is the area where a computer holds and executes programs; *storage* is where one saves files, such as on hard disks, CD-ROMs, or USB drives.

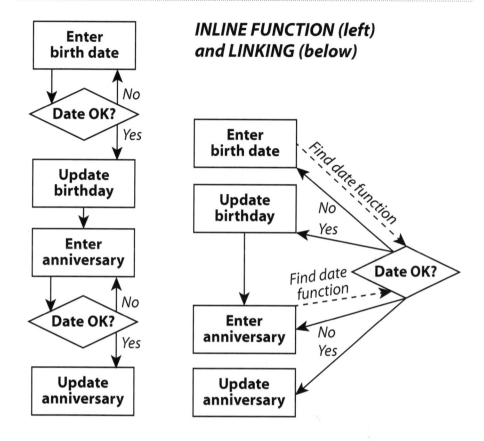

**INLINE FUNCTION (left) and LINKING (below)**

**Figure 2.5** Build of a program that verifies a date

Static linking executes more quickly than dynamic linking. The time it takes for the computer to find, execute, and flush the dynamically linked routine may be very small, but if the computer must do this many times or if the speed of processing is crucial (such as in real-time applications like audiovisual streaming, gameplay, or monitoring operations), dynamic linking can be an unworkable choice. However, static linking takes up more memory because all of the routines must be in memory at once. Static linking can also deteriorate launch times because all of the routines must load into memory when the program starts.

These build techniques are readily interchangeable. The same code can be built in various ways, simply by instructing the build program how to do the build. This is done by a set of commands called a "build script," which contains commands like "Build all of these routines as dynamically linked," or "Build all of these routines as inline," or "Pick and choose for different routines." But modern computer compilers and linkers may not always do what you tell them to do;

some have features that will *optimize* the build of a program by choosing the build method based on efficiency.

## Monoliths and Loadable Kernel Modules

Some operating systems are *monolithic*, meaning that the operating system consists of one big binary. Linux is a *quasi-monolithic* architecture. Most of the elements of a Linux kernel are statically linked and loaded at run time.[6] However, some elements—particularly hardware device drivers—can be implemented as dynamically linked modules. This fact underlies a very important legal question discussed in greater depth in Chapter 8: The GPL 2 Border Dispute.

## Header Files

A header file describes the information that must be passed from one binary file to another so that the two can interoperate. In the date verification routine ("Date OK?"), above, the input might be a date like June 26, 1906, and the output data might be a binary number (0 for OK, 1 for not OK). A header file might look like this:

```
extern int dateOK(int mm, int dd, int yyyy);
```

The presence of the word `extern` in the code means that the routine can be used by routines in other source files; this tells the computer that the information in the interface needs to persist long enough to be captured by the other file. The type `int` means that the function will return a single integer value. In computing, an integer is a whole number, positive or negative. In our routine, this return value will be 1 or 0.[7] That is the output of the function. The function takes three input variables: `mm`, `dd`, and `yyyy`.[8] These input values are sometimes called *arguments*. In our example, each of these variables is of an integer type. `DateOK` is the name of the function; when the calling program wants to invoke this function, it will use a statement like this:

```
if (dateOK(6,26,1906)) [update record] else [go back
to input];
```

---

[6] *Linux Internals,* Section 2.15, **www.cse.unsw.edu.au/~cs9242/11/lectures/08-linux_internals.** pdf.

[7] We could have used a Boolean return value, of course. An integer value is used for simplicity.

[8] We could have used a date type value, of course. But that would be no fun.

The bracketed items represent other programming statements that we need not consider for now, but they follow the logical flow of the diagrams above.

The date verification routine will contain much more processing. For example, it will check that the month is between 1 and 12, that the year is in an expected range, and that the day is within the number of days for the given month. But here is the important point: we don't need to know any of this detail to use the routine. All we need to know is what the function does, the fact that it has been tested and works, and what return value to expect. The header file contains only the information that is strictly necessary to use the function: the name of the function, the number, the type and order of arguments, and the return type. Accordingly, the function is not software code, per se. It is a definition of an interface. (This fact, important in the discussion of the nature of derivative works in software law, is discussed in more depth in Chapter 8: The GPL 2 Border Dispute.)

# Part II

# Basic Open Source Theory and Compliance

Chapter 3

# Common Open Source Licenses

The Open Source Initiative has approved over 60 open source licenses. Some people point to this as a fault with open source licensing—which is odd, because there are many more proprietary licenses, one for each product. In fact, only a handful of the more than 60 approved OSI licenses are in wide use, and many of the others are simply variations on that handful.

The licenses you need to understand are as follows:

- GPL
- LGPL
- Mozilla/Eclipse
- BSD
- MIT
- Apache 2.0

Open source licenses fall into two categories: permissive and copyleft. *Permissive licenses* are very simple: they allow you to do whatever you want with the software as long as you abide by notice requirements. Notice requirements are not complicated to comply with, but for binary distributions, they can be an administrative challenge to implement. (For details on how to do notices, see Chapter 7: Notice Requirements). Like all open source licenses, they provide the software as-is, with no warranties. So permissive licenses can be summarized as follows:

- Do whatever you want with the code.
- Use at your own risk.
- Acknowledge me.

There are many permissive licenses, and for some popular licenses such as BSD and MIT, there are hundreds of variations on them. But because they are permissive, they all generally work the same way.

*Copyleft* is more challenging to understand. In a nutshell, copyleft says, in addition to the above:

- If you distribute binaries, you must make the source code for those binaries available.
- The source code must be available under the same copyleft terms under which you got the code.
- You cannot place additional restrictions on the exercise of the license.

Copyleft falls into several categories:

- Ultra-strong (AGPL)
- Strong (GPL)
- Weaker (LGPL)
- Weak (Eclipse, MPL, CDDL)

The strength has to do with the scope of the software that's subject to the copyleft requirements. GPL is the broadest; it requires that any program that contains GPL code must only contain GPL code. The others draw the line more narrowly: LGPL allows dynamic linking to other code, and the weak copyleft licenses like Eclipse or MPL allow any kind of integration, as long as the Eclipse or MPL code is in its own file.

AGPL is called ultra-strong, but not because of its scope, which is the same as that of GPL. Instead, it is called ultra-strong because AGPL applies its copyleft conditions (access to source code) in some situations where the code is not distributed.

## Dissecting the Open Source License

Open source licenses are conditional copyright licenses. (For a detailed analysis of why this matters and the legal implications for enforcement, see Chapter 5: Conditional Licensing.) All open source licenses grant all the rights of copyright, with no field restrictions or limitations. They do impose conditions on exercise of the license, but if you follow the conditions, you are not limited as to the type of use, location of use, number of copies, and so forth, the way you might be for a proprietary license. To put this in perspective, consider that there is an entire industry that helps companies audit whether they are within the scope of their proprietary licenses. For example, there are tools that allow IT managers to limit the number of users for a company or the number of computers on which a piece of software is installed. None of this is necessary with open source—all you have to do is abide by the conditions. Compared to proprietary software licenses, open source licenses are actually quite easy to comply with.

An open source license contains no obligations for the licensor. The licensor grants licenses but does not promise to do anything. Also, technically, the license does not contain any obligations for the licensee, only conditions to exercise the license.

### Patent License Grants

Some open source licenses contain provisions about patents. The first open source licenses were written back when software patents weren't as prevalent as they are today. Software patents and business method patents (which often claim inventions practiced via software systems) became much more popular in the United States in the 1990s, after some seminal cases that confirmed they contained patentable subject matter.

Open source licenses, for the most part, contain two kinds of patent provisions: licenses and defensive termination provisions.

The license grant in certain licenses (such as Apache 2.0, Eclipse, Mozilla, and GPL 3.0) runs with the license to the software. If a contributor to the code has a patent on the code, that contributor grants a patent license to all recipients of the code to enable them to exercise the open source license.

In addition, almost all open source licenses that contain express patent licenses also have defensive termination provisions. If the licensee asserts a patent, the licensee can lose rights under the open source license.

These provisions are discussed in detail in Chapter 13: Open Source and Patents. However, it is worth noting here that the licensee in an open source license does not grant any patent rights—only the licensor does. There are no grant-backs or cross-licenses in open source because the license is not a contract, does not have an acceptance mechanism, and contains no obligations for the licensee. It contains conditions—one of which may be a defensive termination provision—but no obligations.

### Direct Licensing

Open source licenses are direct licensing models—they do not grant any right to grant further sublicenses. Instead, they allow redistribution of modified or unmodified code. When an author releases code under an open source license, the grant of rights is automatically made to every recipient, regardless of how or when the code is received. Figure 3.1 shows how the grant of rights flows, regardless of whether the author of modifications delivered the modified software to the recipient.

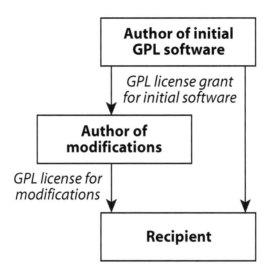

**Figure 3.1** Direct licensing model of open source

The direct licensing model has a few corollaries. If a distributor violates an open source license, then although the distributor may lose his rights, downstream recipients do not. This is because the grant of rights never flowed from the distributor in the first place. Unless the downstream recipient also violates the license, the grant of rights is unaffected.

Moreover, open source licenses are never transferred. GPL version 3 is explicit about this, saying:

> An "entity transaction" is a transaction transferring control of an organization, or substantially all assets of one, or subdividing an organization, or merging organizations. If propagation of a covered work results from an entity transaction, each party to that transaction who receives a copy of the work also receives whatever licenses to the work the party's predecessor in interest had or could give under the previous paragraph, plus a right to possession of the Corresponding Source of the work from the predecessor in interest, if the predecessor has it or can get it with reasonable efforts.

But once you understand the direct licensing model, this is obvious. If a company (Buyer) purchases the assets of another company (Target), and Target delivers to Buyer the open source code Target is using, then after the transaction is done, Buyer is exercising its own license to the code, direct from the author. The license never needs to be transferred because it was granted to all recipients (including Target and Buyer) in the first place. Proprietary licenses, in contrast, must be transferred from one licensee to another—which can be a challenge in mergers and acquisitions (M&A) transactions.

## Common Open Source Licenses

Table 3.1 lists the most common open source licenses. A more detailed list appears in Appendix B: Open Source Licenses.

**Table 3.1** Most Common Open Source Licenses

| License | Copyleft? | Comments |
|---|---|---|
| Affero GPL 3.0 | Yes | Ultra-strong copyleft, like GPL but source code requirements are triggered by SAAS use. |
| Apache Software License (1.1) | No | Apache 1.0 is largely no longer in use; version 1.1 removed the "advertising" clause. |
| Apache License, 2.0 | No | Permissive license but far more detailed terms than BSD, MIT, or Apache 1.0 or 1.1; contains express patent grants. |
| Artistic license | No (though the point has been debated[1]) | Not copyleft, but has more restrictions than most permissive licenses. Many projects under this license are dual licensed under GPL. |
| (New) BSD license | No | Template license—many variants are in use. Major variants are the "3-clause" and "2-clause" variants. Earlier versions contained an advertising clause. |
| Boost License | No | Mostly used for the Boost project as a baseline license; however, some elements of the Boost project do not use it. |
| Common Development and Distribution License (CDDL) | Yes | Based on MPL. Successor to Sun Public License. |
| Common Public License 1.0 | Yes | Successor to IBM Public License. See also Eclipse license. |
| Eclipse Public License | Yes | Successor to CPL |
| GNU General Public License (GPL) version 2 | Yes | Most commonly used license. Strong copyleft. Applies to Linux kernel. |
| Mozilla Public License 1.1 (MPL) | Yes | Weak copyleft. Applied to the Firefox browser. |

---

[1]  en.wikipedia.org/wiki/Artistic_License.

| License | Copyleft? | Comments |
|---|---|---|
| MySQL (GPL + FLOSS Exception) | Yes | Like GPL, but allows linking to open source code. |
| Mozilla Public License 2.0 (MPL) | Yes | Weak copyleft. Applies to the Firefox browser. |
| OpenSSL/SSLeay | No | Permissive licenses, used only for the OpenSSL project. OpenSSLeay contains this provision: "The license and distribution terms for any publically available version or derivative of this code cannot be changed." However, it is generally understood to be a permissive license. |
| Sun Industry Standards Source License (SISSL) | Yes | Deprecated; now largely superseded by CDDL. For more information, see **www.openoffice.org/FAQs/license-change.html**. |
| W3C License | No | Permissive. Note that W3C is a standards organization; this license covers copyrightable material, and standards can cover other types of intellectual property. |
| zlib/libpng license | No | Permissive license |

## GPL

The GPL is the prototypical "free software" or copyleft license. It is generally considered the most widely used open source license.[2]

### GPL Versions

Version 1.0 is no longer in use. Version 2.0 was released in 1991, and version 3.0 was released in 2007.

Versioning of licenses can be confusing. While a small number of projects are released under a single version of GPL (such as GPL version 2 only, which is used for the Linux kernel), most are released under a given version and any subsequent version. A recipient taking code under a given version of GPL (such as version 2) has the option to use the code under that version of the license (version 2) or any subsequent version (currently versions 2 or 3).

The choice to release under a version and any later version betokens great faith in the license steward. If the steward issues a subsequent version that is less favorable to a licensor, the licensor's rights may be compromised. However, this issue is handled with an interpretational sleight of hand—while the recipient can use the license under any version, the licensor is never held to any license grants it did not make. This is probably most meaningful for GPL version 2, which

---

[2] There are many ways to measure use, of course. GPL is applied by the most projects (as measured by various sources), but a measurement weighted by use would doubtless skew more toward Apache 2.0, MIT, or BSD.

contains no express patent license. Theoretically, if an author released code under GPL version 2, it is not held to the patent grants in version 3. The theory, however, is that no subsequent version truly adds grants of rights, only conditions.

### Reading GPL Version 2

Most people who read GPL version 2 complain to me that it is hard or even impossible to understand. In truth, its language is not difficult to understand, but its organization does not help. Of course, there is a big difference in language between GPL and conventional software licenses. GPL version 2 was an attempt at plain-language drafting—something that many lawyers, particularly in the technology practice, favor.

The first portion of the license is a preamble, roughly equivalent to recitals in a conventional license agreement. According to the law governing interpretation of contracts, this portion would probably be considered interpretive background but not part of the license terms.

The first paragraph of the GPL is numbered 0 instead of 1. In computer programming languages like C, ordinal counting begins with 0. For example, the first element of an array is 0—a convention that causes many novice coders to stay up all night debugging code.

The main terms of GPL are divided into three parts: distribution of unaltered source code, distribution of unaltered binaries, and distribution of altered code. This is probably what makes the license confusing to those who are accustomed to conventional licenses, which are almost never written this way.

Several provisions of GPL 2 have nicknames, such as these:

- Section 5 is the "no contract" provision that states that the GPL is a license and not a contract.
- Section 7 is the "Liberty or Death" provision, which states that if the recipient may not distribute the code under the terms of GPL without other restrictions, the recipient may not distribute the code at all. This provision would come into play if there were conflicts between the licensing terms for GPL and proprietary code, for instance, or between GPL and patent licenses or nondisclosure agreements.

The GPL does not have a governing law provision. This is not an omission—it is an attempt to "internationalize" the license and thereby prevent its forking into national versions. While most lawyers consider any choice of law provision better than none, the drafters of GPL placed harmonization with local law above certainty when making this decision. Accordingly, background law will dictate what state's or country's law will be used to interpret the GPL in a particular instance.

### "Special Exceptions"

Generally, GPL only comes in its official form, but there are a few variations of GPL. Each of these has been developed ad hoc and takes the form of a "special exception," or a set of additional permissions, granted by the licensor. Each of these exceptions weakens the scope of GPL. The most popular are listed in Table 3.2.

These exceptions can be idiosyncratic, so if you are dealing with a variation of GPL that applies an exception, you must read it every time and analyze it every time.

**Table 3.2** Special Exceptions to GPL

| Exception | Used For | Meaning |
|---|---|---|
| GCC Runtime Library Exception www.gnu.org/licenses/ gcc-exception-3.1.html | C runtime libraries for the GNU C compiler | Broad exception that removes all requirements of GPL for use of runtime libraries used via any "Eligible Compilation Process." |
| Classpath Exception www.gnu.org/software/ classpath/license.html | GNU Classpath project (reimplementation of Java libraries) and Open JDK | Allows linking to proprietary code. Note that this allows any kind of link, but classpath files are likely to be linked dynamically. |
| FOSS/FLOSS Exception www.mysql.com/about/ legal/licensing/ foss-exception/ | MySQL application interface | Allows linking GPL code to other open source code (including code under permissive licenses). This exception has been revised over time, most recently in 2012. |

Other than the FOSS exception, these exceptions are practical measures to ensure that the licensing of runtime libraries needed by a development tool (like GCC) or a language engine (like Java) does not require the corresponding application to be licensed under GPL. In other words, you can develop proprietary applications with GCC or to run on a Java platform. Note that these exceptions are more permissive than LGPL, which is primarily used to enable the library to be used as a dynamically linked library for an application (such as a plug-in).

## The Lesser General Public License (LGPL)

LGPL is *lesser* than GPL because it has a narrower scope. It is sometimes called the *Library GPL* because it is suitable for use with free software libraries. The preamble to the license says, "We use this license for certain libraries in order to permit linking those libraries into non-free programs." The FSF expressly discourages the use of LGPL because "it does [l]ess to protect the user's freedom than the ordinary General Public License." The FSF believes that some libraries should be available for proprietary development and some should not. "[W]hen a library provides a significant unique capability, like GNU Readline, that's a horse of a different color. The Readline library implements input editing and history for interactive programs, and that's a facility not generally available elsewhere. Releasing it under the GPL and limiting its use to free programs gives our community a real boost. At least one application program is free software today specifically because that was necessary for using Readline" (from its website post "Why you shouldn't use the Lesser GPL for your next library," **www.gnu.org/philosophy/why-not-lgpl.html**). Of course, the other possibility is that this strategy will backfire and the code will not be used much.

LGPL is probably one of the most confusing open source licenses to read. While most companies find it easy to comply with, that is because those companies have adopted a simplified rule of compliance: only use LGPL code as a dynamically linked library. However, those who read the document usually ask, "Where does it refer to dynamic linking?" and in fact, it does not expressly do that.

LGPL is essentially GPL plus additional permissions that allow integration of LGPL libraries with proprietary applications. In version 3.0 of the licenses, LGPL was drafted as an addendum to GPL, which is probably the right way to make it understandable. However, LGPL 2.1, the most common version in use, is a separate document, and it can be hard to track against GPL version 2.

In truth, the terms of the license are more complex. If you want to go beyond this bright-line rule for compliance, take a look at Chapter 9: LGPL 2.1 Compliance.

## Corporate-Style (or "Weak") Copyleft Licenses

There is a category of weak copyleft licenses that are written to implement the copyleft principles of GPL, but with a drafting style more familiar to licensing attorneys. These licenses include the Eclipse Public License (EPL), the Mozilla Public License (MPL), and the Common Development and Distribution License (CDDL).

MPL covered the release of the Netscape web browser in 2002. This software was later improved and released as the Firefox browser, also released under MPL. This license was revised and updated in 2012 and released as MPL version 2.

The IBM Public License was drafted soon after MPL 1.0, but it has since been superseded by the CPL and EPL. The EPL mainly covers the Eclipse development environment.

The Sun Industry Standards Source License was released by Sun Microsystems, but it was superseded[3] by the Common Development and Distribution License (CDDL) in 2005.

These licenses roughly track the substance of LGPL. Although they use different exact wording to describe the scope of their copyleft obligations, none of them is considered as broad in scope as GPL. They are therefore accurately referred to as *weak copyleft* licenses—they allow code libraries released under their licenses to be incorporated into proprietary products. In addition, many of them allow relicensing of binaries under proprietary terms, as long as the source code remains available under the open source license. Therefore, in a sense, the copyleft only applies to source code. This approach is very corporate friendly, obviating the need for the license carve-outs described above for LGPL.

All of these licenses also have express patent licenses and defensive termination provisions. (A summary of these terms is in Chapter 13: Open Source and Patents.)

## Permissive Licenses

There are hundreds of small variations on permissive licenses, but almost all of them are based on the template forms of the BSD (Berkeley Software Distribution) license or the MIT license, or they consist of the terms of Apache 1.1 or 2.0. Most permissive licenses are short and simple. The simplest form of BSD appears below:

* Copyright (c) <year>, <copyright holder>

* All rights reserved.

* Redistribution and use in source and binary forms, with or without modification, are permitted provided that the following conditions are met:

* * Redistributions of source code must retain the above copyright notice, this list of conditions and the following disclaimer.

---

[3] en.wikipedia.org/wiki/Sun_Industry_Standards_Source_License.

* * Redistributions in binary form must reproduce the above copyright notice, this list of conditions and the following disclaimer in the documentation and/or other materials provided with the distribution.

* * Neither the name of the University of California, Berkeley nor the names of its contributors may be used to endorse or promote products derived from this software without specific prior written permission.

* THIS SOFTWARE IS PROVIDED BY THE REGENTS AND CONTRIBUTORS "AS IS" AND ANY EXPRESS OR IMPLIED WARRANTIES, INCLUDING, BUT NOT LIMITED TO, THE IMPLIED WARRANTIES OF MERCHANTABILITY AND FITNESS FOR A PARTICULAR PURPOSE ARE DISCLAIMED. IN NO EVENT SHALL THE REGENTS AND CONTRIBUTORS BE LIABLE FOR ANY DIRECT, INDIRECT, INCIDENTAL, SPECIAL, EXEMPLARY, OR CONSEQUENTIAL DAMAGES (INCLUDING, BUT NOT LIMITED TO, PROCUREMENT OF SUBSTITUTE GOODS OR SERVICES; LOSS OF USE, DATA, OR PROFITS; OR BUSINESS INTERRUPTION) HOWEVER CAUSED AND ON ANY THEORY OF LIABILITY, WHETHER IN CONTRACT, STRICT LIABILITY, OR TORT (INCLUDING NEGLIGENCE OR OTHERWISE) ARISING IN ANY WAY OUT OF THE USE OF THIS SOFTWARE, EVEN IF ADVISED OF THE POSSIBILITY OF SUCH DAMAGE.

Many lawyers are confused by the permission to use software in "source code and binary forms." They wonder whether this distribution must be in both forms or neither. (It would have been more accurate to allow redistribution and use in "source code *or* binary forms.") Some lawyers are also troubled by the lack of a formal license grant. In practice, neither of these issues is a serious concern; BSD is clearly a permissive license and intended to be an irrevocable grant of rights. This is an example of why open source licenses need to be interpreted in context rather than in isolation; any lawyer advising his clients to be concerned about these issues is not seeing the whole picture and not doing his client any favors.

Some readers of this license also wonder why there is an asterisk at the beginning of every line. In many programming languages, asterisks indicate comments—text that will be ignored by the compiler because it is not intended as programming statements. Mostly, this format is an artifact; licenses are usually in their own text files today, but this format allows one to put the license statement in a source code file.

The MIT license appears below:

> Copyright (c) <year> <copyright holders>
>
> Permission is hereby granted, free of charge, to any person obtaining a copy of this software and associated documentation files (the "Software"), to deal in the Software without restriction, including without limitation the rights to use, copy, modify, merge, publish, distribute, sublicense, and/or sell copies of the Software, and to permit persons to whom the Software is furnished to do so, subject to the following conditions:
>
> The above copyright notice and this permission notice shall be included in all copies or substantial portions of the Software.
>
> THE SOFTWARE IS PROVIDED "AS IS," WITHOUT WARRANTY OF ANY KIND, EXPRESS OR IMPLIED, INCLUDING BUT NOT LIMITED TO THE WARRANTIES OF MERCHANTABILITY, FITNESS FOR A PARTICULAR PURPOSE AND NON-INFRINGEMENT. IN NO EVENT SHALL THE AUTHORS OR COPYRIGHT HOLDERS BE LIABLE FOR ANY CLAIM, DAMAGES OR OTHER LIABILITY, WHETHER IN AN ACTION OF CONTRACT, TORT OR OTHERWISE, ARISING FROM, OUT OF OR IN CONNECTION WITH THE SOFTWARE OR THE USE OR OTHER DEALINGS IN THE SOFTWARE.

## Apache

Apache 1.0 was deprecated because of its so-called "advertising requirement," which read as follows: "All advertising materials mentioning features or use of this software must display the following acknowledgement: This product includes software developed by the University of California, Berkeley and its contributors."[4] This requirement was viewed as unworkable and possibly inconsistent with GPL. Very little software is still provided under this license. Apache 1.1, released in 2000, superseded Apache 1.0 and removed the advertising clause.[5] It is very similar to the BSD and MIT licenses.

Apache 2.0, released in 2004, was revised to standardize drafting and add patent provisions. Apache 2.0 has become the template license of choice for many open source projects, including the Google Android project.[6]

---

[4] www.apache.org/licenses/LICENSE-1.0.

[5] www.apache.org/licenses/LICENSE-1.1.

[6] www.apache.org/licenses/LICENSE-2.0.

## Miscellaneous Licenses

There are many other open source licenses, most of which are used on few projects. One category of license that's notable for its amusement value is sometimes called *otherware*. Licenses in this category are generally thought to be permissive, although serious discussions do sometimes crop up over whether they meet the open source definition, due to their tendency to impose odd conditions that may be considered restrictions on use (and therefore inconsistent with the open source definition). Some have described these licenses as social commentary on the length and complexity of the GPL. Some examples of otherware licenses are below:

### The "Beer-Ware" License

# 'THE BEER-WARE LICENSE' (Revision 42)

# <tobez@tobez.org> wrote this file. As long as you retain this notice you

# can do whatever you want with this stuff. If we meet some day, and you think

# this stuff is worth it, you can buy me a beer in return. Anton Berezin[7]

### The BarCamp License (Revision 1)

<tyler@bleepsoft.com> wrote this code. As long as you retain this notice you can do whatever you want with this stuff. If we ever meet at a BarCamp, and you think this code is worth it, you can buy me some tacos in return. -R. Tyler Ballance[8]

### The Catware License

This program is catware. If you find it useful in any way, pay for this program by spending one hour petting one or several cats.[9]

---

[7] www.tobez.org/download/port-tools/port-idea.

[8] tyler.geekisp.com/code/BarCampLicense.txt.

[9] lists.debian.org/debian-devel/1999/01/msg01921.html. Note the query as to whether this qualifies as a "free" software license.

### The Chicken Dance License

This license was intended to "bring humor to the silliness of intellectual property" and is maintained at a GITHUB site: **github.com/supertunaman/ cdl**. The license is based on BSD, with the following condition for redistribution:

4. An entity wishing to redistribute in binary form or include this software in their product without redistribution of this software's source code with the product must also submit to these conditions where applicable:

* For every thousand (1000) units distributed, at least half of the employees or persons affiliated with the product must listen to the "Der Ententanz" (AKA "The Chicken Dance") as composed by Werner Thomas for no less than two (2) minutes

* For every twenty-thousand (20000) units distributed, one (1) or more persons affiliated with the entity must be recorded performing the full Chicken Dance, in an original video at the entity's own expense, and a video encoded in OGG Theora format or a format and codec specified by <OWNER>, at least three (3) minutes in length, must be submitted to <OWNER>, provided <OWNER>'s contact information. Any and all copyrights to this video must be transfer[r]ed to <ORGANIZATION>. The dance featured in the video must be based upon the instructions on how to perform the Chicken Dance that you should have received with this software.

* Any employee or person affiliated with the product must be prohibited from saying the word "gazorninplat" in public at all times, as long as distribution of the product continues.

A license that has been trending upward in popularity in the past few years is the WTFPL:

Do What The Fuck you want to Public License

Version 1.0, March 2000

Copyright (C) 2000 Banlu Kemiyatorn (]d).

136 Nives 7 Jangwattana 14 Laksi Bangkok

Everyone is permitted to copy and distribute verbatim copies of this license document, but changing it is not allowed.

Ok, the purpose of this license is simple and you just DO WHAT THE FUCK YOU WANT TO.

Unfortunately, the terms don't specify what you can do with the code. But one presumes the author does not care enough to challenge you. Also, the FSF considers this license compatible with GPL.[10]

There are also several kinds of public domain dedication, such as the Unlicense and Creative Commons Zero. These are not licenses, of course; they are statements of intent to waive license conditions along with the copyright for the code.

## OpenSSL

This chapter will not attempt to address the many unusual or nonstandard permissive licenses. However, one nonstandard license, the OpenSSL license, is extremely common because it applies to a project in ubiquitous use. OpenSSL is an open source implementation of a secure socket layer toolkit. The OpenSSL license looks like a BSD-style permissive license at first blush, but it contains language that many readers find confusing. The project website says:

> The OpenSSL toolkit stays under a dual license, i.e., both the conditions of the OpenSSL License and the original SSLeay license apply to the toolkit. ... Actually both licenses are BSD-style Open Source licenses.[11]

This is the less common use of "dual license"—that two licenses simultaneously govern the code. Also, the "BSD-style" reference helps clear up some language in the license that seems contradictory:

> The license and distribution terms for any publicly available version or derivative of this code cannot be changed; i.e., this code cannot simply be copied and put under another distribution license (including the GNU [General] Public License).[12]

This confusion illustrates the drawbacks of nonstandard licenses—many readers are concerned that the language above means the license is intended to be a copyleft license.

---

[10] See the list of compatible licenses at **www.gnu.org/licenses/license-list.html#WTFPL**.

[11] **www.openssl.org/source/license.html**.

[12] Spelling and punctuation made to conform to US usage.

## Content Licenses

Software packages contain plenty of non-software materials, such as bit-mapped images (like icons), music files, picture files (GIFs, JPEGs, etc.), and text files—which are sometimes referred to as *content*. When the software is open source, it is helpful to have an equivalent non-software license for these materials. Also, authors who want to make content freely available, independent of software, need licenses to effectuate that release. The most common of these are the GNU Free Documentation License[13] and the Creative Commons licenses.[14]

The GNU Free Documentation License is FSF's equivalent of GPL for a "manual, textbook, or other functional and useful document" or "any textual work, regardless of subject matter or whether it is published as a printed book ... principally for works whose purpose is instruction or reference."[15] Many of this license's terms are specific to documentation and do not apply well to other works. It is not in common use.

Using the Creative Commons licenses is a more popular choice for any kind of non-software copyrightable work. These licenses offer variations to suit the breadth of rights the author wishes to grant; accordingly, not all of them are consistent with the Open Source definition. For instance, there is a "noncommercial" (NC) option that conflicts with the rule that open source licenses must not place any restrictions on fields of endeavor.[16] The licenses include options that disallow modification (*no-derivatives*). All of them require attribution (referred to as *by*), and some contain copyleft conditions (called *ShareAlike*). Each license comes in two verisons—a summary and the *legal code*, which contains the actual license terms. Great care has been taken to make the application of these licenses as international as possible.[17]

The Creative Commons Public Domain Dedication (CC0) is particularly popular for software because it disclaims any waiver of patent rights. This is a handy way for companies to make available copyrightable software for broad use without undue concern about whether any patent rights have been waived. Or, taking the other view, it's a handy way to trick the world into using patented code. But mostly, that is not the intention; it is more to avoid tangential arguments that the company's patents have been licensed free of charge and therefore cannot be

---

[13] www.gnu.org/licenses/fdl.html.

[14] creativecommons.org.

[15] Preamble to GFDL.

[16] "6. No Discrimination Against Fields of Endeavor," opensource.org/osd-annotated/.

[17] The revision 4 licenses in particular contained internationalization terms; see creativecommons.org/version4/.

enforced at all. (For more discussion on this point, see Chapter 16: Open Source Releases.)

Other than the permissive (BY) and public domain (CC0) versions, Creative Commons licenses are generally not a good choice for release of software. The scope of the ShareAlike versions does little to enlighten a licensee about what other code might be controlled as an "Adaptation."[18] In other words, as confusing as the scope of GPL is, CC ShareAlike is even more confusing when applied to software.

## Problematic Licenses

A few licenses are worth noting because they almost always cause compliance concerns. I would put these in the category of my least favorite licenses.

- **ODbL.** An "open data" license with copyleft conditions. (See Chapter 21: Open Hardware and Data.)
- **CPAL.** A "badgeware" license that was approved by OSI while the "Exhibit B" licenses (variations of MPL with badgeware requirements) pioneered by Sugar CRM (and later deprecated by it) became popular. Badgeware licenses cause most companies compliance concerns because their conditions can apply in the absence of distribution. In this respect, they can be considered ultra-strong copyleft licenses similar to APGL.
- **A "public domain" license.** This is on its face a dedication to the public domain, which requires a copyright or licensing notice. This "license" is self-contradictory because no copyright notice is appropriate on a work to which the author has waived copyright protection, and fortunately, it's not very common.

---

[18] For the definition of Adaptations in a ShareAlike Creative Commons license, see, for example, Section 1a, **creativecommons.org/licenses/by-sa/3.0/legalcode/**.

Chapter 4

# License Compatibility

The need for due diligence and the question of license compatibility go far beyond open source licensing. Lawyers have been addressing issues of software license compatibility since software licensing began; the issues have only been brought to the forefront by open source licensing, which has caused compatibility to be a problem for everyone—not just the lawyers. Much of what you will read in this chapter is about software licensing in general, and in the end, you may come to the conclusion that it is proprietary licenses, and not open source licenses, that cause the most problems in due diligence.

## The Awkward Dinner Party

Developing with different kinds of software is like planning an awkward dinner party for your relatives. By duplicating a lot of effort, you can feed everyone: your middle-aged uncle, on his low-carb diet, wants meat and fish; your sister, the vegan, wants only locally grown vegetables; and your teenaged nephew will eat anything as long as it is pizza. But what if your dinner guests not only limited their own diets but also harbored a vehement, polemical disgust for everything they wouldn't eat? It would be hard to bring everyone to the same table.

These woes, like many that populate our world's headlines, come not from the participants being different but from the participants refusing to coexist with others. Software licenses, like people who are certain that they are right and everyone else is wrong, each have their own set of rules. When all the rules conflict, coexistence can be impossible.

## What Is Due Diligence?

Most people who want to learn about open source licensing have a goal of conducting due diligence. This process has many names—audits, due diligence, housekeeping, compliance, and hygiene. But whatever it is called, it is the process of ensuring—as much as possible—that your company is complying with the open source licenses that cover the software it is using. In this chapter, I will refer to this process as *diligence*.

A diligence project can arise for many reasons. It almost always comes up during a corporate transaction—a merger, acquisition, divestiture, or financing deal. But it can also arise because of customer requirements, regulatory audits, or simply an initiative to comply with licenses in order to manage risk or even to do the right thing by respecting the intellectual property of others.

The diligence process is not about perfection; it is about risk management. There is no such thing as perfect compliance; the software landscape, even for a simple product or business, is too complicated for that. The process of diligence is designed to solve the worst problems first, then move to the next set, and then move to the next until one runs out of time, energy, or fear of risk. It is a process of triaging problems and making reasoned decisions.

From an overarching point of view, diligence is the process of making sure your inbound rights are equal to or greater than your outbound rights. By *inbound*, we mean licenses granted to your company, and by *outbound*, we mean rights exercised by your company or granted to others. If you grant, or use, more rights than you have, then you are infringing on someone else's rights.

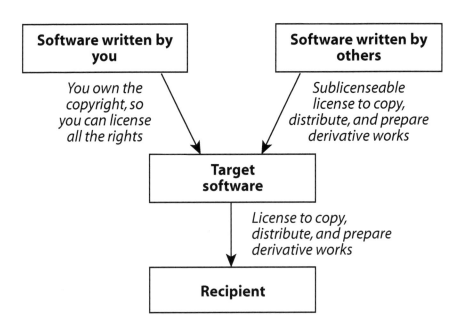

**Figure 4.1** Two common cases governing clearance of inbound rights

Figure 4.1 shows two common cases governing the clearance of rights going into a software code base (i.e., the inbound rights). One is software written by the party creating the target software. As an author, that party has the right to exercise the copyright. The other element is software that is written by others—and that therefore requires a license to exercise the copyright—but that has been provided under a broad inbound license. Each of these inbound cases is sufficient to clear the rights to license out to the recipient—meaning the outbound rights. As long as the outbound rights are less than or equal to the inbound rights, the licensing works.

### Potential Diligence Issues

Problems with clearance of rights can come in many forms, but the most common are license restrictions and license conditions. License restrictions only occur in proprietary licensing; license conditions are more commonly an issue in open source software licensing.

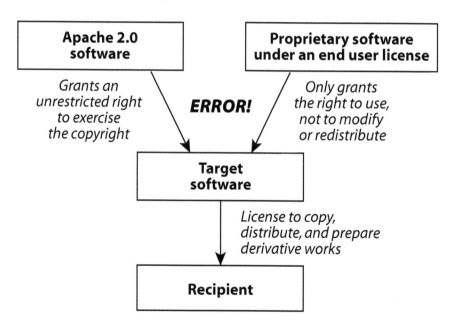

**Figure 4.2** License restriction problems

Figure 4.2 depicts the quintessential diligence problem in proprietary licensing. The scope of the inbound license for the proprietary software is narrower than that of the outbound grant; some of the rights granted out are not granted coming in. Of course, this problem can't happen for open source software components because the open source definition requires that there be no restrictions on the license grant. However, open source licenses can impose conditions that create diligence problems, as Figure 4.3 shows.

In Figure 4.3, the software code base includes a component whose inbound license is covered by GPL. Because GPL is a copyleft license, the copyleft license conditions must be followed when redistributing the software. But here, there has been a mistake; those conditions have not been flowed down to the recipient. This is the quintessential open source diligence problem. Another way to say this is that GPL as an inbound license is not compatible with Apache as an outbound license.

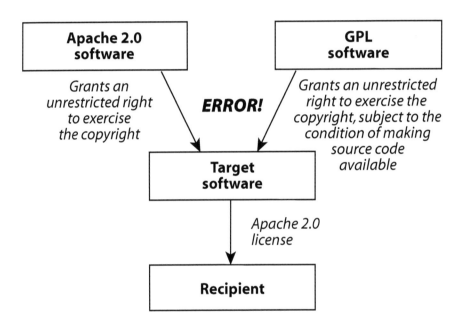

**Figure 4.3** License condition problems

In open source software, conflicts of conditions create many diligence problems. A company that has developed the target code in the figure above would have to change its outbound license to GPL to solve the problem. To create software whose licensing works correctly, we need to use only inbound licenses that are compatible with the outbound license. Accordingly, only inbound licenses with fewer and consistent conditions should be used, as compared with the outbound license. When those in the open source world talk about compatibility, this is what they mean.

In the example in Figure 4.4, many licenses that are compatible with GPL 3 can govern this project. The basic rule is that the outbound license must be the one with the most conditions.

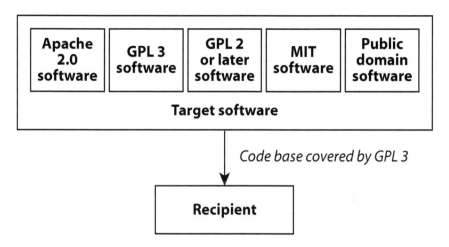

**Figure 4.4** License compatibility

However, components governed by licenses such as AGPL (which has more conditions), Eclipse Public License, or CDDL (which all have different copyleft conditions) could not be included in this software. All of these copyleft licenses are like the guests at the awkward dinner party—their diets are mutually exclusive. This is because all of them exclude placing additional licensing restrictions on the software. Also, because each of them contains slightly different terms, each consists of additional restrictions vis-à-vis the others. For example, Section 6 of GPL 2 says:

> Each time you redistribute the Program (or any work based on the Program), the recipient automatically receives a license from the original licensor to copy, distribute or modify the Program subject to these terms and conditions. You may not impose any further restrictions on the recipients' exercise of the rights granted herein.

A few copyleft licenses are compatible. For example, LGPL code can be redistributed under the corresponding version of GPL because LGPL is merely a set of additional permissions that allow certain kinds of integration with non-GPL software. In the version 3 licenses, this is more obvious, as LGPL 3 is drafted as a set of additional terms to GPL 3; for the version 2 counterparts, Section 3 of LGPL 2.1 contains a specific provision allowing this:

> You may opt to apply the terms of the ordinary GNU General Public License instead of this License to a given copy of the Library. ...

> Once this change is made in a given copy, it is irreversible for that copy, so the ordinary GNU General Public License applies to all subsequent copies and derivative works made from that copy. This option is useful when you wish to copy part of the code of the Library into a program that is not a library.[1]

The above discussion has to do with what I think of as vertical compatibility—given an inbound license, can the software covered by it be redistributed in a code base covered overall by another outbound license? But keep in mind that open source licensing is not a sublicensing regime. The inbound license terms do not change; they are actually passed through directly to all recipients. However, in open source, all of the rights of copyright are granted, so there cannot be any discrepancy between the licenses granted; the only difference is the conditions imposed on exercise of the license. Therefore, as long as the conditions of the inbound license and the outbound license are not mutually exclusive, there is no compatibility problem.

### *"Horizontal" Compatibility Issues*

However, there is a more subtle issue that I think of as horizontal compatibility, and that issue only arises under GPL and LGPL, because those are the only licenses that place limitations on how code can be integrated. There will be more details in Chapters 8 and 9 on GPL and LGPL compliance, but for now, the shorthand rules are as follows:

- If any code in a program is GPL, it must all be provided under GPL.
- LGPL code can be integrated into a program with other code only as a dynamically linked library.

Figure 4.5 shows the problem that can arise from a horizontal incompatibility. In this case, the program contains code covered by inbound terms under various licenses. But the code under the copyleft licenses cannot be redistributed under any other terms, so there is no one license that will work.[2] This is like the dinner table where no one meal will satisfy anyone. The GPL is the diner who not only will not eat the same meal as the others but also will not tolerate the presence of other meals as the same table.[3]

---

[1] opensource.org/licenses/lgpl-license.php.

[2] For discussion of the actual or theoretical incompatibility between Apache 2.0 and GPL 2.0, see below in this chapter.

[3] The same is true for many proprietary licenses as well, of course.

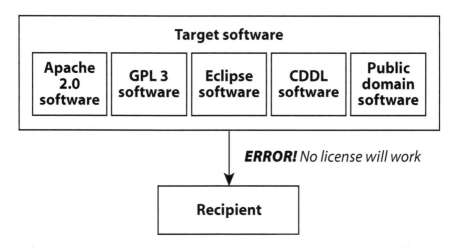

**Figure 4.5** Problem due to horizontal incompatibility

In contrast, software provided under weak copyleft licenses can often coexist in the same program, and of course, permissive licenses place no restrictions on other code. So, the situation shown in Figure 4.6 works.

Because all the licenses shown in Figure 4.6 are copyleft, but weak copyleft, the licensing to the recipient can be achieved by passing through the licensing terms simultaneously. Each component will be governed by its own license, and the code base as a whole has no one license. This is like the dinner table where each visitor eats his own meal, and while the visitors do not share, they can sit at the same table.

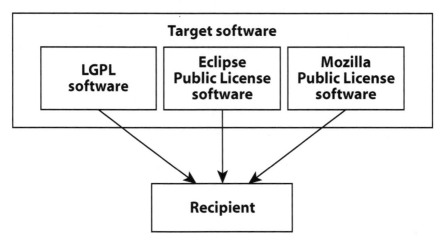

**Figure 4.6** Horizontal compatibility

### How to Avoid License Bugs

All of the above scenarios view diligence from the point of view of a company that is trying to create a software product using components of open source software that are licensed by third parties. In such a case, the developer mostly needs to take the inbound licensing as a given. However, some developers will have the option of releasing their own software under a license not dictated by inbound licensing concerns. (For more discussion of this option, see Chapter 16: Open Source Releases.) The above discussion shows one aspect of why this option is so important. A developer can license his software under whatever terms he likes, but if he makes certain choices—like choosing GPL for a library that must be included in the same program with proprietary or other copyleft components, he may create a situation where other developers cannot reuse the software in other projects. Sometimes, taking this option is a way to force users to buy proprietary licenses, as in a dual licensing model. In such cases, the developer is purposely creating a license bug and a path to resolve it. But if such a choice is made without clear thought, the licensing could backfire and merely create problems.

## Apache 2 and GPL 2

It was noted above that Apache 2 and GPL 2 may be incompatible. On its face, this may seem hard to explain. Permissive licenses are generally compatible with any other open source license. However, after Apache 2 was released, the FSF took the position that Apache 2.0 was incompatible with GPL 2. Information about this difference of opinion—between open source organizations with very different philosophies—is a bit hard to come by. But Apache Foundation posted the following about it:

> After spending a couple hours on the phone with the FSF, we have a better understanding of the particular interpretation of the GPL that might lead one to construe the following: granting an explicit patent license causes any implicit patent licenses to be null and void; revoking that explicit patent license causes the person who is claiming infringement of their patent to lose the patent rights that would otherwise have been attained via the GPL's implicit rights; loss of patent rights means loss of right to use; GPL section 7 allows a patent owner to claim infringement of a patent within a GPL'd work and continue to distribute that work as GPL up until a third party imposes a restriction on the rights of others to distribute (i.e., until a judgment or injunction is placed on the work).

GPL section 6 saying "You may not impose any further restrictions on the recipients' exercise of the rights granted herein" does not apply to patents because the "rights granted herein" are only copyright.[4]

This is our current understanding of the position held by the FSF; whether or not our understanding is correct has not yet been confirmed.

Note that this is contrary to our previously stated belief that the GPL does forbid the continuing use of a GPL'd work by an entity that has claimed the work contains infringement of their own patented technology. Apparently, it is okay for the distribution and use to continue up until a judgment or injunction has been issued because the FSF does not believe a claim of patent infringement amounts to a restriction on the rights of others to redistribute, and the constraint on further restriction applies only to those rights listed within the GPL itself (copyright).

Apache has stated that it "considers this issue to be in legal limbo, at least until we get a definitive answer regarding the survivability of implied patent licenses."[5]

The FSF's position on express patent licenses' taking away implicit licenses—as least as characterized above—is not a foregone conclusion under law; the position is probably advocacy as opposed to objective legal analysis. The issue of patent license termination is more interesting, in light of the so-called "liberty or death" provision in Section 7 of the GPL:

> If, as a consequence of a court judgment or allegation of patent infringement or for any other reason (not limited to patent issues), conditions are imposed on you (whether by court order, agreement or otherwise) that contradict the conditions of this License, they do not excuse you from the conditions of this License. If you cannot distribute so as to satisfy simultaneously your obligations under this License and any other pertinent obligations, then as a consequence you may not distribute the Program at all.

The Apache Foundation points out[6] that even if we accept the FSF's reasoning, an additional restriction will only arise if there actually are patents covering

---

[4] The same is true for many proprietary licenses as well, of course.

[5] people.apache.org/~slive/site/xdocs/licenses/GPL-compatibility.xml.

[6] people.apache.org/~slive/site/xdocs/licenses/GPL-compatibility.xml.

the work that would otherwise be licensed. The Apache Foundation, which is the licensor of a great deal of code under the Apache 2 license, owns no patents,[7] and it is likely that many licensors who release code under Apache 2 are in the same position; most companies that release code under Apache 2 do not choose to do so for code covered by patents the company values.

Note that GPL 3 is understood by FSF to be compatible with Apache 2.0.[8]

## License Proliferation

No discussion of license diligence would be complete without a discussion of *license proliferation*. It is a divisive subject: standardization of license terms unarguably makes the diligence process easier; however, those arguing against proliferation often commit the logical fallacy of equating choice with fiat, assuming that uniformity of licensing terms should turn on their own choice. Those who consider their licenses the best choice for everyone have the right to their opinion, of course, but they do not have the right to choose for other authors, who have the right to choose their own terms.

Anyone who complains about proliferation in open source licensing has probably not spent much time doing diligence on proprietary licenses. Proprietary licenses have a dizzying array of license restrictions—as opposed to licensing conditions—that make diligence expensive and time-consuming. An entire industry of license management and software deployment tools exists to help enterprises comply with proprietary license restrictions. Open source may have over 60 licenses, but proprietary licenses exist in an infinite variety.

Others who take a more nuanced view are not so much against new open source licenses as against new licenses that are difficult to understand. Sadly, many open source licenses are so badly drafted that they are maddeningly difficult to understand, and although proprietary licenses can also be badly written, they tend to get updated and improved over time as they expire and are renegotiated. But open source licenses are forever.

Regardless of your opinion on license proliferation, if you are releasing open source software, you should resist the urge to write a new open source license. Doing so is very unpopular and, especially for copyleft licenses, very challenging. Most companies releasing open source code find that one of the existing licenses works for them (at least moderately well) and that the faults of the existing licenses are outweighed by the goodwill engendered by easing the task of review for those recipients expected to embrace the software.

---

[7] people.apache.org/~slive/site/xdocs/licenses/GPL-compatibility.xml.

[8] gplv3.fsf.org/rationale/.

# Chapter 5

# Conditional Licensing

Open source licenses are conditional licenses. This concept is one of the most difficult for open source novices to grasp, and an insistence on the importance of grasping it is not just pedantry. The opacity of this concept underlines a serious misconception about open source licensing. Like the shadows of Plato's cave, misconceptions about conditional licenses cause far more fear than actual danger. Some people refer to the GPL as "viral," and use of this word is not mere political incorrectness or rhetoric; it exaggerates the risks attendant on using open source software. Eradicating the word *viral* from discussions of open source licensing is long overdue because this word has skewed and limited understanding of open source licensing principles.[1]

## *It's Not a Virus, It's a Bug*

The single most frequent question I hear from clients about GPL is "How can we keep it from contaminating our proprietary code?" The answer is easy: it can't contaminate your proprietary code. There is simply no plausible legal argument as to how it could do that. But in this chapter, we will examine the question in detail, why the misconception persists, and why the conditional licensing model limits the worst-case scenario for GPL violations.

As we know, it is possible to violate GPL by integrating GPL code with proprietary code and distributing that combined code under terms other than GPL. Developers, with visions of viruses dancing in their heads, worry that if GPL and proprietary code are combined into a single program, the GPL licensing terms will "infect" the proprietary code and the proprietary code will be automatically licensed under GPL. The developers then worry that they will be obligated to provide the source code to their own proprietary code.

---

[1] I have heard several stories about how this word began to be associated with free software in general or the GPL in particular, but I can't verify them, so I won't repeat them here.

For most proprietary code developers, this is simply not an option. Not only would doing this violate their fiduciary duty to their shareholders by devaluing their proprietary code, but it would probably make them violate third-party licenses. A company's proprietary product usually contains third-party software that is sublicensed under proprietary terms. The company therefore has no right to convert that product to GPL, even if it wanted to.

But "infection" is not how copyleft works. In fact, if a developer were to combine GPL and proprietary code in a way that violated GPL, then the result would be that GPL had been violated—no more, no less. (And if the developer combined third-party GPL code with third-party proprietary code, then both inbound licenses would have probably been violated.) What that means, legally, is that the author of the GPL code may have remedies for violation of GPL and, if the license is terminated as a result, remedies for unlicensed use of the GPL software. Both possibilities, essentially, are copyright infringement claims. The legal remedies for a copyright infringement claim are damages (money) and injunction (stop using the GPL code).

In fact, there is simply no legal mechanism for GPL changing the licensing terms for other code. For software to be licensed under a particular set of terms, the author has to take some action that reasonably leads a licensee to conclude that the licensor has chosen to offer the code under those terms. In contrast, combining proprietary and GPL code in a single program in violation of GPL is a license incompatibility—meaning the two sets of terms conflict and cannot be satisfied simultaneously. The better analogy for this kind of licensing incompatibility is a software bug, rather than a software virus.

## What Is a Conditional License?

The GPL and almost all other open source licenses grant a copyright license simultaneously to all who wish to take the code under that license. But that license is conditioned on complying with some requirements. Those requirements range from a license notice (for permissive licenses) to copyleft conditions (making source code available, for copyleft licenses). If those conditions are violated, the license terminates.

One reason for the struggle with this idea is that conditional licenses are not very common other than in the landscape of open source. The closest familiar analog for lawyers is probably a unilateral contract. Every law school contracts class starts with this hypothetical: "If you cross the bridge, I will give you $10." When you cross the bridge, the $10 is due. But open source licensing is the opposite. Instead of saying, "Perform this task and I will reward you," it says, "Enjoy this boon until you misbehave." Legally, these are different.

## License or Contract?

You may hear open source advocates say that an open source license is "not a contract." A better analysis is that open source licenses are not necessarily contracts, but this is not the same as saying they are never contracts. To pose the question—License or contract?—oversimplifies the issue. But first, let's understand the distinction between a contract and a conditional license.

A *contract* is a set of promises. Under the law, a contract is formed when there is an offer, an acceptance, and consideration. Consideration is something of value exchanged for a promise. The law will not recognize and enforce a contract unless each party has promised something. (Otherwise, the arrangement is called a *gift*.) The law does not require the bargain to be fair or even,[2] only to be what the parties intended. One form of consideration is forbearance—doing something the party would otherwise have the right to do.[3]

License contracts therefore always involve forbearance because a license is a promise not to sue for intellectual property infringement. The licensor promises not to sue, and the licensee promises something in return, such as the payment of a license fee. Most intellectual property lawyers are accustomed to this model. But open source licenses are subtly different.

In an open source license, there is no consideration per se given by the licensee. Instead, there are conditions for exercising the license. So long as the licensee abides by these conditions, the licensee can continue to exercise the license. If the licensee breaches the conditions, the license disappears, and the licensor is free to sue for infringement.

The difference between a conditional license and a contract is subtle but important. In a contract, each party makes a promise, and if a party breaks the promise, a court can order him to fulfill it. In truth, courts almost never order people to actually fulfill contracts. If someone breaches a contract, the court orders the breaching party to pay damages. In fact, the law almost never supports anything else. Ordering a party to actually perform is called *specific performance*. This is an extraordinary remedy that is only supported in limited circumstances, such as sales of real property. For the most part, breach of contract is considered a purely commercial harm, and accordingly, the only remedy is money. This notion is important, and it actually speaks to a basic premise of political freedom in a common law country. For a civil wrong (as opposed to a criminal one), the pun-

---

[2] In law, consideration is sometimes referred to as a "peppercorn"—in other words, it doesn't matter whether the thing given is of value, so a peppercorn will be enough. Like many legal terms, *peppercorn* has long outlived its original sense. At the time the term was coined, pepper was an expensive, imported luxury. See Restatement (Second) Contracts Section 79.

[3] Such as paying someone for not smoking. See Restatement (Second) Contracts Section 71.

ishment is payment of money or an order to stop doing something. It is an important tenet of our political freedom that courts cannot order us to take positive action except in extraordinary cases.[4]

In a conditional license, the licensee makes no promises to do anything. In fact, an open source license grants you rights whether you intend exercise them or not. I, you, and everyone else are licensed under GPL the moment the licensor releases the code under that license. However, actually exercising that license has conditions: the licensee must abide by the conditions of the license or the license will be lost. As GPL 2 Section 5 says:

> You are not required to accept this License, since you have not signed it. However, nothing else grants you permission to modify or distribute the Program or its derivative works. These actions are prohibited by law if you do not accept this License. Therefore, by modifying or distributing the Program (or any work based on the Program), you indicate your acceptance of this License to do so, and all its terms and conditions for copying, distributing or modifying the Program or works based on it.

But in truth, this is not an attempt to form a contract so much as to explain that the licensee must either abide by the terms or forego the license.

If this view seems tortured, perhaps it is. The "license not contract" position was pioneered alongside GPL 2 during the 1990s. In the early years of that decade, the law about online contract formation was still unsettled. Traditionally, entering into contracts involved a written signature—this was the means of expressing acceptance of the contract's terms. But as the software industry grew, software developers sought to establish the terms of license agreements without the need for paper documents and signatures. The use of "shrink-wrap" or click-to-accept licenses was in common practice by the 1990s, but the efficacy of these methods to form a contract had still not been confirmed by the courts. Then in 1996, a landmark opinion was issued upholding the enforceability of these unsigned agreements.[5] But forming a contract in this way still required the licensor to leap some hurdles, such as implementing an installer or downloader that forced an "I accept" action from the licensee. Open source software is often passed from one recipient to the next without any such technical mechanisms, so the license terms need to have legal traction without the need to form a contract. The conditional

---

[4] In criminal law, courts can imprison or take other actions to curtail personal liberty, but that is different because criminal law seeks to redress harm to society rather than to individuals. It therefore has remedies that are not available in civil law.

[5] *ProCD v. Zeidenberg*, 86 F.3d 1447 (7th Cir. 1996).

license model worked well for this because it drew its power from copyright law, which gave the licensor the power to exclude certain uses of the software regardless of where, when, or how the licensee used it and regardless of the identity of the licensee and the means by which the licensee received the software.

## Implications of the Conditional Licensing Model

The conditional licensing model has two main implications. First, this model offers different remedies from those available under a contract model. Second, the conditional licensing model does not create privity between redistributors and their recipients and therefore places the rights and duties of enforcement on the original author of the software.

### Remedies

The remedies for copyright infringement and breach of contract are quite different. In the United States, the damages for copyright infringement are "the actual damages suffered ... as a result of the infringement, and any profits of the infringer. In establishing the infringer's profits, the copyright owner is required to present proof only of the infringer's gross revenue, and the infringer is required to prove his or her deductible expenses and the elements of profit attributable to factors other than the copyrighted work."[6] The copyright plaintiff can also choose, as an alternative, "statutory damages" of $750 to $30,000 per copyrightable work, "as the court considers just." These damages can be enhanced to $150,000 if the plaintiff proves the infringement is willfully committed. Statutory damages are only available if the work has been registered with the copyright office on a timely basis.

Contract law, in contrast, allows the aggrieved party to seek compensatory damages only.[7] These damages are focused on economic harm and do not include compensation for emotional damages and pain and suffering (which are tort law concepts). If you breach a contract, you might expect to pay expectation damages (profit the other party expected to receive from the contract), consequential damages (lost business or reputation caused by the breach), or restitution (an equitable calculation to avoid unjust enrichment of the breaching party).

Copyright also offers injunction as a remedy. An injunction is an order by the court to cease the infringement. When an injunction is available, as under copyright law, courts use a test with four factors: (1) the likelihood of the plaintiff's success on the merits; (2) irreparable harm in the absence of an injunction (i.e.,

---

[6] 17 USC 504.

[7] Punitive damages are extremely rare in contract law.

the harm cannot adequately be compensated later by money damages); (3) the balance of hardships between the plaintiff and the defendant; and (4) the public interest.[8] In a contract claim, an injunction is an extraordinary remedy that is seldom available.

As you can see, the money damages for copyright violation are at least as broad as those for breach of contract, and copyright adds the possibility of statutory damages and injunction. This is key in open source licensing, where the economic harm may be difficult to prove. Open source licensors give their software away royalty-free, so the harm to the licensor accrues from violation of the conditions, which are primarily notices and the requirement to make source code available. It may be hard to place an economic value on the harm to the licensor for failure to meet these conditions, and copyright law allows the licensor to elect other remedies. Therefore, foregoing the possibility of contract damages is no real loss to the licensor.

The virus model rests on the assumption that specific performance will be available as a contract remedy. For this to happen for an open source license, a contract would need to have been formed, the conditions of source code delivery would need to be interpreted as contractual obligations of the licensee, and most importantly, a court would need to order specific performance of those obligations. But as you can see from the above analysis, this should never happen. No licensee under a copyleft license would be ordered to lay open source code. This kind of specific performance is just not supported by the law. And copyright offers no such remedy at all. So there is no likely basis for such a remedy for breach of an open source license.

## Privity

The second corollary to the conditional licensing model is that the licensor—or copyright owner—will always be the one to enforce the license conditions. This leads to a somewhat counterintuitive paradigm. If someone takes GPL code, modifies it, and refuses to provide the modified source code to a binary recipient, the recipient has no legal claim. Instead, it is the licensor of the GPL code who has the right to pursue a claim.

In the United States, only copyright owners or exclusive licensees have standing to sue for copyright infringement.[9] The conditional licensing paradigm en-

---

[8] See, e.g., *Metro-Goldwyn Mayer, Inc. v. 007 Safety Products, Inc.*, 183 F.3d 10, 15 n.2 (1st Cir. 1999).

[9] 17 USC Section 501(b) says, "The legal or beneficial owner of an exclusive right under a copyright is entitled … to institute an action for any infringement of that particular right committed while he or she is the owner of it." Courts have held this statement to be exclusive under the doctrine of *expressio unius est exclusio alterius*. See, for example, *Silvers v. Sony Pictures Entertainment, Inc.*, 402 F.3d 881 (9th Cir. 2005) (en banc).

ables the licensor to pursue enforcement without identifying licensees in advance. If open source licenses were enforced as contracts, then the copyright holder might need cooperation from the distribution channel to pursue enforcement. Any contract would have been formed between the recipient and the distributor, not the original licensor. Redistributors may have little incentive to enforce license conditions or may selectively do so for commercial gain, so the conditional licensing model also serves to empower the open source author more than the contract model might do.

The analysis above is enough to help you understand the virus fallacy and what you need to know about conditional licensing. The remainder of this chapter contains some more detailed legal analysis, for those interested in the finer points of law surrounding this issue.

## *Contract Formation*

As outlined above, most GPL licensors would refer to cast violations as copyright infringements rather than breaches of contract. But those who say that open source licenses are categorically "not contracts" are probably wrong. Quite the opposite—in many cases, it might be easy to prove that a contract has been formed, but between whom and how might be complicated to prove.

If one sought to establish that a contract had been formed, then there is plenty to support that view. The express terms of most open source licenses suggest that the document is a contract. Most of them contain UCC warranty disclaimers[10] which only apply to sales-of-goods contracts governed by Article 2 of the UCC. GPL 2 Section 5's statement "You indicate your acceptance of this License," if true, forms a contract, assuming that there has already been an offer and consideration. But most important, the circumstances surrounding acceptance of the terms may often be sufficient to support contract formation.[11] It's obvious that there has been an offer if the software is available for download. The consideration is also sufficient—the licensor has offered to forego infringement suits, and the licensee must comply with the conditions. The only challenging plank of formation is acceptance, and the UCC provides that acceptance can be indicated by "including conduct by both parties which recognizes the existence of such a contract." Such conduct is also likely to be easy to prove.

---

[10] For instance, GPL 2 Section 11.

[11] See UCC Article 2, Section 1-204.

### Incentives for Formation Arguments

The obvious question, then, is that if it is so easy to show acceptance via conduct, why was there so much Sturm und Drang leading up to the *ProCD* case. It's important to keep in mind that the scope of open source licenses is quite different from that of EULAs. Accordingly, recipients of proprietary and open source software have very different incentives to avoid license terms.

A person who lawfully possesses a copy of software has the right to create backup copies (under 17 USC Section 1117(a)(2)) and transitory copies as necessary to run the software (under 17 USC 1117(a)(1)). In addition, under background law, someone who purchases a copy of software can invoke the first sale doctrine (17 USC Section 109), create copies as necessary to reverse engineer the software (in some limited circumstances where that use is a fair use),[12] and enjoy certain implied warranties under UCC Section 2-316. However, all this can be altered by contract. So an end user has incentives to avoid the formation of a license contract.

If you read a typical end user license, you will find many or most of these activities are "permitted." Of course, they need not be permitted because the copyright law says they are not violations of copyright in the first place. Remember that a license is no more than the promise not to sue for intellectual property infringement. Most end user licenses prohibit reverse engineering, disclaim liability of the licensor, and limit the warranties enjoyed by the licensee. Therefore, an end user will be in a worse position if he accepts the contract.

But those who want to exercise rights that go beyond mere use are in a different position. There is no background right to distribute or modify software. So, if a recipient of software wants to enjoy these rights, he must receive a license. This is why the formation wars have not materialized for open source, the way they did for EULAs in the 1990s. As we have seen, the licensor has little need for contract claims and the licensee needs the license.

However, it would be unwise to assume that contract remedies are never available under open source licensees. In fact, lawsuits for violations of open source licenses are often brought—rightly or wrongly—as contract claims.[13]

Of course, asking whether the GPL is a license or a contract assumes it must be one or the other. Clearly, it is a license, but it may or may not be a contract. A written document is not a contract by itself; the document may contain the terms of a contract, but a contract is formed by actions. Whether one signs on the dotted line, clicks "I accept," or downloads software, a contract is formed with

---

[12] *Sega v. Accolade*, 977 F.2d 1510 (9th Cir. 1992).

[13] See *Progress Software Corp. v. MySQL AB*, 195 F. Supp. 2d 328 (D. Mass. 2002); and *MontaVista Software, Inc. v. Lineo, Inc.*, No. 2:02 CV-0309J (D. Utah filed July 23, 2002).

offer, acceptance, and consideration—and open source licensing does not change that.

## Eradicating the Virus

I have long been on alert to find any formal legal underpinnings for the virus model. The only ones I have found are *Pickett v. Prince*, 207 F. 3d 402 (7th Cir. 2000) and *Anderson v. Stallone*, 11 USPQ2D 1161 (C.D. Cal. 1989). Both of these cases discuss the principle that an unauthorized derivative work is not entitled to copyright protection.

But these cases both involve very different facts from those of the typical GPL compliance problem. First, in each of these cases, the infringing derivative work probably did not meet a threshold level of creativity necessary for legal protection. The law sets this threshold very low. Any proprietary code with any commercial value would easily meet this threshold. Second, in each of these cases, the putative owner of the infringing derivative work was trying to sue the author of the infringed underlying work—something that requires a fair amount of good old-fashioned chutzpah. These facts cannot reasonably be extrapolated to the situation where the developer of a proprietary software module, which has been inappropriately combined with a GPL software module, tries to enforce its rights in the proprietary code standing alone, against a third party. The analog would be where a proprietary developer takes a blob of GPL code, changes one line of it, and then sues the GPL author for copyright infringement—which would be nonsense.

Finally, these cases, even if they stood for the principle that an unauthorized derivative work is not entitled to copyright protection, would indicate that the proprietary work would be in the public domain, rather than subject to GPL. That is a very scary result indeed—which fortunately is simply not supported by law.

Chapter 6

# What Is Distribution?[1]

The conditions of open source licenses—requirements to deliver notices, make source code available, or relicense on the same terms—are triggered by distribution. For almost all open source licenses, if you don't redistribute the software, you need not meet any conditions to exercise the license. But what is distribution? Twenty years ago, the answer to this question was easy, but it gets more difficult every year.

## An American Term of Art

The GPL is in essence a conditional copyright license, and it has no choice-of-law provision. Therefore, theoretically, only an action regulated by the applicable copyright law can trigger application of its copyleft conditions. In the United States, the core commercial right of copyright is called distribution or publication. Therefore, in the United States, the question of what triggers copyleft conditions is identical to the question of what constitutes distribution under copyright law.

GPL 3, which was released in 2007, attempted to internationalize the license to fit with local variations on this concept, by using neutral words such as "propagate" and "convey." Unlike its successor, GPL 2 specifically named distribution as the trigger for copyleft requirements. GPL 2 remains in wide use—and it particularly is the license applicable to the Linux kernel—so the question of what constitutes distribution under GPL 2 is still alive and well in the open source world.

Distribution, though one of the enumerated rights of copyright under US law, is not defined in the Copyright Act (Title 17 of the United States Code). Title 17 grants a copyright owner the exclusive right to "distribute copies ... of the copyrighted work to the public by sale or other transfer of ownership, or by rental, lease, or lending."[2] The Act states that "offering to distribute copies ... to

---

[1] An earlier version of this chapter appears in "The Gift that Keeps on Giving: Distribution and Copyleft in Open Source Software Licenses," *IFOSSLR* Volume 4, Issue 1 (March 2012). It originally appeared online at **www.ifosslr.org**.

[2] 17 U.S.C. Section 106(3).

a group of persons for purposes of further distribution, public performance, or public display, constitutes publication."[3] But this does not define *distribution*. Where a statute's terms are ambiguous on their face, the rules of statutory interpretation allow us to look to the statute's legislative history. The 1976 House Report[4] also does not define *distribution* but defines *publication* in the negative by saying, "[A]ny form of dissemination in which a material object does not change hands—performances or displays on television, for example—is not publication."[5] Later case law equated distribution with publication.[6]

Section 106(3) of the Copyright Act accords to the copyright owner the exclusive right "to distribute copies or phonorecords of the copyrighted work to the public by sale or other transfer of ownership, or by rental, lease, or lending." Put differently, the copyright owner has the exclusive right to publicly sell, give away, rent, or lend any material embodiment of his work.[7] As the legislative history of this section shows, the definition of *distribution* is "virtually identical with that in the definition of *publication* in section 101."[8] Thus, in essence, exclusive right of distribution is a right to control the work's publication.

### Determining When Distribution Has Occurred

In the United States, therefore, *distribution* means providing a tangible copy to another person. The question of what constitutes distribution therefore devolves to two questions: What is *a tangible copy*, and what is *another person*?

The transfer of the work must be made "to the public" to trigger the definition of distribution under the Copyright Act. In the absence of a statutory definition of the phrase *to the public*, courts have held that a "limited" distribution that "communicates the contents of a manuscript to a definitely selected group and for a limited purpose, and without the right of diffusion, reproduction, distribution or sale," is not distribution to the public.[9]

---

[3] 17 U.S.C. Section 101.

[4] H.R. Rep. No. 94-1476.

[5] *See* House Report at 138, reprinted in 1976 U.S.C.C.A.N. 5754.

[6] *Harper & Row Publs., Inc. v. Nation Enters.*, 471 U.S. 539, 552 (1985).

[7] *National Car Rental Sys., Inc. v. Computer Assocs. Int'l, Inc.*, 991 F.2d 426, 430 (8th Cir. 1993).

[8] Reg. Supp. Rep., p. 19.

[9] *White v. Kimmell*, 94 F. Supp. 502, 505 (S.D. Cal. 1950); *Data Cash Sys., Inc. v. JS&A Group, Inc.*, 628 F.2d 1038, 1042-43 (7th Cir. 1980) (concluding that "a 'limited publication' is really in the eyes of the law no publication at all"); *John G. Danielson, Inc. v. Winchester-Conant Props., Inc.*, 322 F.3d 26, 36 (1st Cir. 2003); *Brown v. Tabb*, 714 F.2d 1088, 1091 (11th Cir. 1983); *William A. Graham Co. v. Haughey*, 430 F. Supp. 2d 458, 470 (E.D. Pa. 2006); *Milton H. Greene Archives, Inc. v. BPI Commc'ns, Inc.*, 378 F. Supp. 2d 1189, 1198 (C.D. Cal. 2005); *Penguin Books U.S.A., Inc. v. New Christian Church of Full Endeavor, Ltd.*, 288 F. Supp. 2d 544, 555 (S.D.N.Y. 2003).

In other words, a distribution is a "general" publication if it is not made (1) to a limited group, (2) for a limited purpose, and (3) "without the right of diffusion, reproduction, distribution or sale." The legislative history of the Copyright Act makes it clear that, "when copies or phonorecords are offered to a group of wholesalers, broadcasters, motion picture theaters, etc., publication takes place if the purpose is further distribution, public performance, or public display."[10] Thus, even if the work is distributed to a single person or entity, the publication would be general if the recipient is free to diffuse, reproduce, distribute, or sell copies of the work.

In the contemporary world of information technology, many activities stray close enough to the transfer of a copy to challenge the boundaries of this definition of distribution. It is these activities that make the question of what is distribution under GPL of such great interest to companies implementing day-to-day strategies for GPL compliance.

Starting at the baseline, the most obvious business case is that of a distributed product. Whether the product is software alone or a hardware product as well, businesspeople understand what it means to sell a product and for it to change hands. Companies trying to comply with open source licenses like GPL 2 therefore have more difficulty assessing activities that they do not consider to be the business case of commercial distribution but that may nevertheless constitute distribution under the law. This chapter discusses those other business cases, from the clearest to the murkiest, as a matter of law.

## *A Clear Case in the Clouds*

Companies often wonder whether software transmissions or remote use—sometimes called the ASP or SAAS model, or cloud computing—constitute distribution.

While this is one of the most controversial aspects of free software licensing, it is not a difficult interpretation question under US law for GPL 2. Advocates of free software have long recognized that if the trigger for copyleft requirements is distribution, increasingly popular cloud computing models will circumvent those requirements. This is sometimes referred to as the "ASP loophole."[11]

During the drafting of GPL version 3, this issue engendered significant controversy. At one point, a variation on GPL 3 was proposed to allow the author to select an option that would cause online use to trigger copyleft requirements. Ulti-

---

[10]   H.R. Rep. No. 94-1476, at 138 (1976).

[11]   The term is often attributed to Richard Stallman, but that may not be accurate. See the April 3, 2007, interview with Mr. Stallman in *Groklaw*, in which he says the term is misleading: **www.groklaw.net/articlebasic.php?story=20070403114157109**.

mately, this variation was removed from GPL 3 and memorialized in an alternative form of the license known as the "Affero GPL." The basic form of GPL 3 makes it clear that ASP or SAAS use does not trigger copyleft requirements. In GPL 3, copyleft is triggered by *conveying* rather than by distribution, and "[t]o 'convey' a work means any kind of propagation that enables other parties to make or receive copies. Mere interaction with a user through a computer network, with no transfer of a copy, is not conveying."[12]

Under US law, distribution requires actual transfer of a copy, in whatever form. Therefore, under US law, SAAS use—which involves accessing software without transfer of a local copy to the user—does not trigger copyleft requirements under GPL.[13]

## The Edge Cases

Leaving aside the two relatively clear business cases of a distributed product (which clearly constitutes distribution) and pure SAAS deployment (which does not), we turn to some of the edge cases that also are common business activities but do not fall so neatly on one side of the distribution coin or the other.

- **Employees.** While companies often worry about this case, it is not a difficult one. Clients often ask whether "internal distribution" within a corporation triggers copyleft requirements. However, under law, there is no such thing as internal distribution because corporations and their employees are considered a single legal person. Therefore, one employee's providing a copy of software to another employee of the same company in the course of performing their duties as employees is clearly not distribution; while it may be a transfer of a copy, it is not a transfer to another person. Free software advocates sometimes refer to this as providing *private copies*.

- **Independent contractors—individuals.** Companies often engage individuals as independent contractors rather than as employees. Emerging growth companies, in particular, do this to avoid the regulatory overhead costs (such as employment taxes) associated with hiring employees. The function of a contractor in such cases is nearly identical to that of an

---

[12] GPL 3, Section 0, "Definitions," **www.gnu.org/copyleft/gpl.html**.

[13] It is worth considering that even in SAAS implementations, some components may be distributed. Today, most SAAS is accomplished only via a browser, so client software is no longer a common requirement to use SAAS. However, there are always exceptions, mostly notably JavaScript or mobile applications. Keep in mind that these are usually clearly distributed and would be subject to copyleft requirements.

employee; however, because a contractor is not an employee, providing a copy of software to a contractor could be considered distribution. This is one of the thornier areas of GPL 2 interpretation, and it is discussed in more detail below.

- **Independent contractors—consulting firms.** Companies often hire small consulting firms to develop, test, or support software. These consultant entities often consist of a few persons working in a team, but their functional relationship to the company is similar to that of an individual consultant or an employee. Individuals in small consulting firms are not, legally speaking, employees of the company, and therefore, providing a copy to them is probably distribution. However, there may be arguments that the copies are not intended for public availability and that, thus, transferring them is not publication and therefore not distribution. This argument has risks, but it is probably supportable under law, particularly if buttressed by a written consulting agreement that recites the parties' intentions. This business case is very similar, in a legal sense, to the engagement of an individual contractor.

- **Independent contractors—outsourcing.** Larger companies often outsource entire business areas such as software development or software support. Outsourcers are clearly separate companies, rather than employees, and therefore, providing a copy to them is clearly providing a copy to a person other than the company. However, some outsourcing companies provide "leased" staff to work on servers and equipment owned or controlled by their customers. In this case, IT companies may reasonably make arguments that copies made available to those persons have not been transferred outside the companies' control. This argument may be less successful, however, for outsourcers who are outside the United States—as most are. The international divide may make it unclear which body of law will determine what is distribution under GPL.

- **Cloud providers.** With the rise of cloud-based computing services such as Amazon Web Services, companies worry about whether uploading software to a cloud service is distribution. Although the question is subject to some debate, the answer is probably not. Although technically this involves the transfer of a copy to the cloud service provider, the virtual space in which the copy resides is under the control of the company user; cloud services agreements generally do not provide the cloud service provider with any control over the information stored in a cloud account. Any transfer of a copy, then, is not "general" under copyright law.

- **Subsidiaries and affiliates.** Companies often create affiliate structures to conduct business for various strategic reasons such as tax planning, the need to do business in other countries through local entities, or creating entities to engage in a particular line of business. For example, a company may use a copy of the Linux kernel, which it has modified for its own purposes, to run an online service. It may provide this modified kernel to a subsidiary or affiliate in Europe or China to offer a local service. For tax, regulatory, or other reasons, it may be important to locate the servers for the business in Europe or China in those territories. If the recipient entity is a wholly owned subsidiary of the company, the company has a good argument that, due to unity of ownership, the copy is a "private copy" that has only been given to the company itself and that therefore, no distribution has taken place. This argument is also reasonably strong for a majority-owned affiliate because the parent effectively exercises control over the affiliate.[14] But if the recipient is a minority-owned affiliate, the company faces a more serious concern over whether distribution has taken place. This scenario is quite common, particularly where companies have little choice but to create minority-owned operating entities in territories, like India or China, that impose significant restrictions on foreign ownership of businesses operating within their borders.

- **Mergers and acquisitions.** US law can be quirky and counterintuitive on the subject of assignments by operation of law in connection with mergers and acquisitions. An assignment of a contract (or a license) occurs when one party to the contract transfers its rights to another. Therefore, for instance, if a corporation enters into an agreement with another party, it may be able to transfer that agreement to another corporation—depending on what the agreement has to say about it. Contracts are generally considered assignable under US law,[15] but intellectual property licenses are subject to different rules. Generally, nonexclusive copyright and patent licenses are not assignable.[16] Therefore, if a corporation takes a nonexclusive license

---

[14] In addition, because the copyleft requirements of GPL only allow binary recipients to seek source code copies, where the recipient is a majority-owned affiliate, the issue may be moot; the recipient would simply never make the request.

[15] Other than special kinds of contracts, where assignment would change the basic nature of the contract, like contracts for personal services or requirements contracts. See Restatement (Second) Contracts, Section 317.

[16] For patent, see *PPG Indus. Inv. v. Guardian Indus. Corp.*, 597 F.2d 1090 (6th Cir. 1979). For copyright, although the law is conflicting see, e.g., *SQL Solutions, Inc. v. Oracle Corp.*, 1991 U.S. Dist. LEXIS 21097 (N.D. Cal. 1991). This is an unpublished decision and arguably contrary to the California Supreme Court's view in *Trubowich v. Riverbank Canning Co.*, 182 P.2d 182 (Cal. 1947).

to a patent, it cannot transfer the license to another corporation unless the license agreement expressly allows transfer. To make matters even more complicated, there are courts that have held that an acquisition—even a transaction such as a reverse triangular merger in which the target entity survives—can be an assignment by operation of law. Even if the licensee is the same corporation before and after the acquisition, the license may not be exercisable after the transaction. This rule of law may also have implications for the definition of distribution. If a change of control is an assignment by operation of law, one might logically conclude that it also constitutes providing a copy to another entity and thus a distribution triggering copyleft obligations. Keep in mind, also, that the effectuation of some forms of M&A transactions, such as asset sales, are clearly assignments and also likely to constitute distribution under GPL 2.

- **Productization.** Although this business case is not complex from a legal standpoint, it is such a frequent trap for companies managing open source compliance that it is worth mentioning in any discussion of distribution issues. Companies that offer SAAS solutions tend to rely on the fact that they are not distributing their products to ensure their GPL compliance. They do this by merely avoiding licenses like Affero GPL that have requirements even in the absence of distribution. However, this can be a dangerous strategy. For a business development manager who is not focused on legal and technical niceties, it is easy to cause transactions to trip over the distribution line. A company with a SAAS offering may, for instance, approach a customer operating in a highly regulated market (such as a health care or financial services) that will insist that the SAAS offering be operated via a private instance on the customer's premises or on servers under the customer's control. This demand usually arises from security or regulatory auditing concerns. From the business point of view, a private instance of a SAAS product is a technical detail. But of course, providing a copy to the customer will likely constitute distribution. If the company's open source compliance strategy hinges on refraining from distribution within the context of a SAAS model, the company may find that it cannot deliver a compliant product in any reasonable amount of time—usually because it has intermixed GPL- and non-GPL-compatible code or has not properly kept track of open source elements in the product.

With these edge cases in mind, we now turn to extrinsic evidence of the meaning of GPL 2 and best practices in managing distribution issues.

## The FSF View

The GPL 2 FAQ, promulgated by the Free Software Foundation (FSF), offers the FSF's insight into what it considers a distribution that would trigger copyleft requirements. For example, one of the FAQs is as follows:

> **Is making and using multiple copies within one organization or company "distribution"?**
>
> No, in that case the organization is just making the copies for itself. As a consequence, a company or other organization can develop a modified version and install that version through its own facilities, without giving the staff permission to release that modified version to outsiders.
>
> However, when the organization transfers copies to other organizations or individuals, that is distribution. *In particular, providing copies to contractors for use off-site is distribution* [emphasis added].[17]

The FAQ also discusses a transfer between an organization and a majority-owned subsidiary:

> **Does moving a copy to a majority-owned, and controlled, subsidiary constitute distribution?**
>
> Whether moving a copy to or from this subsidiary constitutes "distribution" is a matter to be decided in each case under the copyright law of the appropriate jurisdiction. The GPL does not and cannot override local laws. US copyright law is not entirely clear on the point, *but appears not to consider this distribution* [emphasis added].
>
> If, in some country, this is considered distribution, and the subsidiary must receive the right to redistribute the program, that will not make a practical difference. The subsidiary is controlled by the parent company; rights or no rights, it won't redistribute the program unless the parent company decides to do so.[18]

In this FAQ, the FSF acknowledges that, at least in the United States, a transfer to or from a majority-owned and majority-controlled subsidiary may not

---

[17] www.gnu.org/licenses/old-licenses/gpl-2.0-faq.html#InternalDistribution. This same FAQ appears in the GPLv3 FAQ as well (www.gnu.org/licenses/gpl-faq.html#InternalDistribution).

[18] www.gnu.org/licenses/old-licenses/gpl-2.0-faq.html#DistributeSubsidiary. This same FAQ appears in the GPLv3 FAQ as well (www.gnu.org/licenses/gpl-faq.html#DistributeSubsidiary).

constitute distribution. Further, the FSF gives weight to one organization's effective control over another to determine whether the two entities are effectively one entity for the purposes of the analysis.

There is also discussion in the GPL 2 FAQ about providing modifications of GPL code under a nondisclosure agreement:

> **Does the GPL allow me to develop a modified version under a nondisclosure agreement?**
>
> Yes. For instance, you can accept a contract to develop changes and agree not to release your changes until the client says OK. This is permitted because in this case no GPL-covered code is being distributed under an NDA.
>
> You can also release your changes to the client under the GPL, but agree not to release them to anyone else unless the client says OK. In this case, too, no GPL-covered code is being distributed under an NDA, or under any additional restrictions.
>
> The GPL would give the client the right to redistribute your version. In this scenario, the client will probably choose not to exercise that right, but does have the right.[19]

Many companies find the distribution question confusing because they find this FAQ confusing. In this FAQ, the FSF considers two different scenarios: (1) the contractor releases the modified code to the public generally at the direction of the client, and (2) the contractor releases the modified code to the client under the GPL, and the contractor promises not to release the modified code to anyone else. Unfortunately, this FAQ section does not specify whether "a modified version" refers to a modification of the contractor's own GPL code, to GPL code that may have been already modified by the client, or to a modification of third-party code. Clearly, these three situations could be analyzed differently. If the FAQ refers to GPL code owned by either the client or the contractor, it is a trivial question; obviously, the owner of GPL code can choose to deliver that code under GPL terms or not as it sees fit, because an author (as licensor) is not bound by the copyleft obligations of GPL—only the licensee is. If the FAQ refers to modifications to third-party code, it implies that even if the delivery of the original code constitutes a distribution, that distribution does not trigger the copyleft obligations of GPL.

Other information promulgated by the FSF suggests that this FAQ element is not intended to address third-party code. But that is, by far, the most common

---

[19] www.gnu.org/licenses/old-licenses/gpl-2.0-faq.html#DevelopChangesUnderNDA. This same FAQ appears in the GPLv3 FAQ as well (www.gnu.org/licenses/gpl-faq.html# DevelopChangesUnderNDA).

situation: a company wants to use some GPL code but needs modifications, so it finds an expert in the code willing to modify it on a contract basis. In fact, this scenario is so common that it is touted as one of the advantages of open source software. But the company may not plan to ever distribute the software. Therefore, if providing the code to the consultant is distribution that triggers copyleft requirements, the company will likely be unwilling to engage the consultant.

The FSF's view is problematic for a couple of reasons. First, a practical problem: companies that hire consultants simply don't distinguish between the business cases of in-house and contractor development. They do not expect to encounter a completely different GPL compliance landscape based on the distinction. Because FSF's view contravenes business expectations, it is a trap for the unwary. Second, a legal problem: the provision of code for development purposes is more akin to "communicat[ing] the contents of a manuscript to a definitely selected group and for a limited purpose, and without the right of diffusion, reproduction, distribution or sale" (i.e., not publication under copyright law) than it is to common notions of redistribution or publication. Therefore, there is a strong argument that such a transfer is not distribution under the law.

## The International View

It is important to keep in mind that the distribution question as it is analyzed here is largely unique to US law. Because GPL 2 does not have a choice-of-law provision and is a conditional copyright license, it governs only what is protected via local copyright law. A full discussion of the tenets of international copyright law bearing upon this issue is beyond the scope of this chapter, but it seems likely that the question would have different answers outside the United States. The Berne Convention for the Protection of Literary and Artistic Works, as amplified by the WIPO Copyright Treaty, provides for a right to "make available" a literary work. This may be broader than the US notion of distribution, and most importantly, it could include SAAS offerings. Therefore, the triggers for copyleft obligations based on activity outside the United States may have a lower threshold than those based on activity in the United States.

## Best Practices for Contract Drafting and Deal Structuring

As lawyers in private practice await clarity in the common law on distribution issues, they may wish to consider implementing certain drafting and structuring practices to clarify their clients' intent or to minimize the uncertainty of the results should the courts later announce decisions on distribution questions. Such practices cannot address all distribution issues should there be a contrary court pronouncement, but they might help discourage claims, provide evidence of intent, or reduce confusion when those not directly involved in the deal are later asked to assess distribution issues.

### Development Agreements

To avoid confusion about whether development activities constitute distribution, consider adding language such as the following to your development agreements:

- **"Contractor shall conduct development services only on systems and equipment under the control of Customer."** This language limits work to customer-controlled servers. This will address whether a distribution has occurred, the theory being that even though the contractor is a separate person, no copy of the software has been transferred.

- **"Contractor acknowledges that it is performing the development services solely for the benefit of Customer, and solely as directed by Customer, and shall not make any copy of the Software available to any other person or entity."** This language states that copies are intended to be private, thus addressing the situation that the FSF FAQ says constitutes distribution.

These approaches are attractive because they comport with customary confidentiality provisions and "work made for hire" provisions in development agreements, which often recite customer control of the development activities to support treatment of the work as "work made for hire" under *CCNV v. Reid*.[20]

### Mergers and Acquisitions

- **Avoid delivery of GPL software.** Particularly in asset purchase deals, determine if there is a reasonable way to refrain from delivery of open source packages in favor of having buyer download them directly from

---

[20] *Community for Creative Non-Violence v. Reid,* 490 U.S. 730 (1989), held that the factors for determining whether a work of authorship is a work made for hire (owned by the company) or not (owned not by the company but by the author) are, among others, the level of skill required to create the work, the source of the tools used in creating the work, where the work was created, the duration of the relationship between customer and author, the extent of the contractor's discretion over when and how long to work, and whether the work is part of the regular business of the customer or consultant. Therefore, many consulting agreements recite where work will be performed, as well as other facts that might bear on whether distribution has occurred.

the original source or a third-party source. This approach is useful mostly in situations where drivers or other significant original code belonging to the seller is being delivered. It is not useful when the seller is delivering integrated modifications. In that case, the seller would deliver only its additions, and the buyer would receive third-party open source code separately. Clearly, if third-party open source code is extensively modified, this strategy may not be feasible because it would be so difficult to separate the seller's code from the third party's code. However, companies that are very conservative on this issue may deliver only *diffs*, or patches, in an attempt to avoid delivery of any third-party GPL code. Keep in mind that distribution is usually an issue for the seller, not the buyer. Therefore, asset purchases that consist of all the assets of the seller entity may render the concern moot, but a seller's divestiture of partial assets, business lines, or product lines may cause the seller to have concerns about GPL distribution. A seller wishing to sell its own code may find buyers unwilling to pay for that code if the code must be delivered under GPL.

## SAAS Agreements

- **Avoid drafting that confuses SAAS with distribution.** There is some controversy among technology lawyers as to whether SAAS agreements are licenses or merely service agreements. Sometimes, as an artifact of their business antecedents in distributed software, SAAS agreements are drafted so much like distributed software licenses that it is difficult to tell the two apart. Although the distribution question would likely turn primarily on the supplier's actions, not merely on document drafting, it is best not to hurt your position by using a SAAS agreement that reads like it covers a distributed product.

## Intercompany Agreements

- **Recite intent not to distribute.** In software agreements between corporate affiliates, parent entities may wish to clarify that no distribution is intended, much in the same way as recommended above for consulting or development agreements. This may seem obvious, but in fact, intercompany technology licenses are often not drafted by technology lawyers. Instead, they are drafted by tax lawyers or corporate lawyers who are documenting intercompany arrangements for the purpose of managing imputed tax issues, rather than precisely considering intellectual property issues. It is crucial to review these agreements with a view to open source as well as intellectual property issues.

## An Enduring Puzzle

It is unlikely that the federal courts in the United States will answer these distribution questions anytime soon. The open source enforcement actions that have been brought to date have not addressed these questions. Given that other heady issues (such as the scope of derivative works under GPL 2 and the inter-action of patent law and open source licensing) are still unclear in open source law, they may not be ripe for dispute. Also, most authors who release code under GPL 2 are simply not focused on issues like intercompany agreements and mergers or acquisitions. This is because they are primarily technologists rather than corporate strategists. If GPL authors generally do not intend to enforce their rights in these edge cases, there may not be a constituency that is interested in bringing a lawsuit that will make law in this area. It therefore seems likely these questions will persist as long as GPL 2 remains a widely used license, and based on the prevalence of the Linux kernel alone, this will be a long time. Companies assessing open source compliance should be sure they have identified the types of distribution that are most likely to be questioned so they can use open source software with confidence and plan their transactions in a way that comports with their open source compliance strategy.

# Chapter 7

# Notice Requirements

Notice and attribution requirements constitute one of the least intellectually challenging but most important parts of open source licensing. All open source licenses—from the most permissive to the strongest copyleft—require licensing notices. On their face, these requirements are straightforward, but anyone who has tried to create a notice file for a binary product can attest that creating such a file can be challenging and frustrating. How, they think, can such a simple task be so difficult? But one thing is sure: if a redistributor fails to use proper licensing notices, it creates the simplest path for an open source licensor to claim and prove noncompliance. In fact, most litigation concerning open source enforcement is based on failure to provide notices.

## *What Is a License Notice?*

The requirement to deliver notices is merely that—a requirement to deliver a text file informing the recipient that certain open source software, which is available under the noticed license, is included in the software being delivered to the recipient. Sometimes, that notice also acts as the operative licensing terms, but not always.

For example, if a product is distributed under an end user license agreement and contains some elements of third-party open source software that are available under the BSD license, the licensor must give a copy of the BSD license to the recipient of the software. However, the software as a whole is not licensed on those terms. Effectively, this license notice serves to inform the recipient that the recipient is receiving a license to that element directly from the licensor and also that the software may be available to the recipient under those terms. Of course, permissive licenses do not have source code delivery requirements, so the recipient may not know where to get a copy of the source code. Nevertheless, the recipient may choose to look for a copy independently.

For copyleft licenses, the license notice serves to inform the recipient that the software is provided under those license terms, directly from the licensor—or in the case of the weak copyleft licenses like Mozilla Public License or Eclipse Public License, that the source code is available under those terms. In the case of licenses like GPL and LGPL, binaries must be provided only under those terms, so the licenses serve as the operative licensing terms for the software.

Most licenses also include a copyright notice, such as Copyright 2015 XYZ, Inc. The copyright notice is usually at the top of the license, but some open source authors omit the copyright notice. The license notice requires one to reproduce what was provided—no more, no less.

## How to Create a License Notice

Creating the exact form of a license notice can also be challenging. Almost all open source licenses only require the text file of the license to be delivered. Typically, the license notice is delivered in plain text format.

Different licenses require delivery of notices in different circumstances. Here are some examples:

- MIT. "The above copyright notice and this permission notice shall be included in all copies or substantial portions of the Software."

- BSD. "Redistributions in binary form must reproduce the above copyright notice, this list of conditions and the following disclaimer in the documentation and/or other materials provided with the distribution."

- GPL 2:1. "You may copy and distribute verbatim copies of the Program's source code as you receive it, in any medium, provided that you conspicuously and appropriately publish on each copy an appropriate copyright notice and disclaimer of warranty; keep intact all the notices that refer to this License and to the absence of any warranty; and give any other recipients of the Program a copy of this License along with the Program."

- Apache 2. "(1) You must give any other recipients of the Work or Derivative Works a copy of this License ... (3) You must retain, in the Source form of any Derivative Works that You distribute, all copyright, patent, trademark, and attribution notices from the Source form of the Work, excluding those notices that do not pertain to any part of the Derivative Works; and (4) If the Work includes a "NOTICE" text file as part of its distribution, then any Derivative Works that You distribute must include a readable copy of the attribution notices contained within such NOTICE file, excluding those notices that do not pertain to any part of the Derivative Works, in at least one of the following places: within a NOTICE text file distributed as part of the Derivative Works; within the Source form or documentation, if provided along with the Derivative Works; or, within a display generated by the Derivative Works, if and wherever such third-party notices normally appear. The contents of the NOTICE file are for in-formational purposes only and do not modify the License. You may add Your own attribution notices within Derivative Works that You distribute, alongside or as an addendum to the NOTICE text from the Work, provided that such additional attribution notices cannot be construed as modifying the License.

There are variations of these requirements. For example, some forms of the BSD license do not require delivery of a license notice with binaries, only with source code.

However, because a product often has many open source components, it is unmanageable to have a different license notice process for every license. There-fore, most companies seeking to comply with open source notice requirements develop an internal process for preparing notices that is consistent with the most stringent common notice requirements; GPL is usually the model.

The notice requirement almost always requires delivery of an entire copy of a license. Some licenses allow a form of abbreviated notice. But it is not practical to implement different internal processes for different licenses, so most compa-nies provide a copy of the entire license for every open source license, whether it is required or not.

If a software product is delivered in source code form, the notices are usually "baked in." If a developer downloads an open source component for his product, the license file is usually contained in a text file called *license.txt* or *copying.txt*, which is included in the download package along with the source code files for the com-ponent. If the developer simply redistributes all of the source code files along with the product, there is often no need to create a separate license notice. This is the best and easiest approach.

However, many companies do not want to deliver source code up front. There are many reasons for this. Often, it is impractical to do so. In some cases, the company objects to the requirement to deliver the source code when the licens-es don't require them to, such as with permissive licenses like BSD or MIT. When the license imposes no condition to deliver source code, doing so is a choice, not a requirement. In the case of copyleft licenses like GPL and LGPL and weak co-pyleft licenses such as Mozilla Public License, there is no requirement to deliver source code with every binary. However, there is a requirement to inform the re-cipient that the source code is available under the terms of that copyleft license. In such cases, the developer has a choice whether to include the source code up front with binaries or not, but when he elects not to do so, he must prepare a separate notice file. It is creating this extra file of licensing notices that causes companies so much distress.

Accordingly, the easiest and best practice is always to deliver source code up front. Not only does this ease or eliminate the task of preparing licensing notices, but it also will deflect requests for source code that must be made available under copyleft licenses, the failure to complete which results in noncompliance.

If the product is a hardware product, and if the software is embedded or has no user interface, then delivery of notices can be particularly difficult. Companies continually insist that they should be able to deliver notices via the Internet instead of with a product distribution. Unfortunately, although that might be a convenient solution, it does not comply with the notice requirements of most open source licenses. The open source license almost always requires that an entire copy of the license be delivered with the product. If the product is a software product, this usually means the notice files are in the product download or on the distribution media (such as CD-ROM). If the product is a hardware product, there may be no user interaction screen suitable for displaying the notices, and even if there is a screen, a small screen will make reading the notices unpleasant. Ironically, this is usually a compliant approach, although it may not serve the user in a practical sense. If you have a smartphone, for instance, you can probably easily find the open source license notices in it. However, you will find reading hundreds of pages of notices on a very small screen very difficult. Companies often argue—not unreasonably—that it would be better to point the user to any web page where notices could be provided in a more digestible format. Unfortunately, this is not what most of the licenses require.

The theory behind disallowing online notices and requiring reproduction of the entire license (even though open source licenses are almost always readily available online) is that when most of the licenses were originally written, most people did not have Internet access. Of course, in the twenty-first century, Internet access is ubiquitous. So the reason for the original requirement to deliver the entire copy of the license may be anachronistic, but open source license terms do not change. Therefore, for many years in the future, much legacy code will be distributed under licenses that require notices to be delivered in ways that do not take advantage of modern technology.

There is one circumstance in which it is reasonable—and probably compliant—to deliver licensing notices via the Internet, and that is when delivering licensing notices for an Internet product. For example, JavaScript—a language that executes in the user's browser in source code form—is often distributed in connection with SAAS and web services. Much JavaScript is under open source licenses. When pushing JavaScript out via a web browser, it is reasonable to provide a link where the user can go to find licensing notices. In such a case, the JavaScript could not possibly be distributed to the user unless the user has access to the link. Though this may or may not comply with the letter of some open source notice requirements, it complies with the spirit.

A similar edge case might exist for a device that only works with an Internet connection—particularly a device that has no user interface. In this case, delivering notices via a web link would be an alternative to delivering a set of paper notices or notices on electronic media such as a CD-ROM—both which are expensive to do.

Finally, once a company decides on its procedures for delivering notices, it must take care to keep them current. Notices must be updated as open source components to the products change over time. Unfortunately, outdated license notices are very common.

## *Attribution and Advertising Requirements*

Some open source licenses have more troublesome notice requirements, such as requirements to deliver notices "in the user manual"—which made sense 20 years ago but not nowadays, when the creation of separate user manuals is becoming less popular every year. In addition, a certain set of licenses contained what are called advertising requirements. Apache 1.0 Section 3 contained this provision:

> The end-user documentation included with the redistribution, if any, must include the following acknowledgment: "This product includes software developed by the Apache Software Foundation (www.apache.org). Alternately, this acknowledgment may appear in the software itself, if and wherever such third-party acknowledgments normally appear."[1]

This kind of "advertising requirement" has been deprecated, not only because it is costly and difficult to implement but because it is incompatible with GPL.

One popular piece of software that is still under such a license is OpenSSL, whose license says this in Section 3:

> All advertising materials mentioning features or use of this software must display the following acknowledgment:
>
> > "This product includes software developed by the OpenSSL Project for use in the OpenSSL Toolkit. (www.openssl.org)"[2]

Requirements like this can be difficult to interpret. What constitutes advertising material? Does any product listing noting that the product is compatible with SSL meet this definition? What does it mean to mention "features"? In the

---

[1]  www.apache.org/licenses/LICENSE-1.1.

[2]  www.openssl.org/source/license.html.

case of a package like OpenSSL that implements a protocol (SSL) with other implementations, is this requirement triggered by mentioning SSL or only the features particular to the OpenSSL implementation? Provisions like this are unpopular—and not a best practice in open source licensing—because of their vagueness and quick obsolescence.

## Noting Modifications

Some notice requirements of open source licenses are often forgotten. For instance, many open source licenses require the developer to note his own changes. For example, GPL version 2 says, "You must cause the modified files to carry prominent notices stating that you changed the files and the date of any change." In practice, this only requires a name and date, not a description of the changes.

Some other licenses have different and broader modification notice requirements. These requirements may seem burdensome on their face; they were historically considered good programming practice, regardless of the license requirement. Today, however, most information about changes to software is stored as metadata in a concurrent versioning system, rather than in source code comments. So including this as a notice requirement is not popular among engineers.

## Automation

There is some good news in the grim task of notice creation. Clearly, it is an area ripe for automation. Some build systems (such as Debian Linux and the Android system) contain functionality that helps gather information for notice files. Reports generated by code scanners like Black Duck Software or Palamida can often be culled for license notices.

Although not intended primarily to address notice delivery, the SPDX (Software Package Data Exchange) project also promises to assist in the automation of the delivery of licensing information. This project works under the aegis of the Linux Foundation. As of this writing, version 2.0 of the specification is in the works.[3] SPDX is a standardized format for communicating licensing information. SPDX contains interesting information about licensing that can be useful for generating or checking notice files for end users, but it is primarily intended to address the delivery of information in supply chains—from one developer to another. This is an issue that goes beyond notices or even the SPDX project. As it currently stands, business users of open source software waste much effort when creating information disclosures at every level of the supply chain. (For more on this, see Chapter 17: Mergers & Acquisitions and Other Transactions.)

---

[3] For more information, see **spdx.org/about-spdx**.

David Marr eloquently describes this issue as follows:

> FOSS exists in all levels of a supply chain, from the first software developer creating software all the way to the final packaged product that is sold to end users. However, in the context of a commercial supply chain, the current FOSS ecosystem is broken. If a supply chain can be compared to a stream or a river, as software flows down the supply chain—i.e., when software is delivered from one company to the next—each successive downstream company is redoing portions of the compliance work already done (or what should have been done) by the upstream company. This is all done at unnecessary cost and inefficiency, and it often delays time-to-market.[4]

The challenge of conveying license notices and the challenge of conveying licensing information are, of course, related. License notices are required for all distribution—and that includes every intermediate distribution within the supply chain. So, every supplier in the chain has the obligation under the applicable open source license to convey license notices and the business necessity to deliver the substance of the licensing information to its customers. Although one is a license compliance issue and the other is an information management issue, the resolution to these issues should dovetail in a standardized and compliant process.

---

[4] Email, on file with author. Mr. Marr is a well-known open source legal expert and currently vice president of legal at Qualcomm Inc.

# Part III

# Advanced Compliance

Chapter 8

# The GPL 2 Border Dispute

The single most difficult and controversial legal issue in open source licensing is the scope of GPL version 2. When clients ask about this issue, they usually use words like "tainting" or refer to the "viral" nature of GPL. But in an effort to use more neutral language, I call it the *border dispute* because the basic issue is this: What does GPL cover, and what does it not cover? In the language of the license, what is a "work based on the Program" versus something entirely separate that does not need to be covered by GPL?

The copyleft conditions of the GPL apply to the original work released under the license (the "Program") and works "based on the Program." But the GPL does not seek to control other works that are "mere aggregations" with the Program. In law school, we learned that any use of the word *mere* signaled that a conclusory statement was about to follow, and analysis of the GPL is no different. There has been a fair amount written about the border dispute, but much of it is not well reasoned because it's advocacy rather than analysis. In analyzing issues of GPL's scope, it is necessary to know who says what about this topic, and why. But a reasoned discussion of this topic tests one's understanding of what principles guide the law in a way that few other topics do.

Developers of proprietary software are extremely concerned with this issue—and rightly so, if they want to avoid breaching the GPL. But free software advocates have a tendency to dismiss the angst this topic generates in proprietary software developers. Some believe that developing proprietary software is morally wrong to begin with and that proprietary developers bring these concerns upon themselves—therefore, they believe that such concerns shouldn't trouble the pure of heart. But at the risk of being labeled a free software "denier," I will simply point out that we live in a world where open source and proprietary software must coexist. Also, many of the biggest open source projects today are supported largely by industry players who develop proprietary software. These players need to know where they stand—where to draw the line between what must be GPL and what need not—and they are often frustrated at the GPL's lack of clarity on this question. But perhaps more importantly, justice demands that the rules of a society be clear and understandable, or else only those with arcane knowledge can fully participate in society. GPL is a kind of constitution for the free software world, so its lack of clarity is a continuing concern for those working in that world—even those who want to promote free software.

Speaking from experience, I have almost never heard a client say it wanted to violate GPL, but I have heard hundreds of clients say they were confused about what is necessary to avoid violating GPL. Responding to this concern by suggesting that all these companies should not worry about the rules and simply release all their software under GPL is neither realistic nor the best result for open source software. Private enterprises usually could not do this if they wanted to; they owe a duty to their shareholders to make money. Those who feel this is morally wrong and that all software companies should be not-for-profit entities don't believe in the inventive value of private enterprise, and thus, they play into the stereotype that allowed anti–open source factions to get traction in the 1990s. In fact, most open source developers, proponents, and supporters are fairly neutral about this topic and understand that open source is a great model for some software and not such a great model for other software. Just as judges have long pondered the balance of intellectual property protection and public domain that will best foster innovation, there is a balance of scope to open source licenses that will result in maximum contribution to open source by the technology industry. Lack of clarity in the rules of the road imposes a risk tax on the technology industry, and private companies consider pondering GPL's scope to be one of the hidden elements of the total cost of ownership of open source software.

## *Libraries and Other Standard Elements*

To understand how all the other scope issues are analyzed, take the case of a humble but useful software routine: a time function. If an application wants to find the current time, it might make a call like this:

```
Time_t t=time(NULL);
```

Don't worry if the syntax looks odd to you. This code is doing something very simple. The program that uses this line of code is defining a variable called t that will be populated with the current time, using the function time. Once the program gets that information, it can display the time on the user interface screen, make calculations using the time, or do whatever else it wants with time information. Obviously, many application programs might need to use this basic function. To do so, the application needs to make the system call (time) using the library of code containing the time function, while the application program is running. Suppose you are writing a calendar application (the "Application")—clearly, you will need to know the current time and date and update it frequently during the running of the application. Your calendar application will make frequent use of this library function time (the "Library"). Translating this into the context of the question of GPL scope, we would ask, "Under GPL, are the calendar Application and the time function Library two programs or one?"

Now, this is in fact a trick question. By answering this question, we will see the border dispute of GPL in action. In other words, we are seeking, based on the language of GPL, to determine which of the following is true:

> Case One: The Application and the Library are part of the same program and thus must both be covered by GPL.
>
> Case Two: The Application and the Library are different programs, and thus if one of them (the Library) is covered by GPL, the other (the Application) need not be covered by GPL.

### What the GPL Says[1]

The language of GPL that governs this question centers on the phrase "work based on the Program." The *Program* means the software released under GPL. GPL imposes conditions that govern the distribution of the Program or any work based on the Program.

Paragraph 0 says, "This License applies to any program or other work which contains a notice placed by the copyright holder saying it may be distributed under the terms of this General Public License. The 'Program,' below, refers to any such program or work, and a **'work based on the Program' means either the Program or any derivative work under copyright law: that is to say, a work containing the Program or a portion of it, either verbatim or with modifications and/or translated into another language.**"

Paragraph 2 says, "You may modify your copy or copies of the Program or any portion of it, **thus forming a work based on the Program.**"

Paragraph 2(b) says, "You must cause any work that you distribute or publish, that **in whole or in part contains or is derived from the Program or any part thereof,** to be licensed as a whole at no charge to all third parties under the terms of this License." This can be thought of as the copyleft provision of GPL, because it imposes the condition of relicensing under the same terms.

Paragraph 2 also says, "These requirements apply to the modified work as a whole. If identifiable sections of that work are **not derived from the Program, and**

---

[1] In this section, all emphasis in quotations from the GPL has been added by the author.

can be reasonably considered independent and separate works in themselves, then this License, and its terms, do not apply to those sections when you distribute them as separate works. But when you distribute the same sections as part of a whole which is a work based on the Program, the distribution of the whole must be on the terms of this License, whose permissions for other licensees extend to **the entire whole, and thus to each and every part** regardless of who wrote it.

"Thus, it is not the intent of this section to claim rights or contest your rights to **work written entirely by you;** rather, the intent is to exercise the right to control the distribution of **derivative or collective works based on the Program.** In addition, [this section] does not bring the other work under the scope of this License."

Paragraph 5 says: "You are not required to accept this License, since you have not signed it. However, nothing else grants you permission to modify or distribute the Program **or its derivative works.**"

## *How Courts Interpret the Language of Contracts*

At this point, do you know the answer to our "time" question? Of course not. The language of GPL requires interpretation.

When lawyers interpret documents such as contracts, statutes, or regulations, they use rules that are old and well settled. These rules seek to determine the intent of those who wrote the documents, at the time they were written. Though some claim the GPL is a license and not a contract, there is no reason to think that the rules of interpretation would be different from those applied anywhere else in the law.[2]

The most basic rule of contract interpretation is the *four corners rule*, which holds that one first tries to discern the meaning of the document from the language within its four corners. (Think of it as WYSIWYG). Another important rule is the *parol evidence rule*, which holds that if a written document exists, prior or contemporaneous oral statements are not evidence of intent. Also, where possible, a document is interpreted as a whole, giving effect to all parts of the document. We can't just pick and choose the parts we want to use; we have to assume that the whole document—every phrase of it—has meaning.

This leads us to an important idea. One's interpretation of a document depends primarily on the objective meaning of the words of the document, not on what others think or say about them. Interpretation goes through a series of steps:

---

[2] Below, I apply these rules as articulated in the Restatement (Second) of Contracts and the Uniform Commercial Code. While a contract would normally have a law selection clause that applies the law of a specific US state, GPL does not have a governing law–selection clause. Licenses of software are generally considered to be covered by UCC Article 2, and those rules are consistent with contract common law on interpretational rules.

First, the exact words in the document are assigned their ordinary, plain meaning (such as the meaning they would have in a dictionary). If the dictionary definition still leaves the meaning ambiguous, then we use other rules of contract construction to resolve the ambiguity.

Those rules look outside the four corners and dictionary definitions. For example, a meaning given to a word by a trade or profession will trump the dictionary definition of the word, if that makes sense in context. In computer software licenses, obviously, technical meanings are very important. For example, GPL has this to say about source code:

> For an executable work, complete source code means all the source code for all modules it contains, plus any associated interface definition files, plus the scripts used to control compilation and installation of the executable. However, as a special exception, the source code distributed need not include anything that is normally distributed (in either source or binary form) with the major components (compiler, kernel, and so on) of the operating system on which the executable runs, unless that component itself accompanies the executable.

Words like *kernel* and *scripts* obviously have special meanings here. They don't refer to wheat bran and movie dialogue.

Beyond this, there are two other interpretational rules that are often confused with each other: course of performance and usage of trade.[3] *Course of performance* (sometimes called course of dealing) describes how the parties to an agreement perform the agreement. For example, if you agree on paper to pay your rent on a monthly basis, but if the paper does not say what day of the month you will pay and you pay on the first of the month for six months, then the paper will be interpreted to require you to pay on the first of the month because of the way you have performed the contract so far. *Usage of trade* describes how the industry generally operates. So for instance, if you write a contract to buy a wooden beam that is a "finished two-by-four" and the supplier delivers to you a beam that is slightly smaller, you will not have a legal claim. It is customary in the trade to call such beams two-by-fours even though after finishing, they are slightly smaller.

Finally, if the rules of contract construction fail to resolve the ambiguity, then under the rule of contra proferentem, any ambiguity must be construed

---

[3] The Restatement describes "course of performance" as "repeated occasions for performance by either party with knowledge of the nature of the performance." "Usage of trade" is defined in the UCC as "any practice ... having such regularity of observance in a place, vocation, or trade as to justify an expectation that it will be observed with respect to the transaction in question."

against the drafter of the contract. This rule is meant to protect those who don't wield the drafter's pen.

Moreover, if a particular party to a license makes a statement against his own legal interest, then as a matter of fairness, the courts will not sustain legal claims against those who reasonably rely on that statement. For instance, suppose the author of the Library said publicly, "I have licensed this software under GPL, but I don't intend ever to enforce its terms against anyone in schools or nonprofit organizations." Then, any lawsuit by the author against a school or nonprofit for violating the GPL would probably not be successful. This principle is known as waiver or estoppel—the author has waived his rights, or as a matter of fairness, he should be stopped from suing for infringement.

## Applying the Four Corners Rule to GPL 2

Now we have a question, a set of language to interpret, and a set of rules to make our interpretation. This is what lawyers do, and even if you are not a lawyer, you can do it, too. You just need to think carefully and precisely about the language and think of all the meanings it might have.

The GPL is not a traditional legal document. If it were, the term *work based on the Program* would be capitalized whenever it is used and defined once, and only once, at the beginning of the document. When we lawyers draft legal documents, this is how we seek to minimize the ambiguity of language. It is also, of course, how ambiguities are avoided in programming languages: variables are defined at the beginning and should only be used in a consistent way, or there will be bugs. If the GPL's omission of definitions of important terms like *work based on the Program* seems ironic to you—well, it does to me, too.

Taking the language of GPL at face value, we would need to assess the boundary or overlap between, on the one hand, "works written entirely by" the licensee, works combined by "mere aggregation" on the same storage volume or medium, and works that "can be reasonably considered independent and separate works in themselves" and, on the other hand, a work "that in whole or in part contains or is derived from the Program or any part thereof." Keep in mind that we do not have the option of discarding any of these phrases if they don't seem necessary or useful to us. Every term in the document must have meaning.

This is why attorneys who read the GPL quickly come to the conclusion that the phrase "work based on the Program"—upon which entire companies and development projects depend—is irretrievably vague. To illustrate this point, Figure 8.1 provides a Venn diagram of the various definitional phrases of the language of GPL 2 that I drew once in a moment of philosophical contemplation.

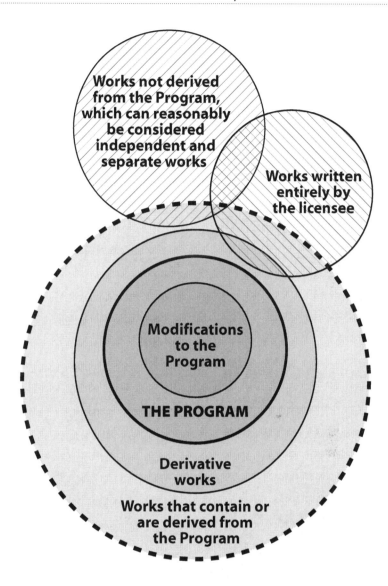

**Figure 8.1** Venn diagram of code covered and not covered by the GPL

In a properly drafted document, the area within the heavy dashed line, which represents code covered by the GPL, would not overlap with the crosshatched portions, which represent code that is not covered by the GPL.

The ambiguity of these terms is undeniable. The FSF itself, author and steward of the document, has published extensive FAQs on GPL 2. Now that we know that the four corners rule will not give us an answer, we have to look elsewhere.

One observation: if a lawyer ever offers to write you a long analysis of GPL's language on its face, it is not worth the fees you will have to pay. GPL needs to be interpreted in its technical and social context, the importance of which far eclipses the language on its face. In this respect, interpreting GPL is no ordinary legal task.

In this sense, the GPL is more like a statute than a contract—it's a single document applied to many persons and many software projects. The traditional approach to contract interpretation via course of performance evidence is seldom relevant. If FSF is viewed as a legislative body setting the rules for its community, then what it says about the contract may be paramount. But FSF is not a legislative body, whose powers would be limited by the Constitution or whose position of authority would depend on a political process like elections or appointments. It is a self-appointed group. Statutory enactments have the power to affect many people's lives, and this is why the government that makes them has limited powers. The FSF is, after all, only a not-for-profit corporation, which ultimately is not bound to answer to an electorate. Therefore, its statements about interpretation should not necessarily be given the weight of law—though we will find them useful and interesting, as described below.

### Applying the Rules of Contract Construction to the Border Dispute

We now have several (not necessarily mutually exclusive) alternative methods to interpret GPL:

- Look to trade usage.
- Look to the statutory meaning of the term *derivative work* (discussed below).
- Use a "legal realism" approach—focus on the risk of enforcement instead of pure interpretation.

One reason the language of GPL may seem opaque is that it uses a term of art from US copyright law: a *derivative work*. Under US law, copyright covers *works of authorship*, which include a variety of works such as books, music, videos, and software. A *derivative work* is a variation of the work that is close enough so that it is governed by the rights of the original author, but not close enough so as to be identical. Outside the software context, a derivative work might be a revision (such as a new edition of a book), a translation (such as a translation of a book into another language), or an incorporation of a work into a larger work in a creative way (such as into a medley that uses parts of other songs).

This is good for us in our task of interpreting GPL; it means we have a whole body of law to draw on for the meaning of this important phrase. The FSF has publicly declared that it considers the definition of work based on the

Program to be identical to that of a derivative work under copyright law. Unfortunately, while the term *derivative work* is clearly ensconced in copyright law, the law says almost nothing about what a derivative work of software might be. Copyright law is much more robust on works like books, music, and films. After all, software is relatively new compared with copyright law, which has been around for centuries—copyright is even mentioned in the US Constitution as one of the powers of the federal government.[4] On the other hand, software has only been around since the 1940s, and it was not clearly considered a copyrightable work of authorship until much later.

## The "Derivative Works" Question

To be precise, it is not accurate to call the border dispute a question of what is a derivative work. If you look at the case law, you will find many cases that discuss how much variation in the original work is required to make a derivative work. This is not the question we are asking at all. We are asking what constitutes an infringing work versus a separate, noninfringing work. However, the question is usually cast as whether the Application and Library are a derivative work of the Application, or a collective work.

The Copyright Act says this:

> A "derivative work" is a work based upon one or more preexisting works, such as a translation, musical arrangement, dramatization, fictionalization, motion picture version, sound recording, art reproduction, abridgment, condensation, or any other form in which a work may be recast, transformed, or adapted. A work consisting of editorial revisions, annotations, elaborations, or other modifications which, as a whole, represent an original work of authorship, is a "derivative work."

The Copyright Act also defines a *collective work* as "a work . . . in which a number of contributions, constituting separate and independent works in themselves, are assembled into a collective whole."

Copyright law allows a copyright owner to exclude others from making derivative works; however, it does not allow him to exclude others from creating collective works.

---

[4] "The Congress shall have Power . . .[t]o promote the Progress of Science and useful Arts, by securing for limited Times to Authors and Inventors the exclusive Right to their respective Writings and Discoveries," United States Constitution, Article I, Section 8.

In the language of GPL, some things are derivative works (i.e., they require one to exercise copyright in the original work) and some are *mere aggregation* (i.e., a compilation of separate works). The difference between these two is the crux of the border dispute. These two possibilities map to the difference between a derivative work and a collective work.

Before we delve into this, we can isolate one easy case. Most modern programs are delivered in *packages*. These packages can have different names. In Java programming, they are called JAR files. In Linux system programming, they are often called tarballs. They are also sometimes called images—particularly when an entire system is delivered in binary form. Putting software in the same JAR, tarball, or image as GPL code does not mean that software has to be licensed under GPL. In other words, if we deliver our Application and the time function Library in the same tarball, that doesn't mean—by itself—that the Library must be governed by GPL. That question depends on more detail about how the two elements of software interact when they are running. The packaging only governs how they are delivered.

Returning again to our "time" question, do you know which case is right— one or two? Of course not. To answer this question, we need to determine which work is at issue: Is it the Application and the Library as a whole, or is it only one of the components?

US copyright law offers little guidance on the difference between a single work and a collective work. There is an area of the law that is instructive, however—the law of statutory damages. Under US copyright law, an author can choose to sue for actual damages (the actual economic harm to the copyright holder) or statutory damages. The law sets a maximum amount of statutory damages for each work of authorship. "[W]here separate copyrights have no separate economic value, whatever their artistic value, they must be considered part of [a] ... work for purposes of the copyright statute" (*RSO Records, Inc. v. Peri*, 596 F.Supp. 849, 862 n. 16 (S.D.N.Y.1984)).

The economic value test would yield different results in different cases. In the cases of the Application and the Library, it seems fairly clear that they have separate markets. Obviously, the Library has uses for many Applications. The Application may not run without the Library, but it might also be useful on other operating systems that use other similar time libraries. So they do seem to be separate works. But the rule we have extracted from statutory damages law is hardly clear-cut, so we still need to consider how to analyze our question if we have no clear answer on this point.

Essentially, there are three possibilities:

1. The Application and the Library are one work.
2. The Application and the Library are separate works, and taken together, they form a collective work.
3. The Application and the Library are separate works, but when they are run together, they form a single work.

If we assume the Application and the Library are one work, our analysis is done. The Library is the Program, and the new work consisting of the Library and the Application is a work based on the Program. But what if they are separate works? This is a much more complicated question.

## The Curious Case of the Software Under Copyright

Let's start by assuming that the Application and the Library are two separate copyrightable works and that we, as the Application developer, plan to distribute only our Application and not the Library. (Assume that the Library will be publicly available, so we can reasonably expect our customers to already have it.) We would then ask whether the Application is substantially similar to the Library. What do they have in common? They have a programmatic interface in common—an API.[5] Can this make the Application a derivative work of the Library?

Copyright protects artistic expression. For a book, a movie, or a song, it is easy to understand what that means, but for a computer program, it is not so easy. Copyright does not protect functional elements. This principle is called the *idea/expression dichotomy* or the *merger doctrine*. Source code is not as flexible as natural language, and there are fewer creative ways to use it. For example, in most programming languages, there is only one way to put a value into a variable (such as a=1;); therefore, this element cannot be copyrightable. The more difficult question is how complicated the code must become to enjoy copyright protection. For example, say there are many such statements:

```
a=1;
b=1;
c=1;
```

Is this copyrightable? Probably not. But the more we add, the more likely there are many ways to write the code, some of which may be more elegant or expressive

---

[5] If you are unfamiliar with APIs, header files, and the concept of linking, please read Chapter 2: A Tutorial on Computer Software.

than others. Many languages will allow you to write the same code with different white space, such as:

```
a=1; b=1; c=1;
```

And in other languages you may be able to write:

```
a=b=c=1;
```

And as a functionally equivalent alternative, you could always write:

```
c=1;
b=1;
a=1;
```

or:

```
a=6/6;
b=.5*2;
c=SQRT(1); [using the square root function]
```

All these look a bit different, but is the choice to write these, rather than the first example, expressive or merely trivial? Conceptually, the problem with analyzing software copyright is that each statement like a=1; on its own is probably not protectable, but at a certain point, all of the unprotectable elements put together become protectable. It is not a bright line at all.

We must add to this the idea that much of software is dictated either by efficiency or the constraints of the programming language. Anything that is dictated by language syntax rules, technical requirements (such as hardware requirements), or functional needs is not copyrightable. If you put all this together, any work of software is a patchwork of copyrightable and uncopyrightable elements, yet the whole may be protectable. It is like music—each note is not protectable, but a phrase or line of music probably is protectable. For software, though, there are many discontinuities in protection, so the law has special rules for analyzing the protectability of software.

### What Does US Law Say?

To find out what US law has to say about our question, we look to the language of the Copyright Act and cases that have been decided by judges based on that Act. In our system of law—called a *common law* system—we have to consider both the statute and the cases that comment on it. The Copyright Act says, "In no case does copyright protection for an original work of authorship extend to any idea, procedure, process, system, method of operation, concept, principle, or discovery, regardless of the form in which it is described, explained, illustrated, or embodied in such work" (17 USC 102(b)). The notion embodied by this statute is sometimes referred to as the doctrine of *merger* or the *idea/expression dichotomy*. On its face, this spells grave news for software, which clearly is at its core a procedure, process, and method of operation. However, software is squarely covered by the copyright law as a "literary work."

The US Supreme Court has stated, "There are, and can be, few, if any, things which, in an abstract sense, are strictly new and original throughout. Every book in literature, science and art, borrows and must necessarily borrow, and use much which was well known and used before" (*Emerson v. Davies*, 8 F.Cas. 615, 619 (D. Mass. 1845)). This applies to software more than to any other kind of copyrightable work. Therefore, to build a framework for analyzing software copyright, some courts have adopted the "abstraction, filtration, and comparison" (AFC) test. This test determines whether one work accused of infringement actually does embody the copyright of another work. If it does, it is infringing (or derivative); if not, it is a separate work. Under the AFC test, the court goes through the following process:

- Abstract all expressive elements of the programs from their ideas.
- Filter out all unprotectable elements.
- Compare any remaining elements of creative expression.

If the remaining elements are substantially similar, then the accused work is infringing.

Unprotectable elements could include high-level program architecture, algorithms, or data structures. These elements are filtered out of both the original work and the accused work, and the remaining expressive elements remain. Then original work and the accused work are compared. If they are substantially similar, then the accusing work is a derivative work of the original and therefore infringes its copyright.

The Ninth Circuit (which is the US appeals court that has jurisdiction over California and therefore much of the software industry) uses the Analytic Dissection test. This test is similar, but not identical, to AFC. The test distinguishes between "intrinsic" and "extrinsic" components. *Intrinsic* or *expressive* elements are assessed "from the standpoint of the ordinary reasonable observer, with no expert assistance." The steps used in this assessment are as follows:

- Identify the source of the alleged similarity between the works (similar to the comparison step of the AFC test).

- Determine whether any of the allegedly similar features are protected by copyright (similar to the filtration step in the AFC test).

- Decide whether similar and protectable elements enjoy broad or thin protection (facts and ideas get thin protection).

- Decide whether the works are substantially similar as a whole.

The cases on this test do not involve computer software and are hard to apply to computer software. The analytic dissection test comes from *Sid & Marty Krofft Television Productions, Inc. v. McDonald's Corp.* and was later used in *Apple Computer, Inc. v. Microsoft Corp.* The *Apple* case concerned infringement by the Microsoft Windows GUI of the Apple Macintosh desktop GUI. *Sid & Marty Krofft* involved the infringement by the MacDonald's Hamburglar character of the characters in the television show *H.R. Pufnstuf.* For these, the viewpoint is that of an "ordinary reasonable observer, with no expert assistance." For software, of course, this viewpoint is just not useful. The ordinary reasonable observer has no idea what an API is at all. Also, it is sensible that an ordinary, reasonable observer would be able to make a reasoned judgment about whether puppets or GUIs look the same. For software, the question is not how the code looks but how expressive it is. The average person could not tell an expressive line of code from an unexpressive one.

The question of whether a programmatic interface, standing alone, is copyrightable is an unsettled matter of law. As this book goes to press in 2015, the *Oracle v. Google* case, centering on this issue, is still in the appeals process. Resolution of that case may clarify this issue, but until then, the case law on the question is laid out below.

In the *Worlds of Wonder* cases, the plaintiff sold a talking, dancing bear named "Teddy Ruxpin." The plaintiff held a copyright on the toy. The programming for the bear's movement and voice was stored on cassette tapes built into the toy. The defendants had changed the tapes, thereby changing the programming. The Ninth Circuit held that third-party tapes were infringing derivative works, even though the third-party tapes did not contain any part of the recordings from the original tapes. However, the copyright in this case subsisted in the toy as an audiovisual work. Software code is a literary work. It is easy to see why the test for similarity for audiovisual works would be different and why the entire work could be infringing even though the cassettes were entirely different. The test for substantial similarity of an audiovisual work is to compare the "total concept" of the accused work with that of the original. Moreover, the court observed that children were the primary audience for the work and based its analysis on a child's point of view.

*Micro Star v. Formgen*, or the Duke Nukem case, involved the popular first-person shooter video game *Duke Nukem 3D*. The distributed game included a build editor that allowed users to create their own levels. Micro Star created a CD-ROM from 300 user-created levels and distributed them. These levels did not incorporate any code or artwork from the game, but they used MAP files created by the build editor to instantiate levels using art libraries from the game. The court said, "A copyright owner holds the right to create sequels ... and the stories told in the N/I MAP files are surely sequels, telling new (though somewhat repetitive) tales of Duke's fabulous adventures. A book about Duke Nukem would infringe for the same reason, even if it contained no pictures." The court held the work to be infringing. Even though this case involved software, the analysis in the opinion compared the audiovisual displays of the game, rather than the software code. Again, the focus was on an audiovisual work, not a literary work.

These cases hold that a work can be infringing even if it contains no part of the original, despite the clearly enunciated rule that an infringing work "must substantially incorporate protected material from the preexisting work" (*Micro Star v. FormGen Inc.* 154 F.3d 1107 (9th Cir. 1998)).

If all this seems very complicated and unlikely to answer our question, it might be a relief to look at the case law in the First Circuit. The seminal case on copyright in computer software is *Lotus v. Borland*, 49 F.3d 807 (1995). In this case, the accused work was a computer menu command hierarchy. The court said, "When faced with nonliteral-copying cases, courts must determine whether similarities are due merely to the fact that the two works share the same underlying idea or whether they instead indicate that the second author copied the first author's expression." The court found the command menu hierarchy to be an uncopyrightable "method" as described in 17 USC 102(b):

> The Lotus menu command hierarchy ... serves as the method by which the program is operated and controlled. ... The Lotus menu command hierarchy is also different from the Lotus screen displays, for users need not "use" any expressive aspects of the screen displays in order to operate Lotus 1-2-3; because the way the screens look has little bearing on how users control the program, the screen displays are not part of Lotus 1-2-3's "method of operation." The Lotus menu command hierarchy is also different from the underlying computer code, because while code is necessary for the program to work, its precise formulation is not. In other words, to offer the same capabilities as Lotus 1-2-3, Borland did not have to copy Lotus's underlying code (and indeed it did not); to allow users to operate its programs

in substantially the same way, however, Borland had to copy the Lotus menu command hierarchy.

*Lotus v. Borland* remains the most instructive case for analyzing questions of protectability of APIs. The menu structure was, in fact, a kind of API—though between the macro writer and the spreadsheet program instead of between two programs.

Stepping a bit further afield into analogies, the LEXIS/Westlaw cases also analyze the bleeding edge of copyright. LEXIS and Westlaw are two leading companies in the field of reference books containing the published opinions of law courts. The texts of the opinions are not protected by copyright because they are works produced by the US government and therefore in the public domain. When Westlaw sued the owners of LEXIS for copying its material, it based the claim on the pagination of the cases in Westlaw's books. Mead had added a feature to its online products enabling the user to skip to a particular page in the opinion, as it would appear in the West reporter. In an initial decision in 1986, the Eighth Circuit found the use to be infringing. However, in light of the 1990 Supreme Court case *Feist Publications, Inc. v. Rural Telephone Service Co.*, which rejected the "sweat of the brow" doctrine in assessing copyright infringement, the same issue was later otherwise decided by the Second Circuit. As a consequence, use of West's paging is probably not considered infringement.

Even if a computer software interface is theoretically protectable under copyright, the reuse of small amounts of code for purposes of interoperability is often fair use. *Sega v. Accolade* held that copying an initialization code in software for Sega Genesis game cartridges was fair use. *Vault Corp. v. Quaid Software, Ltd.* held that copying and decompilation of a software program key and fingerprint was fair use. APIs are close to initialization codes and program keys in this respect—they are needed for interoperability. In fact, APIs are the very definition of interoperability.

### Summary

Overall, the law points to the notion that programmatic interfaces are likely to be functional and therefore not copyrightable. This, in turn, would point to the conclusion that the Application does not contain any protectable part of the Library, that it is therefore not a derivative work of the Library, and that the Application could therefore be distributed separately under a different license without violating GPL.

In sum, copyright law suggests that the Application and the Library are separate works, that neither is a derivative work of the other, and that the two taken together—regardless of whether they are integrated by dynamic linking, static linking, or otherwise—are a collective work rather than a single derivative work. However, as we will see below, the answer we get from a pure copyright analysis may not work in the real world of risk assessment.

## International Interpretations

The above derivative-works analysis presumes the application of US law. However, because the GPL has no choice-of-law provision and relies for its power on background copyright law, the scope of derivative works can be different in different jurisdictions. A thorough analysis of this question is beyond the scope of this book. However, the answer to the border dispute might differ across jurisdictions.

## The Approach of Legal Realism

The above analysis is important to understand—if only to know how complicated the legal questions surrounding GPL might be in an actual lawsuit. But businesses, faced with making decisions about how to comply with GPL every day in a murky legal landscape, don't usually rely on this kind of legal analysis. They make decisions based on their estimate of real-world risk. We now leave behind the pure legal analysis and examine best practices in a world where we assume the answer to the border dispute is unclear and is not likely to be cleared up anytime soon.

Quite a bit has been written on the Web about the border dispute, but much of it is confusing, uninformed, or mere rhetoric without logic. Keep in mind that the most important opinion about the application of GPL to any code belongs to the owner of the copyright in the code. If the copyright owner says that a particular practice—like linking the code to proprietary applications or using it as a library with proprietary code—is acceptable, then both the legal question and the risk question are resolved. But we might also consider the opinions of others, primarily because they reflect industry practice and community norms. Those offering the most frequent or useful opinions on this topic are the FSF. Recall that under a pure legal analysis, the statements we read by thought leaders the in the open source world are only of limited value as evidence of trade usage. But these statements matter a great deal to assessing real risk.

The FSF takes a functional approach to this question. Though that approach may seem arbitrary, at least it is useful. You may have heard that linking is the crux of this issue. That is not exactly true, but understanding linking is important to assessing the issue. (If you don't know what linking is, please take a few minutes to read Chapter 2: A Tutorial on Computer Software.)

Under this functional approach, the Application and the Library would either be considered part of the same Program or not, depending on how they interact but not on how they are packaged—including whether the Application developer is actually distributing the Library or not.

Even if the two are delivered separately, if they are considered part of the same work, the Free Software Foundation expressly states they must both be under GPL. The FSF has released a FAQ on the interpretation of GPL 2, and that FAQ says this:[6]

> *Q:* You have a GPL'ed program that I'd like to link with my code to build a proprietary program. Does the fact that I link with your program mean I have to GPL my program?
> *A:* Yes.

But the FSF also says:

> *Q:* If a program released under the GPL uses plug-ins, what are the requirements for the licenses of a plug-in?
> *A:* It depends on how the program invokes its plug-ins. If the program uses fork and exec to invoke plug-ins, then the plug-ins are separate programs, so the license for the main program makes no requirements for them.
> If the program dynamically links plug-ins, and they make function calls to each other and share data structures, we believe they form a single program, which must be treated as an extension of both the main program and the plug-ins. This means the plug-ins must be released under the GPL or a GPL-compatible free software license, and that the terms of the GPL must be followed when those plug-ins are distributed.
> If the program dynamically links plug-ins, but the communication between them is limited to invoking the "main" function of the plug-in with some options and waiting for it to return, that is a borderline case.

Many people find this discussion of linking confusing. While programmers may find it less so, it is still misleading. First, linking is a concept that only exists for certain kinds of programming languages, like C. When you are programming in languages like PERL, PHP, or HTML (so-called scripting languages), the concept of linking is meaningless or nearly so. The bottom line here is that for GPL

---

[6] www.gnu.org/licenses/gpl-faq.html#TOCLinkingWithGPL.

interpretation, the method of linking is a distinction without a difference. This makes sense because in a program build, it is usually possible to either dynamically or statically link any code of your choosing, depending on how you think the program will best perform. Static linking makes the program larger but eliminates processing time used to find the linked code. Dynamic linking makes more efficient use of memory while slowing down processing speed.

At one time, there was a notion floated in the open source world that dynamic linking mattered. In other words, in our example, if the Application and the Library were dynamically linked, they were two different programs, and if they were statically linked, they were the same program. Clearly, if they are statically linked, they are in the same binary file, but not if they are dynamically linked. But in practice, this is not a useful distinction.

Eric Raymond—one of the pioneers of open source and one of the founders of the Open Source Initiative—discussed this in a Web exchange regarding Linus Torvalds's views on whether LKMs create derivative works of the Linux kernel under the GPL. Someone commented that "Linus's opinion on this is irrelevant," and Raymond said:

> [I]n fact, I agree with his assessment. The key question is whether the particular kind of linking involved with loading binary modules propagates derivative-work status under copyright law. This is a legal question a court may rule on someday. Until one does, anyone who relies on such linking is taking a legal risk. … [But it] is not quite right that Linus's opinion is irrelevant. It is irrelevant to the underlying legal question, but not to the associated business risk.

And this is exactly so.

## The FSF's View

The FSF has made the most, and the most thoughtful, public commentary on the border dispute. Therefore, we take their position as a baseline best practice. Their position is as follows:

- Any linking (dynamic or static) to GPL code creates a single, derivative work of that code that falls within the boundary.
- Software that interacts via communications protocols such as pipes and sockets is not a derivative work.

- Software programs that interact only via shell commands and exec statements are separate works.
- User space is outside the boundary of the GPL applied to the kernel.
- Source code for a GPL program does not include standard Linux system or language libraries.

The FAQ on the GPL 2 says this:

> *Q:* What constitutes combining two parts into one program?
>
> *A:* This is a legal question, which ultimately judges will decide. We believe that a proper criterion depends both on the mechanism of communication (exec, pipes, rpc, function calls within a shared address space, etc.) and the semantics of the communication (what kinds of information are interchangd).
>
> If the modules are included in the same executable file, they are definitely combined in one program. If modules are designed to run linked together in a shared address space, that almost surely means combining them into one program.
>
> By contrast, pipes, sockets, and command-line arguments are communication mechanisms normally used between two separate programs. So when they are used for communication, the modules normally are separate programs. But if the semantics of the communication are intimate enough, exchanging complex internal data structures, that too could be a basis to consider the two parts as combined into a larger program.

According to FSF, therefore, anything that is linked in the same executable as GPL code must be covered by GPL. If our Application developer adheres to this rule, he will be safe. But in fact, there are exceptions to this rule, and the exceptions can be challenging to understand, particularly for non-engineers.

But in fact, the above rule does not fully enunciate the FSF's view—it is merely an expedient to avoid having one's coding practices fall outside FSF's approval. The FSF often refers to how "intimately" programs are integrated, and clearly this notion is an ad hoc or fluid one.

Because, in this sense, there is never a clear answer to the border dispute question, it is a good idea to follow the spirit of GPL, even when you can't tell whether you are following its letter. The spirit of the GPL is freedom—anyone who gets binaries should be able to get source code. Anyone who uses a binary should be able to fix it, study it, and change it. If you are pondering the border disputes because you are trying to hide functionality in proprietary modules, that is not the spirit of GPL. However, if the interface between proprietary modules and GPL modules is transparent, simple, well documented, and a true black box, then even if you have violated GPL, fewer people are likely to complain about it. And that, in a phrase, is risk management. Moreover, simple, clear interfaces are good engineering. So the best approach to comply with GPL is to do the right thing in engineering your software.

## Loadable Kernel Modules (LKMs)

The border dispute of GPL crystallized in the controversy over loadable kernel modules. For the most part, the Linux kernel is *monolithic*, meaning it is a single binary that loads when the computer boots up. But it can also support dynamically loaded modules. The poster child for this debate is a company called Nvidia, which has proprietary Linux drivers for its graphics card drivers—causing Richard Stallman to nickname the company "Invidious."[7]

However, other free software advocates and other Linux developers—such as Linus Torvalds—have expressed other views on the border dispute, particularly as it relates to LKMs. Torvalds's comments are particularly interesting:

> There are (mainly historical) examples of UNIX device drivers and some UNIX filesystems that were preexisting pieces of work, and which had fairly well-defined and clear interfaces and that I personally could not really consider any kind of "derived work" at all, and that were thus acceptable. The clearest example of this is probably the AFS (the Andrew Filesystem), but there have been various device drivers ported from SCO too.[8]

Torvalds is, of course, taking a fact-specific and practical view of the question. Linux was originally written to implement the interface specification of UNIX, so Torvalds naturally had assumed that the interface was free to use. He has also said this about the exception for system libraries:

> Well, there really is no exception. However, copyright law obviously hinges on the definition of "derived work," and as such anything can always be argued on that point.

---

[7] A caveat: It's hard to find evidence of this epithet on the Web. Some links on the topic appear to be broken.

[8] Quotes from Torvalds in this section are all from **www.win.tue.nl/~aeb/linux/lk/COPYING-modules.txt.**

I personally consider anything a "derived work" that needs special hooks in the kernel to function with Linux (i.e., it is _not_ acceptable to make a small piece of GPL-code as a hook for the larger piece), as that obviously implies that the bigger module needs "help" from the main kernel.

Similarly, I consider anything that has intimate knowledge about kernel internals to be a derived work.

What is left in the gray area tends to be clearly separate modules: code that had a life outside Linux from the beginning, and that do[es] something self-contained that doesn't really have any impact on the rest of the kernel. A device driver that was originally written for something else, and that doesn't need any but the standard UNIX read/write kind of interfaces, for example.

He has also said this:

Well, see above about the lack of exception, and about the fundamental gray area in _any_ copyright issue. The "derived work" issue is obviously a gray area, and I know lawyers don't like them. Crazy people (even judges) have, as we know, claimed that even obvious spoofs of a work that contain nothing of the original work itself, can be ruled to be "derived."

I don't hold views that extreme, but at the same time I do consider a module written for Linux and using kernel infrastructures to get its work done, even if not actually copying any existing Linux code, to be a derived work by default. You'd have to have a strong case to _not_ consider your code a derived work.

He has also observed that the more complex Linux gets, the less likely it is that an LKM should be considered a separate work:

The Linux kernel modules had (a long time ago), a more limited interface, and not very many functions were actually exported. So five or six years ago, we could believably claim that "if you only use these N interfaces that are exported from the standard kernel, you've kind of implicitly proven that you do not need the kernel infrastructure."

That was never really documented either (more of a guideline for me and others when we looked at the "derived work" issue), and as modules were more and more used not for external stuff, but just for dynamic loading of standard Linux modules that were distributed as part of the kernel anyway, the "limited interfaces" argument is no longer a very good guideline for "derived work."

So these days, we export many internal interfaces, not because we don't think that they would "taint" the linker, but simply because it's useful to do dynamic run-time loading of modules even with standard kernel modules that _are_ supposed to know a lot about kernel internals, and are obviously "derived works."

Torvalds takes the practical view that published interfaces support the existence of a separate work.

It's an issue of what a "plug-in" is—is it a way for the program to internally load more modules as it needs them, or is it _meant_ to be a public, published interface.

For example, the "system call" interface could be considered a "plug-in interface," and running a user mode program under Linux could easily be construed as running a "plug-in" for the Linux kernel. No?

And there, I obviously absolutely agree with you 100%: the interface is published, and it's _meant_ for external and independent users. It's an interface that we go to great lengths to preserve as well as we can, and it's an interface that is designed to be independent of kernel versions.

But maybe somebody wrote his program with the intention to dynamically load "actors" as they were needed, as a way to maintain a good modularity, and to try to keep the problem spaces well defined. In that case, the "plug-in" may technically follow all the same rules as the system call interface, even though the author doesn't intend it that way.

So I think it's to a large degree a matter of intent, but it could arguably also be considered a matter of stability and documentation (i.e., "require recompilation of the plug-in between version changes" would tend to imply that it's an internal interface, while "documented binary compatibility across many releases" implies a more stable external interface, and less of a derived work).

All of this underscores that there is no clear, identifiable difference between the way a program operates through a "standard" interface and any other kind of interface. This is part of the reason the border dispute remains so intractable—what constitutes a platform interface, a language interface, or a "standard" interface is fact specific and sometimes, ultimately, a matter of industry consensus. Moreover, it changes over time, as computing becomes increasingly layered.

## *Export Symbol*

The "Export Symbol" method of determining GPL compliance is probably less popular than it once was, but it remains an interesting window into the expression of an author's intent on difficult license interpretation questions, particularly for a complex project like the Linux kernel. The kernel contains a "MODULE_LICENSE" macro. An author of a module of Linux can include code so that invoking the macro will return a certain value if queried—it is a way to "hard code" licensing information into the software. For instance, if a module contains the statement MODULE_LICENSE("GPL"), it means the author intends that the license for any module being coded to that interface should be GPL. In other words, this is a way for the author to express his intent that the interface is part of the "Program" covered by GPL. Historically, Linux programmers have often followed these signals—LKMs coded to such an interface would be licensed under GPL. Compile/build systems can be set to generate errors if the wrong kind of licensing information applies to a module being used.

Here is an interesting discussion entitled "On the value of EXPORT_SYMBOL_GPL":[9]

> When a loadable module is inserted, any references it makes to kernel functions and data structures must be linked to the current running kernel. The module loader does not provide access to all kernel symbols, however; only those which have been explicitly exported are available. The export requirement narrows the API seen by modules, though not by all that much: there are over 6,000 symbols exported in the 2.6.13 kernel.
>
> Exports come in two flavors: vanilla (EXPORT_SYMBOL) and GPL-only (EXPORT_SYMBOL_GPL). The former are available to any kernel module, while the latter cannot be used by any modules which do not carry a GPL-compatible license. The module loader will enforce this distinction by denying access to GPL-only symbols if the module's declared license

---

[9]  lwn.net/Articles/154602/.

does not pass muster. Currently, less than 10% of the kernel's symbols are GPL-only, but the number of GPL-only symbols is growing. There is a certain amount of pressure to make new exports GPL-only in many cases.

It is a more difficult question, though, as to whether the absence of a GPL-only symbol means the interface could be used by a proprietary LKM. Silence may not be consent. In legal terms, an express statement that linking to proprietary code is allowed could be viewed as waiver or estoppel. However, that doesn't necessarily mean the converse: that failing to object to such integration means it is allowed. Moreover, with each new release of Linux, more modules are coded as GPL-only. Therefore, relying on EXPORT_SYMBOL analysis to analyze the border dispute is not a stable model and should be approached with caution.

Chapter 9

# LGPL 2.1 Compliance

LGPL version 2.1 may be one of the most abstruse licenses ever written. While its best practices for compliance are less difficult to understand than those of GPL, mapping those practices onto the text of LGPL is difficult.

The Lesser General Public License was written to enable authors to release libraries under a GPL-style license. Because GPL would require all code integrated into the same program as the library to be licensed under GPL, GPL does not work for libraries intended for use in proprietary applications. LGPL, therefore, was intended to relax some of the requirements of GPL to allow the license to be applied to libraries. LGPL 2.1 is an entirely separate license, so it is not obvious on its face that LGPL 2.1 is intended to be a variation of GPL.[1]

The basic rule of LGPL compliance (as understood by everyone) is that in proprietary applications, LGPL should be used only for dynamically linked libraries. But that rule is a best practice more than a requirement. The core terms in Section 6 of of LGPL 2.1 are as follows:

> As an exception to the Sections above, you may also com-
> bine or link a "work that uses the Library" with the Library
> to produce a work containing portions of the Library, and dis-
> tribute that work under terms of your choice, provided that the
> terms permit modification of the work for the customer's own
> use and reverse engineering for debugging such modifications. . . .
> Also, you must do one of these things:
> a) Accompany the work with the complete corresponding
> machine-readable source code for the Library including whatever
> changes were used in the work ... and, if the work is an execut-
> able linked with the Library, with the complete machine-readable
> "work that uses the Library," as object code and/or source code,

[1] In the version 3 licenses, this was done in a more understandable way—LGPL 3 is a set of additional permissions that apply as a supplement to the terms of GPL 3.

so that the user can modify the Library and then relink to produce a modified executable containing the modified Library.

b) Use a suitable shared library mechanism for linking with the Library. A suitable mechanism is one that (1) uses at run time a copy of the library already present on the user's computer system, rather than copying library functions into the executable, and (2) will operate properly with a modified version of the library, if the user installs one, as long as the modified version is interface-compatible with the version that the work was made with.

The well-known compliance rule regarding dynamic linking comes from section (b) above—dynamic linking is a shared library mechanism. Most companies, as a best practice, limit their use of LGPL code to dynamically linked libraries.

There is another way to comply, but most companies consider it riskier and less attractive. You can, for example, statically link LGPL code to your application if you both

- provide the source code for the Library; and
- provide complete machine-readable "work that uses the Library," as *object code and/or source code.*

This requires delivery of unlinked objects for proprietary software. While this would not normally require disclosure of proprietary code or information, it is an administrative burden to create such a package to deliver—a package unlikely to be used in precisely that form, even by the code developer. Also, lawyers are troubled by the "and/or" because they are concerned it will be interpreted as "and" and require delivery of source code for the application. It's likely that the better interpretation is that it does not require delivery and is thus intended to be a Boolean "or." But this ambiguity of "and/or"[2] is a drafting lesson that lawyers learn the hard way. In any case, the application developer usually does not wish to make the proprietary objects available for relinking or doesn't have the rights to do that due to upstream licensing restrictions for third-party proprietary objects.

Other complexities of LGPL compliance include the question of reverse engineering. LGPL 2.1 contains a provision that can conflict with most end user licenses. Section 6 says this:

---

[2] I am compelled to comment here that, like many lawyers, I hate this construction and never use it. I would rather include interpretive guidance that "or" is considered inclusive rather than exclusive (the exclusive form being, in programming, XOR), if the distinction must be made.

[Y]ou may also combine or link a "work that uses the Library" with the Library to produce a work containing portions of the Library, and distribute that work under terms of your choice, provided that the terms permit modification of the work for the customer's own use and reverse engineering for debugging such modifications."

Most proprietary licenses restrict reverse engineering, and they therefore conflict with the provision of LGPL 2.1 that requires the entire application to be provided on terms that "permit modification of the work for the customer's own use and reverse engineering for debugging such modifications." If a proprietary application is properly integrated with the LGPL code, then the interface is a black box and no such reverse engineering should be necessary. Therefore, this may not be a significant substantive concern for developers of proprietary applications, but it is a trap for the unwary—it's easy to violate LGPL by forgetting to carve out reverse-engineering restrictions to the extent necessary to allow this.

To comply with LGPL, the end user license must be revised to make an exception for the LGPL code. Practically speaking, this is not difficult, because any end user license for a product that includes LGPL code must contain carve-outs; LGPL code cannot be sublicensed and must be licensed only on the terms allowed by LGPL. For a discussion of how to resolve the two, see Chapter 17: Mergers & Acquisitions and Other Transactions.

Anyone responsible for compliance with LGPL should also note that some technology platforms, such as iOS and Android, do not support dynamic linking. Therefore, LGPL code is seldom appropriate for mobile applications.[3]

Finally, there is the 10-line limit on source code macros. LGPL limits the use, via static linking or "include" statements, to 10 lines. (For more explanation of in-line functions, see Chapter 2: A Tutorial on Computer Software.) This restriction is very limiting. Contemporary compilation techniques not only make use of more static linking and in-line compilation (because more weight is given to processing speed than memory limitations), but the 10-line limit may be based on a urban legend that anything under 10 lines of software is not subject to copyright.[4] While this 10-line limitation is potentially a thorny issue, it is pretty much ignored in practice.

---

[3] This is a conservative rule. It is possible to comply with LGPL in ways other than using the code via dynamic linking. Moreover, some authors of libraries that are useful in mobile applications make public statements that they approve the use of the code in mobile applications via static linking.

[4] There is no such rule under law per se; however, 10 lines is often given as an example threshold below which use would constitute fair use (a defense to infringement), or the 10 lines would not be protectable (and therefore there would be no infringement).

# GPL 3 and Affero GPL 3

GPL version 2 was released in 1991. As the 21st century approached, it was clear that a revision was in order. In the interim, the license had gained impressive traction, the software industry had changed, and some laws affecting software licensing had changed as well. The revision process was long and involved many stakeholders. The revised licenses have been in existence for some years now. This chapter outlines the differences between the new, version 3 licenses and their predecessors, and it describes how they apply to the current software landscape.

## GPL Version 3.0 (GPL 3)

Version 3 of the GPL was released on June 29, 2007. Since that time, its adoption has been relatively slow. Although many software projects have been released under GPL 3—or GPL 2 or a later version, which allows use under GPL 3—many projects remain under GPL 2 only.

The reluctance to follow FSF's lead in moving to the new version demonstrates that the revision happened at a time when the free software movement had lost traction to more practical voices, particularly those from private industry. Although private industry had, somewhat reluctantly, embraced free software, it had not embraced free software ideals or the leadership of the FSF. The GPL 3 revision project was long and difficult. During the process, there were acrimonious public arguments between key players—for instance, FSF and Linus Torvalds (and the kernel maintainers), who were unconvinced of the need for a new license. James Bottomley and others wrote:

> Since GPL has served us so well for so long, and since it is the foundation of our developer contract which has helped propel Linux to the successes it enjoys today, we are extremely reluctant to contemplate tampering with that license except as bug fixes to correct exposed problems or updates [to] counter immi-

nent dangers. So far, in the whole history of GPLv2 ... we have not found any bugs serious enough to warrant such correction.[1]

These disputes were ostensibly resolved by the time the final draft was issued, but they signaled deep philosophical differences in the open source community.

Also, during the redrafting project, Microsoft and Novell announced a patent deal. The terms of this deal were disclosed on a confidential basis to the SFLC,[2] and the terms were soon thereafter filed in connection with Novell's 10-K. This delayed the final draft and resulted in the so-called "Anti-Microsoft" and "Anti-Novell" provisions described below.

There is no doubt that GPL 2 needed to be improved and updated, but several of the new features that were added to GPL 3 were met with lukewarm acceptance, particularly among commercial enterprises. On the other hand, GPL 3 added some useful and clarifying terms. A detailed explanation of many of the changes embodied in GPL 3 appears in the FSF's rationale document for the last discussion draft.[3]

## *Versioning of Licenses*

Most copyleft licenses have versioning rules baked into them. Section 9 of GPL 2 said:

> The Free Software Foundation may publish revised and/or new versions of the General Public License from time to time. Such new versions will be similar in spirit to the present version, but may differ in detail to address new problems or concerns. Each version is given a distinguishing version number. If the Program specifies a version number of this License which applies to it and "any later version," you have the option of following the terms and conditions either of that version or of any later version published by the Free Software Foundation. If the Program does not specify a version number of this License, you may choose any version ever published by the Free Software Foundation.

---

[1] James Bottomley et al., "GPLv3 Position Statement," September 22, 2006, **lkml.org/lkml/ 2006/9/22/217**.

[2] Tom Sanders, "Novell opens legal books to GPL pundits,"Vunet.com, **www.vnunet.com/vnunet/ news/2168151/novells-opens-microsoft** (no longer available).

[3] Available at **gplv3.fsf.org/gpl3-dd4-rationale.pdf**.

Most software that had been released under GPL prior to the publication of version 3 was licensed under "GPL version 2 or any later version." At that point, all such software was available under either version, at the recipient's choice. The Linux kernel, however, was mostly under version 2 only.

In 2001, Torvalds wrote:

> I don't trust the FSF. I like the GPL a lot—although not necessarily as a legal piece of paper, but more as an intent. Which explains why, if you've looked at the Linux COPYING file, you may have noticed the explicit comment about "only _this_ particular version of the GPL covers the kernel by default". That's because I agree with the GPL as-is, but I do not agree with the FSF on many other matters. ... The FSF has long been discussing and is drafting the "next generation" GPL, and they generally suggest that people using the GPL should say "v2 or at your choice any later version." ... The "v2 only" issue might change some day, but only after all documented copyright holders agree on it, and only after we've seen what the FSF suggests. From what I've seen so far from the FSF drafts, we're not likely to change our v2-only stance, but there might of course be legal reasons why we'd have to do something like it (i.e., somebody challenging the GPLv2 in court, and part of it to be found unenforceable or similar would obviously mean that we'd have to reconsider the license).[4]

As Torvalds accurately pointed out, those who choose to license their software—even optionally—under any later version are placing a great deal of trust in the license steward.

In fact, because the kernel development project was run without a contribution agreement, it would probably be impossible to reconsider the license.[5] GPL 2 and GPL 3 are not compatible—a program has to be under either one or the other.[6] Therefore, it is possible to combine in one program code that is under GPL 3 and "GPL 2 or any later version"—this would mean the whole program would be licensed under GPL 3. However, it is not possible to combine software under GPL 3 and "GPL 2 only."

---

[4] lkml.org/lkml/2003/6/15/67.

[5] For more on why, see Chapter 16: Open Source Releases.

[6] Richard Stallman, "Why Upgrade to GPL Version 3?" a communication distributed to the comment committee distribution list on May 31, 2007.

Assuming a project had been available under either version, the project could, at any point, have chosen only the later version. This "migration" was not undertaken by many projects after the release of GPL 3; it was undertaken by the projects run by FSF, such as GCC and other GNU tools.

## GPL 2 Versus GPL 3

GPL 3 was an entire rewrite of the license; little of the original text remains. However, there are only a handful of significant substantive differences; most of the changes were intended to clarify the original intent of GPL 2 and update it to meet the legal and technical context of the twenty-first century. The substantive differences, roughly in order of importance, are as follows:

- Derivative works (or scope) definition
- Definition of copyleft trigger
- Patent licensing
- Other patent provisions
- Obfuscation and disabling ("anti-Tivoization")
- DRM provisions
- DMCA provisions
- Effect of corporate transactions

## The "Derivative Works" Issue

The biggest question for most business users of GPL software has to do with its scope: What software must be made available under GPL? GPL 2 caused great confusion on this issue.[7] GPL 3 took positive steps to clarify this question.

Whereas GPL 2 treated this subject primarily as a question of what is a derivative work, GPL 3 moved away from that calculus; the term *derivative work* is mainly drawn from US law, and one object of GPL 3 was to internationalize the license.

GPL 3's formulation of scope turns mainly on the definition of *Corresponding Source*, which includes "definition files associated with source files for the work, and the source code for shared libraries and dynamically linked subprograms that the work is specifically designed to require, such as by intimate data communication or control flow between those subprograms and other parts of the work." Whereas GPL 2's inclusion of dynamically linked files within its scope was left to external interpretive evidence, GPL 3 incorporated some of the language of the

---

[7] For a detailed analysis, see Chapter 8: The GPL 2 Border Dispute.

FSF's prior FAQs on this issue for GPL 2. While "intimate" communication may still be subject to interpretation, GPL 3 has clarified that dynamically linked files are required.

GPL 3 also clarifies that standard language libraries need not be covered by GPL even if they link to GPL code. In the intervening time between GPL 2 and GPL 3, computing became more layered: today's computing environment usually includes multiple language platforms or virtual machines. Rather than drawing a single line between user space and operating system space, GPL 3 allows integration of multiple platform layers without requiring a single licensing paradigm to cover them all.

## Copyleft Triggers

The trigger for copyleft conditions for GPL 2 was distribution. (See Chapter 6: What Is Distribution? for more detail on this issue.) However, the term *distribution* is somewhat specific to US copyright law. Because GPL 3 was intended to internationalize and clarify the license, its language was greatly changed to avoid turning on a definition drawing from US law. During the drafting process, opinions differed greatly on whether to close the *ASP loophole*—the ability to provide software on a SAAS basis and not make source code available. In the years between the publication of GPL 2 in 1991 and the drafting project of GPL 3 in 2007, the software industry had undergone a sea change away from on-premises installation of software and toward SAAS. Some felt that this allowed free riders to make significant commercial use of GPL software without sharing source code; others thought that changing this rule would create havoc in an industry that had based compliance processes on whether software was distributed.

In GPL 3, two new terms of art were introduced: *conveying* and *propagating*. Only *conveying* triggers copyleft requirements. GPL 3 specifically states that "[m]ere interaction with a user through a computer network, with no transfer of a copy, is not conveying." *Propagating* is a broader term that might include what some refer to (confusingly and inaccurately) as *internal distribution*, or SAAS use.

## Patents

GPL 2 contains no express patent licenses. Between the time GPL 2 was released in 1991 and the GPL 3 revision process in 2007, many other open source licenses were revised to contain express patent licenses. During that time, software patents became more common. FSF took the position that although there was no express patent license in GPL 2, there was an implied license. Because the law of implied licensing is unclear, the scope of that license was unclear.

The scope of the express license in GPL 3 was a compromise; the patent terms were lightning rods of controversy in the drafting discussions. In the end, GPL 3 contained express licenses that were similar to, but probably slightly broader than, those of other copyleft licenses and Apache 2. Like the terms of the other licenses, the patent grant in GPL 3 only inured to contributors to the software. Thus, a "mere redistributor" granted no right under the express license. The license extended to a contributor's "essential patent claims," which are patents "owned or controlled" by the contributor "whether already acquired or hereafter acquired."

Most other open source licenses with express patent grants contain defensive termination provisions. GPL 3 does not, exactly, but contains terms with a similar effect in Section 10:

> You may not impose any further restrictions on the exercise of the rights granted or affirmed under this License. For example, you may not impose a license fee, royalty, or other charge for exercise of rights granted under this License, and you may not initiate litigation (including a cross-claim or counterclaim in a lawsuit) alleging that any patent claim is infringed by making, using, selling, offering for sale, or importing the Program or any portion of it.

Accordingly, any patent claim by a licensee accusing the GPL 3 software will be a breach of the license and terminate not only the patent license from others but the copyright license as well.

The patent license grant was not terribly controversial in the end. It was customary given similar terms in other open source licenses that had been in practice for years. The controversy centered on the patent provisions added in the final draft—the so-called "Anti-Microsoft" and "Anti-Novell" provisions. These provisions were added to the draft with little community input, near the end of the drafting effort, and they therefore did not benefit from much mindshare of the community on whether they made sense from either a substantive or a drafting perspective. Most readers of GPL 3 find them bewildering.

The Microsoft/Novell deal involved a promise to grant a patent non-assert by Microsoft for software distributed by Novell, for which Novell (and presumably its customers, ultimately) paid a fee. In this case, Microsoft avoided distributing GPL code—thereby avoiding a patent license being implied—but received a fee for granting the right and also benefited from the related marketing deal with Novell. Apparently, FSF wished to make such arrangements inconsistent with the exercise of a license under GPL 3.

Section 11 of GPL 3 says this:

> If you convey a covered work, knowingly relying on a patent license, and the Corresponding Source of the work is not available for anyone to copy, free of charge and under the terms of this License, through a publicly available network server or other readily accessible means, then you must either (1) cause the Corresponding Source to be so available, or (2) arrange to deprive yourself of the benefit of the patent license for this particular work, or (3) arrange, in a manner consistent with the requirements of this License, to extend the patent license to downstream recipients. "Knowingly relying" means you have actual knowledge that, but for the patent license, your conveying the covered work in a country, or your recipient's use of the covered work in a country, would infringe one or more identifiable patents in that country that you have reason to believe are valid.

This paragraph is hard to understand at first blush but relatively easy to comply with by taking option (1) and making the Corresponding Source "available for anyone to copy, free of charge and under the terms of this License." Theoretically, causing the Corresponding Source to be available allows recipients of the software to more easily engineer around patent infringement claims. The provision's usefulness is questionable, but it does not present any thorny problems of interpretation. Anyone who conveys a work under GPL 3 has an obligation to make source code available; this provision only requires the source code to be available to any taker; the easiest route to compliance is to post the code on a publicly available website.

Another paragraph of Section 11 says this:

> If, pursuant to or in connection with a single transaction or arrangement, you convey, or propagate by procuring conveyance of, a covered work, and grant a patent license to some of the parties receiving the covered work authorizing them to use, propagate, modify or convey a specific copy of the covered work, then the patent license you grant is automatically extended to all recipients of the covered work and works based on it.

Of course, if the licensee ("you") does not have the right to grant a patent license to every recipient, this provision cannot make it so; presumably, the licensee that is unable to grant such broad rights will be in breach of the license. Therefore, a licensee ("you") who conveys a GPL 3 work must either clear patent rights for all recipients or for none. Of course, this excludes business models that might do otherwise, but few companies are interested in such strategies. This is the probably most troublesome provision of GPL 3. Many patent licenses are granted to settle end-patent litigation. A defendant (licensee) who receives a patent license in settlement will almost never be able to negotiate a broad enough right to comply with this provision. Therefore, faced with a third-party patent claim, the licensee may have to choose between settling the litigation and conveying the GPL 3 software. That is a business risk; it could cause the licensee to have to cease the use of the GPL 3 software, through no fault of its own.

Finally, Section 11 contains this language:

> A patent license is "discriminatory" if it does not include within the scope of its coverage, prohibits the exercise of, or is conditioned on the non-exercise of one or more of the rights that are specifically granted under this License. You may not convey a covered work if you are a party to an arrangement with a third party that is in the business of distributing software, under which you make payment to the third party based on the extent of your activity of conveying the work, and under which the third party grants, to any of the parties who would receive the covered work from you, a discriminatory patent license (a) in connection with copies of the covered work conveyed by you (or copies made from those copies), or (b) primarily for and in connection with specific products or compilations that contain the covered work, unless you entered into that arrangement, or that patent license was granted, prior to 28 March 2007.

This provision is clearly an attempt to prevent deals like the one Novell entered into with Microsoft; Novell had done roughly what was described here. However, the date at the end of the provision grandfathers in that deal. This was the date of the first discussion draft of GPL 3 that included language addressed at the deal, but the deal was entered into before that time.

## DMCA

The Digital Millennium Copyright Act (DMCA) went into effect in 1998—between the publication of GPL 2 and GPL 3. Discussion of the DMCA can be confusing because the law covers several distinct subjects.[8] The element of concern for free software is the part that gets the most attention in the news: an

---

[8] The DMCA also provides a safe harbor for online service providers—a separate subject that sometimes gets tarred with the same brush.

odd addition to the copyright law that provides for civil and criminal penalties for the act of reverse engineering to circumvent copyright protection. The provision is odd because it covers actions not regulated by the main provisions of the copyright law. It was quickly invoked in the law to prevent actions that may never have been anticipated by its passage.[9] It was passed in part to enable the entertainment industry to implement digital rights management technology, or DRM.

Although the free software community tends to oppose DRM,[10] that is more an issue around content than software. However, a time-honored functionality of open source software is to hack all kinds of security measures. The anti-DRM provisions of GPL 3 went through quite a bit of revision in the drafting process and caused much disagreement among stakeholders. Some were concerned that any such provision would have to be so general that it would exclude legitimate security functionality. The Open Source Definition requires nondiscrimination as to all fields of endeavor, so it would not have been acceptable to exclude DRM— or any other kind of functionality—from being licensed under GPL 3, nor would it have been acceptable to exclude modifications to add that functionality. The final provision in GPL 3 is seldom invoked and was watered down to the point of non-controversy.

Section 3 of GPL 3 says this:

### Protecting Users' Legal Rights From Anti-Circumvention Law

No covered work shall be deemed part of an effective technological measure under any applicable law fulfilling obligations under article 11 of the WIPO copyright treaty adopted on 20 December 1996, or similar laws prohibiting or restricting circumvention of such measures.

When you convey a covered work, you waive any legal power to forbid circumvention of technological measures to the extent such circumvention is effected by exercising rights under this License with respect to the covered work, and you disclaim any intention to limit operation or modification of the work as a means of enforcing, against the work's users, your or third parties' legal rights to forbid circumvention of technological measures.

---

[9] See *Chamberlain v. Skylink*, 381 F.3d 1178 (Fed. Cir. 2004) and *Lexmark Int'l, Inc. v. Static Control Components, Inc.*, 387 F.3d 522 (6th Cir. 2004).

[10] www.gnu.org/philosophy/opposing-drm.html.

In other words, a redistributor under GPL 3 cannot simultaneously claim the enjoyment of the license and bring claims under this section of the DMCA; the two positions would be antithetical, and doing so would, arguably, have been a prohibited "further restriction" under Section 7.

## Disabling and Obfuscation[11]

Section 6 of GPL 3 contains provisions intended to solve the so-called Tivoization problem. Free software advocates were concerned that, while GPL required the delivery of source materials, it did not exactly require the redistributor to enable the recipient of the software to change and install the software in a product in which the software is embedded. On its face, it can be challenging to comply with GPL in a meaningful way for software in embedded systems. Suppose you distribute a toaster that includes GPL software. The software is not written or debugged on the toaster. It is written in a development environment, possibly including an emulator debugging tool that mimics the operation of the toaster but runs on a standard computer system. How can you give the recipient the means to revise the software? At a certain level, it may be impossible, or it might require you to deliver prototype devices—which is clearly not a requirement of GPL. Most embedded system developers comply with GPL by providing source code that compiles in a standard environment.

In addition, enabling users of physical devices to modify embedded software can cause serious support or security issues. Some vendors lock down their devices by introducing technical blocks that will disallow operation or connection to communications networks if the software has been changed. This is not a problem with an obvious solution. How can the freedom of the recipient to change software be balanced against the need to prevent software bugs that would cause physical damage or security breaches?

Section 6 only applies to certain kinds of products. It defines a *User Product* as (1) a consumer product or (2) anything designed or sold for incorporation into a dwelling.[12] It requires the distributor to provide installation information.

> "Installation Information" for a User Product means any methods, procedures, authorization keys, or other information required to install and execute modified versions of a covered work in that User Product from a modified version of its Corresponding Source. The

---

[11] This is sometimes called the "Tivo problem." I make no claims about Tivo or its practices; this is simply a shorthand phrase common in the free software world.

[12] Note that the focus is on the product rather than the user; the open source definition disallows making distinctions between users. See **www.opensource.org/docs/definition.php**.

information must suffice to ensure that the continued functioning of the modified object code is in no case prevented or interfered with solely because modification has been made.

The requirement to provide Installation Information does not include a requirement to continue to provide support service, warranty, or updates for a work that has been modified or installed by the recipient, or for the User Product in which it has been modified or installed. Access to a network may be denied when the modification itself materially and adversely affects the operation of the network or violates the rules and protocols for communication across the network.

Notwithstanding the carve-out, which was added to allay concerns expressed by many parties during the drafting discussions, many consumer electronics companies are reluctant to use code under GPL 3. They find delivering this information to be too potentially risky to their business.

## Affero GPL

Because the threshold for copyleft triggers did not change in the move from GPL 2 to GPL 3, FSF released a variation of GPL 3 to close this loophole. Before that time, several licenses had set SAAS (or ASP) use as a threshold for triggering copyleft issues. The most notable of these was the Affero GPL, which was created by Affero Inc. The version of Affero GPL that existed prior to GPL 3 said this:

If the Program as you received it is intended to interact with users through a computer network and if, in the version you received, any user interacting with the Program was given the opportunity to request transmission to that user of the Program's complete source code, you must not remove that facility from your modified version of the Program or work based on the Program, and must offer an equivalent opportunity for all users interacting with your Program through a computer network to request immediate transmission by HTTP of the complete source code of your modified version or other derivative work.[13]

FSF incorporated this idea into a variant of GPL called Affero GPL 3, which is identical to GPL 3 except that making the software available over a net-

---

[13]  www.affero.org/oagpl.html.

work triggers the copyleft conditions that require source code to be made available. It contains this provision:

> **Remote Network Interaction; Use with the GNU General Public License.**
>
> Notwithstanding any other provision of this License, if you modify the Program, your modified version must prominently offer all users interacting with it remotely through a computer network (if your version supports such interaction) an opportunity to receive the Corresponding Source of your version by providing access to the Corresponding Source from a network server at no charge, through some standard or customary means of facilitating copying of software. This Corresponding Source shall include the Corresponding Source for any work covered by version 3 of the GNU General Public License that is incorporated pursuant to the following paragraph.

Note that these requirements only exist if you modify the software. Mere users need not make source code available. In part because this license is not very commonly used, it is still unclear what constitutes *interaction*. For instance, if this license covered a language engine and you made changes to that engine and made a program executing in that language available to users online, would the language engine be interacting remotely with the users? Or does this require direct interaction, such as with a GUI or application? No one knows. The main program available under AGPL is MongoDB, a database engine. MongoDB is available under dual licensing, so anyone who worries about this issue simply buys an alternate license; therefore, this question is unlikely to be tested or resolved anytime soon.

Affero GPL 3 also says this:

> Notwithstanding any other provision of this License, you have permission to link or combine any covered work with a work licensed under version 3 of the GNU General Public License into a single combined work, and to convey the resulting work. The terms of this License will continue to apply to the part which is the covered work, but the work with which it is combined will remain governed by version 3 of the GNU General Public License.

GPL 3 contains a counterpart in Section 13:

> **Use with the GNU Affero General Public License.**
>
> Notwithstanding any other provision of this License, you have per-

mission to link or combine any covered work with a work licensed
under version 3 of the GNU Affero General Public License into a single combined work, and to convey the resulting work. The terms of
this License will continue to apply to the part which is the covered
work, but the special requirements of the GNU Affero General Public License, section 13, concerning interaction through a network
will apply to the combination as such.

This allows the two licenses to be horizontally compatible; it's possible to combine GPL 3 code and Affero GPL 3 code in a single program.

## *Apache 2 License Compatibility*[14]

After the kerfuffle about whether Apache 2 and GPL 2 were compatible, the GPL 3 drafting project aimed to bury that hatchet. Apache 2 and GPL 3 were declared compatible—though given that many people did not understand the compatibility argument in the first place, the solution to the problem seemed a bit too easy. In any case, FSF apparently determined that the addition of patent and other provisions to GPL 3 reconciled the two.[15]

---

[14]  See Chapter 4: License Compatibility.

[15]  www.gnu.org/philosophy/license-list.html#apache2.

# Chapter 11

# Open Source Policies

Today, it is considered a best practice for a company to have a written open source policy. In some areas of law (such as employment law), the fact of having a written policy has a direct bearing on liability, but for open source, the policy is entirely functional. Copyright infringement is largely is a *strict liability* regime—meaning that intent is not an element of infringement.[1] Therefore, a company will not be able to avoid liability for the infringing acts of its employees merely because it has a written policy. A written policy that everyone disregards is worthless and, in fact, can be counterproductive because it sends a signal that the company will look the other way when violations occur.

Written policies need not be long or complicated. But having them in writing is useful, particularly when a company has multiple development teams who may be in different countries and may speak different languages. Having a written policy gives these teams the time and opportunity to read and understand the policy, ask questions, and refer to the policy when necessary.

A model open source policy appears in Appendix A. However, there is no one-size-fits-all policy. Here are some things to consider if you are contemplating an open source policy for your business.

## *Start Small*

Your company may not need all the topics in the model policy at the outset; the policy is drafted to allow you to remove the "extras" easily. The most important elements of the policy are the compliance elements, which make up most of the policy. Topics like contributions, code releases, and transactional terms can be added when the company is ready for them; before that time, these elements are usually handled ad hoc.

---

[1] Willful infringement can lead to a higher statutory damages award, but that is a relatively minor enhancement compared to what occurs in other areas of law.

## Business Processes

The corollary to the policy is the process that attends it. The policy only describes certain checks and processes; the business then has to implement them. For example, if using GPL code in a product requires the approval of an engineering manager or the legal department, the company may want to implement an automated way to generate that request. Also, every company needs to consider how it will capture and store the information about the open source software it is using. Using spreadsheets is a fairly bad way to do this, and any method is only useful if it is easy to update and if updating it is incorporated into the development and release cycle. A company should also consider when in the development cycle the open source "seal of approval" needs to be applied. The closer to release it happens, the more likely that any remediation or substitution of code to comply with open source licenses will delay release or simply be abandoned in favor of meeting the release date.

## Staffing

The title of the person designated to approve requests to use open source software in the business will differ from company to company. Some companies want to conserve the resources of their legal department and delegate some decisions to engineering management; some take the opposite approach and delegate the question to legal; some have a committee to deal with open source matters (usually composed of representatives from legal, engineering, and management areas); some hire a specialist paralegal or lawyer to handle open source matters. Most open source compliance matters can be handled by someone with minimal, but solid, engineering and legal training. As the volume of approvals at a company goes up, decisions need to be pushed down to an operational level so senior management is not tasked with making routine or recurring decisions. Recurring requests to use the same open source software are frequent because code that works well in one company product may very well work well in all of them.

## License-Based Review

The model policy focuses on review of software based on the license that covers it, and this is the way most companies review their potential use of open source software. However, there are good reasons to take a more nuanced approach. Some companies review and approve the use of open source software package by package; this is most common when the company has heightened security concerns or exacting product qualification requirements from their customers. Some companies create a "sandbox" from which all open source software used in the company must be drawn, and they forbid downloading directly from the Internet. Some companies review open source software for patent infringement or other legal matters (such as export restrictions) as well. Accordingly, the model policy takes a lightweight approach to review, based only on the license.

## Use Cases

A policy for an SAAS company may not fit a consumer electronics company, and vice versa. They are at opposite ends of the spectrum of open source risk. Depending on the company's appetite for risk, it may require much less review of open source risks than do other companies. However, SAAS companies should keep in mind that basing an open source compliance policy on the absence of distribution can lead to terrible results. Most SAAS companies eventually distribute their products—whether to customers who want a private instance of the software to manage regulatory or security issues, to corporate partners or affiliates, or to successors in interest. So don't start what you can't finish—interleaving GPL code with proprietary code in the same program, particularly at a granular level, will likely lead to problems someday. Also, companies that assume they are immune to open source risk will be tempted to ignore record keeping. Taken together, these practices can mean the software can never be distributed. Then, when the company decides that distribution is its next business initiative, no one will want to deliver the news that it can't be done without a massive reengineering and audit effort.

Chapter 12

# Audits and Due Diligence

While most audits are conducted at the time of an investment, corporate sale, or other such transaction, other audits are conducted in connection with customer sales or simply as a process of establishing responsible internal business controls that manage intellectual property hygiene. Today, many customers who are buying licenses for software insist on a full disclosure of open source components. In fact, if the product is to be distributed to the customer, the vendor has an obligation to provide this information to the customer—in the form of the license notices required by the applicable open source licenses.

Open source compliance can be easy to forget and can suddenly become a major concern. It is best to be ready for this challenge before you need to make guarantees that your company is compliant.

## *The Challenges of Open Source Compliance*

Open source compliance is not especially difficult—particularly compared to compliance requirements for proprietary licenses, which might require constant tracking of the software's users, servers, or use cases. In fact, on a conceptual level, open source compliance is easy in most cases. Only a small number of use cases raise the potentially complex legal issues discussed in Chapter 6: What Is Distribution? and Chapter 8: The GPL 2 Border Dispute. But open source compliance does involve some information management challenges, and when people say open source compliance is difficult, they are usually referring to this issue.

The information management challenge arises because open source software tends to circumvent normal business processes. In contrast, if you must license software from a proprietary vendor, then you must first pay a license fee. Most businesses have internal controls that capture the payment of fees: if you must write a check to a licensor, you must sign a license agreement, and the license agreement must undergo legal review, which causes a lawyer or contract negotiator to consider whether the uses contemplated by the company will be compliant and whether the fees to be paid are reasonable in light of the licensing terms. However, open source is always free of charge and can usually be downloaded freely from the Internet without signing any agreement or paying any fee. This means that for most organizations, there are no internal controls that capture the initial use of the software and, therefore, there is no advance consideration of whether the company can comply with the licenses. Open source compliance is left as a "cleanup" matter for a later time.

As a consequence, many companies wake up one day to discover that they do not know what open source software they are using or whether they are compliant with open source licenses. When this happens, companies may initiate an audit. Alternatively, companies are often forced to initiate an audit when a potential buyer or customer demands it.

## Snapshots, Surveys, and Title Searches

There are two kinds of audits—the snapshot and the ongoing business review. If you have been asked to undertake an audit to support a transaction like an investment or acquisition, you are probably taking a snapshot. The snapshot identifies the open source software in your code base at a particular moment in time; for an acquisition, that would be the moment of closing the transaction. However, companies that are more sophisticated about open source compliance want to make sure that they are always compliant—not just when someone else demands it. Therefore, they conduct diligence on an ongoing basis as code is added or changed in the code base of their products.

An open source audit is like any other audit, in the sense that one is looking for problems but one can never be sure that all problems have been found. The art of auditing involves engaging in efforts that are financially and technically practical to eliminate the most significant problems. The proper level of effort depends on how risky you think a mistake will be, and that in turn depends on the use case for the software you are auditing and your assessment of the existing internal controls used to manage open source licensing compliance.

There is no one right way to conduct an audit. Lawyers are often asked to make a decision about whether to hire a code-scanning consultant to examine the code. It is never wrong to do this. However, hiring a consultant is like buying insurance: it may be useful, but it may be too expensive. It's possible to spend all the money you like on managing risk, but it only makes sense to spend money on activities that actually reduce risk.

Economically speaking, the equation is this:

```
AC < R * L,
```

where AC = Audit Cost, R = Risk of a problem, and L = Loss that would occur if the problem occurred.

Thus, a problem with a small likely loss is not worth spending a great deal of money to find. Risk and loss depend on use case and your assessment of the company's internal controls. If a company has no internal controls on open source software use, R will be higher. If the software is distributed in a consumer electronics product, both R and L will be higher than they would be for an SAAS product.

It is not difficult to tell whether a company has internal controls for open source compliance processes in place—all you have to do is ask. For instance, if you ask for a list of open source code that is in a product, and if the company doesn't have such a list (or doesn't understand the question), then the company likely has no compliance process in place. In such a case, hiring a code scanner is a great idea. However, if the company provides a list of open source code and licenses that looks reasonably professional, you may decide that hiring a code scanner is unlikely to yield additional information that is material to risk.

There are two overarching approaches to automated auditing: forensic matching and string searching. Companies like Black Duck Software, Palamida, nexB, and OpenLogic perform services known as forensic matching. In other words, they examine the source code for a particular code base and match it against known open source code. They identify the known open source code by its tools. The other approach is to run a string-matching program, which programmers often call a *GREP*.[1] This kind of program compares *strings* (which in programming language means text characters) in the source code against *regular expressions*—meaning target strings, sometimes with wild cards—to find indicia of licensing terms such as copyright notices and licensing statements. Using GREPS is a bit like typing a query into a search engine. So for instance, if you searched the code base for "copyright," "Copr.," or "license," you would find copyright notices, licensing notices, and probably a lot of extraneous items as well. Programs like FOSSology, an open source utility for compliance, use this basic approach.

Alternatively, you may be asked to conduct an audit based on the external records kept by the company. Most often, self-disclosures are in the form of spreadsheets or text lists, and they list software and licenses. The difference between these two approaches is like the difference between a land survey and a title search. Forensic matching is like a survey—it looks at what is actually there and tries to map it onto known information. String matching or self-reporting is like a title search—it looks at what people have recorded about the licensing of the code and assumes that the information is reliable.

---

[1] GREP, the name of an old UNIX routine that does string searching, stands for "globally search a regular expression and print."

In truth, neither of these approaches is foolproof, nor is either without its challenges. Forensic matching is less prone to false negatives—it can find open source for which the copyright and licensing notices have been removed from the software being audited. This removal of licensing notices is considered poor programming practice, but it happens. However, forensic matching is prone to false positives in that it finds potential problems that are not actual problems. On the other hand, a GREP approach will not identify code for which licensing information has been removed or not properly preserved. Therefore, the GREP approach is very useful at identifying entire packages, files, or libraries of open source code, but it may not be successful in identifying fragments or snippets of code.

In an auditing effort, false negatives are more dangerous than false positives. Therefore, proper auditing techniques should tend toward zero false negatives and minimal false positives. To understand better how this works, consider the following seeming paradox: Most people who test positive for a serious disease probably don't have it. Does this mean the test is wrong? No, it means the test is properly designed to avoid false negatives. If the test is positive, more accurate tests will be done, and these tests are intended to weed out the false positives. The first level of testing is performed on a much larger population than subsequent tests, so it produces many more false positives than the true positives found in later testing. Any kind of audit of testing works in this way.

But as a result, reports that are generated by auditing efforts can be maddeningly difficult to review. They tend to include a lot of false positives, or "noise." Every code base will have small fragments of code that may be taken from elsewhere, but not all such fragments constitute infringement. For very common code lines, it may be difficult to tell the original source. Also, the copyright law will not protect what it calls *de minimis* use of copyrighted material.

The upshot of all this is that audit reports give you information, not answers.

## Setting the Rules

Once you perform such an audit, you must determine whether the information you have found meets the criteria that you have set for compliance. For many companies, these criteria are embodied in an open source software policy. (For more on open source policies, see Chapter 11: Open Source Policies.) Different companies have different levels of tolerance for risk, and different use cases have different risk profiles. However, one thing is certain: you cannot tell whether an audit has passed your criteria if you don't have criteria to apply.

Today, most companies conducting audits consider permissive licenses to be of little concern. Of course, distributing code that includes open source software licensed under permissive licenses requires the delivery of a notice, so some basic compliance is always necessary. However, delivering notices is almost always possible, even if administratively burdensome. Mostly, in audits a company is looking for copyleft software—particularly copyleft software under licenses like GPL and LGPL—because it is concerned that the audited software may have been engineered in a way that causes compliance to be impossible, even if all of the information is known and the license notices are applied. For example, if a proprietary application uses a GPL library, it may be impossible to comply simultaneously with both licenses.

## The Perils of Self-Disclosures

Self-disclosures are often skeletal, inaccurate, and misleading. They generally contain correct information about the open source code that is included—at least at a package level. A list of open source components can usually be generated by the build instructions for the software. This package-level information is reasonably reliable because the compiler must be given this information in order to build the product. But this information does not include any license information. In a typical open source self-disclosure, license information is prepared manually. However, it is often very inaccurate due to any or all of the following issues:

- Lack of license information
- No versions for licenses
- Conflicting license information
- Lists software that is not open source

Here is a hypothetical self-disclosure:

| | |
|---|---|
| Linux | GPL |
| Jboss | LGPL |
| GCC | GPL |
| XYZ | GPL/MIT |
| Java | GPL |
| Adobe | public domain |

The problems with this self-disclosure are that there are no license version numbers, one of the items is clearly inaccurate (Adobe is not a specific piece of software and is likely neither open source nor public domain), one item references a dual license without explanation (which usually, but not always, means the licensor has a choice), one item (GCC) is a development tool that is unlikely to be in a product, and Java is generally under GPL+ exception. Correcting self-disclosures is a long-standing pastime in auditing. Those who do audits for a living see all manner of weird self-disclosure. One of my personal favorites was "GNU BSD." Therefore, if you are conducting an audit based on a self-disclosure, you should not rely on the licensing information you have been given, unless you trust that the source of the information knows how to locate and vet the information.

This means that those conducting audits spend a lot of time researching licensing terms, starting from a list of packages. Researching licensing terms can be tricky. For instance, if you have been told that code base includes a piece of software called FOOBAR, your first step would be to search for FOOBAR in a search engine. If you're lucky, you will find a FOOBAR project page that indicates the license terms. At this stage, several things can go wrong: there may be more than one project called FOOBAR, there may be no project called FOOBAR, or the licensing information for FOOBAR may not be clearly indicated on the project web page. Moreover, if you take the trouble to download the FOOBAR source code, you may find that the licensing notices in the project are not the ones that are indicated on the project web page.

Therefore, researching licensing terms is more of an art than a science. Projects that are competently run will clearly indicate licensing terms on the web page, and the licensing terms will match the license notices that are actually in the code when you download it. Projects that are not competently run may have no license terms or inconsistent license terms. The cloud development platform GITHUB is especially known for projects with no licensing terms. Unfortunately, if no licensing terms are applied, the default is that no rights are granted to use the software. In such cases, there is no way to be compliant.

If you are presented with conflicting licensing terms, such as one license identified on the web page for a project and another in the source code COPY-ING file, you should make a reasoned judgment as to which set of terms is right. If a project seems not to have taken proper care with upstream rights, you may need to try to determine where the code came from to determine which licenses must apply. Generally, the license that is actually in the source code will be the more reliable indicator. But there is no magic to this inquiry. Assuming the licensor has made his own due diligence mistakes, you can rely on any license that the author has applied to the software. Placing a license notice on the software is usually enough to indicate that the author has intended to apply those licensing terms.

## Versioning

Occasionally, the license terms that are provided to you in an audit process may be inaccurate because the project has changed its license terms. In other words, the license in the software notices for the code you are auditing may be correct, but it may not match the license terms in the currently available version of the software. One way to avoid this problem is to ask for version numbers in the disclosure to be audited. License changes almost always coincide with the release of a major update, so it is usually possible to check the licensing from publicly available sources if you have the software version number. It is most common for a project to change to more permissive licensing terms rather than less permissive licensing terms, so this phenomenon does not usually cause audit problems. In fact, if the license that applies to the version of the software in the audited code base is too restrictive, it is possible that moving to a later release will solve the problem.

## Solving Problems

If you identify a problem in an audit, you should always think about a solution. (This comment is mostly for the benefit of lawyers. Engineers always think about solutions; lawyers sometimes seem to think their job is to find problems and stop there.) Almost every audit problem has either an engineering solution or a licensing solution, or both. Always consider all of these possibilities:

- **Remove.** In any code base, quite a bit of code goes unused. There are various explanations, but the most common is that the code was used in testing but not in the final product. The actual binary of a software product need not contain all the code in the source code repository from which the product is built. Therefore, if you find a licensing problem, your first questions should be "Is this code really in the product? If so, can we remove it?"

- **Replace.** Open source packages are often created as alternatives to popular proprietary software, or vice versa. Therefore, if the open source terms are a problem, you may be able to find a proprietary alternative that you can substitute for the open source package with minimal engineering effort. Often, proprietary substitutes are not expensive—after all, there is a substitute good that is free of charge.

- **Reengineer.** This is the option everyone wants to avoid because it is expensive and time-consuming. Of course, it is rarely necessary unless the issue involves GPL or LGPL, because these are the licenses whose conditions rely on the means of integration of software.

- **Relicense.** If the open source software is provided under license terms that you cannot comply with for the use case you are auditing, you may ask the author if he or she is willing to grant an alternative license. Clearly, this approach will not work with most major projects, such as the Linux kernel or Apache web server, which have set licensing terms based on the project's philosophy. Relicensing works best for individual authors. Keep in mind that if a project has more than one author and you seek an alternative license, you may have to locate and make an agreement with all the authors.

## Audits and Mergers & Acquisitions

Anyone who has ever been involved in a mergers and acquisitions (M&A) transaction knows that open source audits can be frustrating to accomplish within the confines of such a transaction. Despite the fact that it is more popular than ever to conduct code scans for M&A deals, most due diligence in M&A is still based on self-disclosure. Unfortunately, these disclosures tend to come late in the deal process and be extremely inaccurate, so they tend to create issues too late to do much about them. If you are running a startup business, you can effectively streamline investment transactions and corporate sales by engaging in at least basic open source compliance and keeping records of the open source software you are using. Preauditing your own products can save you a lot of time and trouble and make your company look more professional in the due diligence process. (For more on this, see Chapter 17: Mergers & Acquisitions and Other Transactions.)

# Part IV

# Intersection with Patents and Trademarks

Chapter 13

# Open Source and Patents (Grants, Defensive Termination)

Software patents come with plenty of political baggage—of all the articles I have written, the ones about software patents have gotten me the most hate mail. But whether software patents are good policy or bad policy, they are part of our law.[1] And because it can be hard to find objective and practical analysis of the intersection between open source software and patents, businesspeople need a framework in which to make rational decisions about software patents based on the current rule of law.

This chapter covers two topics. The first is the question of how third-party patents—patents owned by parties who are not engaged in open source licensing—can affect the community's freedom to use open source software. The second is the question of how open source licenses affect the patents of those who are engaged in open source licensing. The first is largely a policy question. The second is a question of license interpretation and intellectual property strategy.

---

[1] Many people are fond of saying software patents only exist in the United States, but that is not quite accurate. In the United States, it is not so much that software patents exist as that they have not been excluded, because Congress did not so limit the patent law ("Whoever invents or discovers any new and useful process, machine, manufacture, or composition of matter, or any new and useful improvement thereof, may obtain a patent therefor, subject to the conditions and requirements of this title" (35 USC. § 101)), which can cover "everything under the sun made by man" (*Diamond v. Chakrabarty*, 447 US 303 (1980)). Only Congress has the power to change this law. So although software patents are less common in Europe than in the United States, the difficulty of drawing a bright line excluding software patents plagues both sets of law. The European Patent Convention (EPC), Article 52, paragraph 2, excludes "programs for computers" from patentability, but paragraph 3 says, "The provisions of paragraph 2 shall exclude patentability of the subject-matter or activities referred to in that provision only to the extent to which a European patent application or European patent relates to such subject-matter or activities as such." However, the EPO considers an invention patentable if it provides a new and nonobvious "technical" solution to a technical problem, and that invention can be embodied in software.

## *The Great Patent Debate[2]*

The Internet teems with discussion about whether software patents pose a particular threat to open source—as opposed to a threat to software in general—as well as about whether software patents are right or wrong. Some of this discussion is interesting and thoughtful, and some of it is laced with profanity and rage (and therefore may be interesting but not particularly useful). But one thing is clear: the open source community hates software patents. For instance, the preamble to the GPL contains a statement that "any free program is threatened constantly by software patents," and the FSF and other free software organizations actively engage in lobbying and other efforts to defeat particular patents or software patents in general.

Whether or not you agree that software patents are immoral, you should understand that this attitude is ubiquitous among today's software engineers. In practical terms, therefore, it can be difficult to involve software engineers in patent portfolio management. Historically, patent lawyers worked closely with engineers to prepare patent disclosures and applications; today, some engineers refuse to engage in the process. In 2012, Twitter published an "Innovator's Patent Agreement"—a pledge to inventors that their employer will not use their patents for offensive purposes:[3]

> It is a commitment from Twitter to our employees that patents can only be used for defensive purposes. We will not use the patents from employees' inventions in offensive litigation without their permission. What's more, this control flows with the patents, so if we sold them to others, they could only use them as the inventor intended.

Other companies have also signed on to an informal pledge saying: "No first use of patents against companies with fewer than 25 people."[4]

Reading between the lines, companies may think that unless they promise not to use their patents for offensive purposes, they won't be able to retain the best and brightest engineers or secure their assistance with the company's patent prosecution efforts. Many other companies have made similar decisions or promises—usually less publicly. In technology companies, engineers are the star talent, and management caters to the political leanings of the stars.

---

[2] An earlier version of this discussion appeared in "The Fuzzy Software Patent Debate Rages On," *Linux Insider,* February 25, 2005. This is the one that generated so much hate mail!

[3] github.com/twitter/innovators-patent-agreement.

[4] www.thepatentpledge.org.

## More or Less at Risk?

The open source community will certainly not resolve the larger patent debate, because the policy decision to limit the scope of patentable subject matter goes far beyond open source software. But there is a narrower question—which is perhaps more interesting because it is more likely to be answered—as to whether open source software is more or less vulnerable to claims of patent infringement than is proprietary software.

GPL 2 says, "Any free program is threatened constantly by software patents." But there is a difference between being threatened and being thwarted. The question of whether open source is particularly risky to use—in the sense that it is vulnerable to patent claims—is of great practical importance to those using open source software in business. This is an open source issue, not just a free software issue. But the ability of a third party to bring patent claims has nothing to do with the outbound license terms applied to software—and that, in part, is the key to answering this question.

One of the most difficult concepts in intellectual property law is this: patents are rights, and nothing but rights. Owning a patent gives the owner nothing but the right to exclude others from practicing the invention claimed in the patent. A patent is sometimes referred to as a *non-enabling right*. It does not enable its owner to make any product or engage in any business. Enforcing a patent by bringing a patent infringement suit does not require the patent owner to engage in any business he is trying to protect. This is why patent "trolls" can exist—companies that do not engage in any business except suing others for patent infringement. Patents are negative rights only.

Under copyright law, in contrast, an author has to actually create something to own the rights to it. The same is true under the other intellectual property regimes—trade secret and trademark; in each case, one must actually create something to own the rights to it. Trade secrets arise because someone has created confidential business information. Trademarks arise because someone has used them in trade to designate the source or origin of goods.

This non-enabling nature of patent rights is part of what makes people hate patents. They view patents—not unreasonably—as being a net loss for society because their owners can stop others from engaging in innovation without engaging in any themselves. But the premise of patent law is that the publication of the patent is intended to advance the useful arts by disclosing inventions—making them "patent"—to the world. Perhaps the reason the patent system seems broken today is that people no longer consider patents to be a good means of teaching innovation. This, in turn, probably stems from a perceived failure of the patent office to limit patents to inventions that are truly innovative and not obviously based on the state of the art. When half of the patents that are enforced are invalidated, mostly due to obviousness, it's hard to disagree.

Moreover, under other intellectual property regimes, independent authorship is a defense to a claim of infringement. Under copyright and trade secret, if one takes the time and trouble to reinvent the wheel without copying or using the proprietary material of others, one can use the wheel. The fact that someone else used a wheel first makes no difference, though the defendant may be hard-pressed to prove that he created the idea of the wheel independently rather than mimicking it. Independent invention is not a defense to patent infringement, and as a result, one can easily infringe a patent without knowing it, even if one has created the invention without "stealing" others' ideas.

The theory is that an issued patent, which is free for anyone to read and learn from, is constructive notice to the world of the invention and how to practice it. The word *patent* means open for inspection, but in practice, searching for a patent that covers an invention one might want to practice is expensive, time-consuming, and complex—and therefore functionally impossible. In fact, the law creates a disincentive for doing this research (sometimes known as a freedom-to-operate study) because being aware of potential patent infringement only exposes one to "willful" infringement, which makes one potentially liable for treble damages and attorneys' fees. So in sum, patent law has become a minefield, and the winners often seem to be companies that don't innovate at all.

As a consequence of the non-enabling nature of patent rights, software can be developed in any way and still be vulnerable to patent claims. Even code written completely from scratch, line by line—if any such code exists—could infringe a patent, and the developer would not know this until he got sued. That code could be proprietary or open source—it doesn't matter.

So the GPL's assertion that all free software is constantly threatened by software patents is true—but it is only part of the truth. Any software is constantly threatened by software patents, and yet we still have software. In fact, open source software and software patents have grown up together; the decision in *Diamond v. Diehr*, 450 US 175 (a landmark case allowing a software patent), was handed down in 1981; GPL was written in 1991; and the decision in *State Street Bank v. Signature Financial Group*, 149 F.3d 1368 (allowing a business method patent) was handed down in 1998. Both software patents (and their sisters, business method patents) and open source have enjoyed tremendous success in the 1990s and the early twenty-first century.[5]

---

[5] For a very good summary history of software patentability in the United States, see **www.bitlaw.com/software-patent/history.html**.

If we peel back another layer of this onion, the question of whether open source software is particularly vulnerable to software patents becomes more interesting. Those of you who have negotiated software agreements know that, given the impossibility of knowing whether software infringes third-party software patents, liability for patent infringement is a difficult issue to address in software transactions. Neither side—licensor/licensee nor assignor/assignee—wants to bear this uncontrollable and potentially expensive burden. A pure open source software license is different from a proprietary license in this respect. Software provided under a pure open source license is provided as-is, with no warranty, and that means the licensor is not bearing any risk for claims of patent infringement. Proprietary software is often—though not always—supported by a licensor indemnity covering patent infringement claims.

But this is not as simple as it seems. A great deal of proprietary software comes with no indemnity for patent infringement. (Next time you click to accept an end user license, you may see an example of this.) Or perhaps there is an indemnity limited to the price of the software, which will be inadequate compared to defending a patent infringement claim. Even preparing a simple response to a patent infringement lawsuit costs many thousands in legal fees. So it's not true that proprietary software always comes with an indemnity.

And sometimes, open source software does. Above, I referred to *pure* open source licensing, meaning getting software under an open source license with no additional business terms. Although the license itself provides no indemnity, a vendor whose products include open source software can agree to a contract for an indemnity, usually as a quid pro quo for maintenance and support or services fees. The important thing to remember about indemnities is that they have an economic cost, so no one gives them for free. Open source software is more likely to be free, so it less frequently comes without an indemnity. (For more detail on this question and what is reasonable and customary for the bearing of risk in commercial transactions, see Chapter 17: Mergers & Acquisitions and Other Transactions.)

To understand the risk of patent infringement liability, we need to consider the motivations behind patent infringement claims. If patent infringement exists, nothing will come of it unless a claim is brought by the owner of the patent. To assess the risk that a patent owner will bring a claim, we must understand why the owner would want to do so. After all, patents are expensive to prosecute; filing an initial application for a software patent costs $10,000–$20,000 on average in legal fees, plus additional legal fees to respond to the objections of the patent examiners before the claims are actually allowed and the patent issues. So no one gets patents just for fun. In addition, patent infringement claims are not only expensive to defend—they are expensive to bring. So why spend all that money?

The three reasons to own patents and thus pay the attendant fees are

- suing people for money,
- counteroffensive claims, and
- disrupting competitors.

## Money

The first reason is the most straightforward: a plaintiff in a patent action can sue for monetary damages. Patent infringement claims are economic weapons. One lawyer joke is that rule number one is: don't sue anyone poor. Open source projects make bad targets for damages claims because they usually do not have any money. Companies using open source software to make money, however, can be more promising targets. But few companies make money directly on open source, so overall, open source should be less vulnerable to patent claims than is proprietary software.

As for the amount of money one can hope to get by suing, patent damages can be complex to calculate, and litigation over the methods used to calculate them is often fierce. But essentially, damages are (a) at a minimum, a reasonable royalty rate for a license to the patents (35 USC 284),[6] and (b) lost profits of the patent holder.[7] Neither of these measures is particularly attractive in the open source landscape because open source software tends toward backbone, commoditized, or unprofitable functionality, where there is not much room for profit and therefore not much room for patent royalties.

## Counteroffensives

Counteroffensives are key motivators for patent enforcement. Most companies that own patents do not engage in proactive enforcement (also known as *licensing programs*); they build *defensive patent portfolios* to enforce in the event a patent suit is brought against them. Before the rise of the patent troll, this was the norm; many large companies entered into cross-licenses that provided a kind of nuclear stalemate discouraging patent claims among big players. Anyone who did not participate hoped that the value of its own patent portfolio was enough to discourage third-party claims.

Counteroffensive claims are common in proprietary software, but not in open source. That is because most companies with proprietary products seek pat-

---

[6] *Georgia-Pacific Corp. v. United States Plywood Corp.*, 318 F. Supp. 1116 (S.D.N.Y. 1970), mod. and afford, 446 F.2d 295 (2d Cir. 1971), cert. denied, 404 US 870 (1971).

[7] *Panduit Corp. v. Stahlin Bros. Fibre Works, Inc.*, 575 F.2d 1152, 197 U.S.P. Q. 726 (6th Cir. 1978).

ent protection but open source projects rarely have patent rights to enforce. If the open source provider does not bring a patent claim, there is no reason for a counteroffensive.

A counterexample is a community defense program such as the Open Invention Network (OIN).[8] Such programs seek to build patent portfolios to defend open source. This requires obligating patent owners such as proprietary software companies, who may have patents with useful counteroffensive claims, to bring lawsuits in response to a claim accusing an open source project, even if the claim is not brought against the patent owner itself. But gauging the success of such efforts is difficult, because for them, success is the absence of lawsuits. Many people are skeptical that these pledges to "defend" Linux are effective—though they do result in some useful publicity for their supporters.

However, when people complain about patent enforcement, they are not usually talking about defensive enforcement. Indeed, as described in the second part of this chapter, even some open source licenses acknowledge the necessity of bringing defensive claims—even if those claims accuse open source software.

## Competitive Disruption

The final motivation for bringing a patent infringement claim is to disrupt competition. This is the most likely motivation for a patent claim in the open source landscape; if a company is competing with an open source product, it has potentially serious competitive concerns and its motivation to levy patent rents on competing open source product is high. After all, open source software is free of license fees and can therefore easily undercut sales of competing proprietary products. For example, Microsoft has engaged in an aggressive and successful program of patent licensing for embedded Linux and Android products, presumably to disrupt competition with its Windows and Windows mobile platforms. However, in practice, few companies bring patent claims accusing open source software. It is wildly unpopular to bring such claims, and doing so is a scorched-earth public relations strategy. Leaving aside trolls (who don't need goodwill because they have no products to protect), only two companies are active in patent enforcement against open source software: Microsoft and Oracle. Both are so large and entrenched in their markets that they can afford some derision by the open source community.

On the other hand, the poster child for destroying a business by bringing an open source lawsuit is *SCO v. IBM*. Arguably, SCO was a dying company before it went on the warpath against IBM and Linux, but if it had any business

---

[8] The OIN involves both a patent pool and defensive pledges. See **www.openinventionnetwork. com/about.php.**

to preserve, it put the last nail in its own coffin with this landmark lawsuit. The SCO case was not a patent lawsuit, but it was the first major litigation relating to open source. (See the discussion in Chapter 19: Enforcement and Obstacles to Enforcement.) If nothing else, it showed how spectacularly unpopular it was to bring a suit accusing open source software. The media circus that resulted did not help SCO's case. Most major technology companies, including those with significant patent portfolios, are more interested in preserving their goodwill than in any gain they could realize from bringing patent lawsuits accusing open source software—even if those lawsuits might disrupt the businesses of their competitors.

Based on these assumptions about the motivation for bringing patent lawsuits, we can now turn again to the question of whether open source software is more or less vulnerable to patent challenges. Overall, my analysis shows that open source software is less vulnerable than proprietary software. However, the question is a difficult one with no simple answer. The reasoning is below.

### Discovery

One significant difference between open source and proprietary software is that open source software is freely available to review. This means a potential patent plaintiff does not have to engage in the legal discovery process—asking the court to mandate delivery of evidence—to investigate whether potentially infringing software actually infringes the plaintiff's patent.

This easier means of identifying potential infringement cuts both ways for our question. On the one hand, if a potential plaintiff truly cannot tell whether proprietary software is practicing certain inventions, said potential plaintiff will be less likely to identify the infringement but more likely to bring an actual lawsuit to compel discovery. On the other hand, if a potential plaintiff can easily review potentially infringing software, said potential plaintiff may be more likely to determine that a claim has no merit or to bring the claims sooner rather than later.

This is probably, overall, favorable to the defendant. The longer software has been on the market, the more potential damages in an infringement suit and the harder it may be to engineer around the issue. Moreover, if accused software has been available in source code form for a long time, the defendant may claim that the plaintiff should have brought a suit sooner because it had constructive notice that the invention was being practiced. This is a legal doctrine called *estoppel* or *laches*, which discourages plaintiffs from sitting on their rights and allowing infringement to accumulate in order to seek more damages.

Also, those analyzing this issue should beware of making simplistic assumptions about the ability to determine whether binary code is practicing certain inventions. Some software patents have claims that describe inventions at a very high level. There is no need to examine source code to determine whether software practices such inventions—only to know what the software does. Moreover, those skilled in the art may be able to examine binary code to determine what kind of functions it performs. Languages like Java can easily be decompiled. Software written in high-level scripting languages such as Ruby, Perl, or JavaScript is always in source code form, regardless of whether it is licensed under open source terms or proprietary terms. Don't just assume that anything distributed in executable form is hidden from curious eyes—it may be, but it may not be.

### Work-arounds

Just as the open source community can easily cooperate on fixing bugs and software, it can easily cooperate on engineering around patent claims. This happened, for example, in the *Jacobsen vs. Katzer* case, in which volunteers from the community assisted Jacobsen in locating prior art and suggested reengineering to avoid the patent claims brought by Katzer.[9] Organizations such as PUBPAT, the Electronic Frontier Foundation, and the Software Freedom Law Center sometimes coordinate volunteers to thwart patent claims that accuse open source software. Overall, this means that open source software, even if accused of patent infringement, can be more easily changed to avoid ongoing infringement and thereby reduce potential damages and avoid injunction.

### Obviousness

Approximately 50 percent of all patents are invalidated when they are enforced. Mainly, this happens when the defendant identifies prior art that was not disclosed during the patent application process and that renders the patented invention obvious in light of prior art. An invention must be both *novel* and *non-obvious* to be the subject of a successful patent prosecution. This nomenclature is confusing to most people who are unfamiliar with patent law. The novelty requirement is easy to meet; it only requires that the invention be something new. However, to form the basis for a successful patent, the invention must not be obvious based on prior art. Therefore, if an invention is a new but is a small innovation that would be obvious to someone skilled in the art at the time the invention was created, it should not form the basis of a patent.

---

[9] For a fuller discussion of this case, see Chapter 19: Enforcement and Obstacles to Enforcement.

One complaint about software patents is that there are not sufficient repositories of prior art to assist patent examiners in eliminating obvious patent claims.[10] This was a more compelling argument when software patents were a more recent development. However, in the 30 years since the *Diamond v. Diehr* case, a great deal of patent prior art in the software world has been developed. In any case, because open source software is freely available for anyone to examine, it is also a huge store of publicly available potential prior art. Open source software therefore has a tendency to reduce the ability to successfully prosecute patents. This does not protect open source software from patent claims per se, but in some cases, the open source software could predate the patent that is being used to accuse it. This would raise an obviousness defense that might easily defeat a patent claim.

### No Champion

A countervailing argument—that open source software is riskier—is based on the premise that while proprietary products tend to have defensive patent portfolios to back them and that the consequent potential of counteroffensive claims discourages patent lawsuits, open source projects do not have defensive portfolios. See the discussion above regarding counteroffensive measures as a motivation to bring patent claims.

## Patent Grants and Provisions in Open Source Licensing

Now we turn away from policy and toward licensing technicalities. Many open source licenses have patent licensing built into them. However, these licenses look quite different from traditional patent cross-licenses, and interpreting them requires an understanding of how and why such clauses were developed. Many who are learning about open source licensing find the patent terms of open source licenses hard to understand. While traditional patent licenses usually seek to slice the patent rights granted into the narrowest slivers possible, open source patent licenses are purposely broad—and some would argue, purposely vague. That said, most patent grants in open source licenses are roughly similar in scope and not so difficult to understand.

---

[10]  Also, patent examiners are overworked and the US Patent and Trademark Office is underfunded, but that is a separate policy argument about which much has been written.

## Implied Patent Licenses

Even in the absence of an express patent grant, all open source licenses grant some patent rights, by implication. Case law on the doctrine of *implied license* is vague and sparse. The doctrine broadly rests on the premise that it would be unfair for a patent owner to grant a copyright license for software and then sue the licensee for patent infringement for engaging in the activities already licensed.

Implied license is actually a pastiche of several legal doctrines: legal estoppel, equitable estoppel, and patent exhaustion (or *first sale* doctrine).[11] Reading the case law on this question can be challenging, but it helps to keep in mind that courts may be reasoning backward to try to avoid unfair results and may be less concerned about distinguishing the doctrine under which they are righting wrongs. Under *Wang Lab. v. Mitsubishi Elecs. Am.*, 103 F.3d 1571 (Fed. Cir. 1997), the federal circuit held that under legal estoppel, a licensor cannot use patent infringement claims to take away a right that the licensor has already granted to the licensee. *Equitable estoppel* allows a licensee to rely on actions of the licensor that cause the licensee to reasonably believe the licensee has a license to the patent.[12] The foundation of this doctrine is old,[13] but its application to software is too new to draw a bright line around the scope of an implied license. For instance, the federal circuit has said, "Generally, when a seller sells a product without restriction, it in effect promises the purchaser that in exchange for the price paid, it will not interfere with the purchaser's full enjoyment of the product purchased. The buyer has an implied license under any patents of the seller that dominate the product or any uses of the product to which the parties might reasonably contemplate the product will be put."[14] It is true that open source licensing is "without restriction," but this case was not about software, and generally no price is paid for an open source license.

To avoid licenses implied by equitable estoppel, a patent holder can communicate that a separate patent license is necessary. Doing this in open source licensing can be challenging because open source licenses do not contain any reservation

---

[11] Nimmer & Dodd, *Modern Licensing Law*, §§4:2–4:3 (2007). David B. Kagan gamely tries to harmonize the doctrines in this article: "Honey, I Shrunk the Patent Rights: How Implied Licenses and the Exhaustion Doctrine Limit Patent and Licensing Strategies," **www.lesusacanada.org/docs/hts/exhaustion-and-implied-license-paper-for-les-aerospace.pdf.**

[12] For a more thorough discussion, see "Potential Defenses of Implied Patent License Under the GPL" by Adam Pugh and Laura A. Majerus, available at **www.fenwick.com/FenwickDocuments/potential_defenses.pdf.**

[13] "Any language used by the owner of the patent, or any conduct on his part exhibited to another from which that other may properly infer that the owner consents to his use of the patent ... constitutes a license." See *De Forest Radio*, 273 US 236 (1927).

[14] *Hewlett-Packard Co. v. Repeat-O-Type Stencil Mfg. Corp., Inc.*, 123 F.3d 1445 (Fed. Cir. 1997).

of rights[15] and copyleft licenses prevent placing "additional restrictions" on the exercise of the license. However, it is not clear under many open source licenses whether requiring a separate patent license would be such a restriction.[16] A patent license is more likely to be implied where no express patent license exists—so even for open source licenses that contain an express patent grant and no reservation of additional licenses, it is possible that no additional license will be implied.

Some of the basic principles of patent licensing depend on how we define certain terms in the patent license, such as these:

- Definition of licensed patents (*capture*)
  - Patent owner
  - Time period of capture (which may include forward capture)
  - Listed or particular patents
  - Geographic limitations
- Definition of products licensed (the object of the grant)
- Field or territory definitions for the license grant (*scope limitations*)

A full discussion of patent licensing is beyond the scope of this book, but a couple of these elements are key to understanding patent grants in open source licenses.

While traditional patent licenses often capture only a specific patent or list of patents, an open source patent grant capture always consists of any "necessary claims" of the patent owner. The concept of a necessary claim is an old one in patent licensing, particularly in standards licensing and patent pools. That is unsurprising because the purpose of a patent license in an open source license is to create a kind of "patent commons" covering the software.

A *patent claim* is the part of the patent that describes the invention covered by the patent. A *necessary claim* is a patent claim without which it would not be possible, or perhaps feasible, to engage in an activity—such as practicing a standard or using a piece of software. In other words, if you can feasibly use the software without practicing the invention described in the claim, the claim is not necessary and therefore not licensed. Imagine, for instance, that a patent claim covers purple user interfaces and that a piece of software allows you to build interfaces in many colors. In this case, the claim covering the purple interface would not be a necessary one.

---

[15] There are some exceptions. Mozilla Public License 2.0 contains a reservation of rights in Section 2.3. Also, Creative Commons Zero, a public domain dedication, expressly disclaims the granting of any patent right (Section 4.a); see **creativecommons.org/publicdomain/zero/1.0/ legalcode.**

[16] GPL 3 does make clear that it is a violation of the license, under Section 10.

To assess the breadth of the capture, one must also understand who is considered an owner. For example, the grant may capture patents owned by a company and all its subsidiaries or affiliates, or it may capture patents owned by only a single entity. Capture provisions that include affiliates are intended to avoid licensors' creating loopholes by setting up separate companies to own patents—something that is often done for tax and other reasons. These entities are sometimes referred to as IP holding companies. Most open source licenses, however, only capture the patents of one legal entity. A capture that includes parent companies can be a poison pill in an acquisition—a company may want to think twice about encumbering all its patents merely by buying another company that has contributed to open source software.

Also, the capture sometimes only includes patents owned by the licensor and sometimes captures all patents licenseable by that entity. For instance, the definition of "Patent Claims in Mozilla Public License 1.1" is this: "Any patent claim(s), now owned or hereafter acquired ... in any patent Licensable by grantor." This could include patents not owned by the grantor but for which the grantor has the right to sublicense.

An open source license patent grant has only one field limitation, which is that the right is granted only in connection with the exercise of the copyright licenses granted for the software. So, if a contributor to an open source project grants rights in patents, those rights only extend to use of the software under the open source license and not to separate embodiments of the invention. Any other field limitations—such as territory, commercial or technology fields, or commercial vs. noncommercial use—conflict with the Open Source Definition and therefore are never included.[17]

The time capture for an open source license patent grant is usually infinite and forward looking. Therefore, if the license captures any patents owned by the licensor, it will encumber any patent owned on the date of the grant and on any date in the future, such as if a patent is later prosecuted or acquired by the grantor. This is usually a concern for companies who expect to acquire other companies or technology; as soon as the acquisition closes, a patent license may spring into being. Most traditional patent licenses treat this subject in great detail, but in open source licensing, the capture is treated in a broad and shorthand manner.

To understand how patent licensing works in open source licenses, we will look at the patent provisions of Apache 2.0, which are both simple and customary for the open source context. Here are the relevant provisions from Section 3:

> Grant of Patent License. ... Each Contributor hereby grants to You a perpetual, worldwide, non-exclusive, no-charge, royalty-free, ir-

---

[17] opensource.org/osd-annotated. See items 5, 6, 8, and 10.

revocable (except as stated in this section) patent license to make, have made, use, offer to sell, sell, import, and otherwise transfer the Work, where such license applies only to those patent claims licensable by such Contributor that are necessarily infringed by their Contribution(s) alone or by combination of their Contribution(s) with the Work to which such Contribution(s) was submitted. If You institute patent litigation against any entity (including a cross-claim or counterclaim in a lawsuit) alleging that the Work or a Contribution incorporated within the Work constitutes direct or contributory patent infringement, then any patent licenses granted to You under this License for that Work shall terminate as of the date such litigation is filed.

This provision has two parts: a patent license and a defensive termination provision. The patent license runs from every Contributor (i.e., the author of a contribution) and captures patents "necessarily infringed" by the Contribution.

In this paradigm, *mere redistributors* who do not contribute to the code base do not grant any patent rights. Therefore, a company that is using open source software and not redistributing, or that is redistributing but not redistributing any of its own modifications, need not wonder whether it is granting any rights.

In GPL 3, the scope of the patent grant is broader. Although its patent license, too, only must be granted by contributors, it covers all patent claims infringed by the software contributed to—not merely the patent holder's own code contribution.

Remember that the purpose of the patent grants in open source licenses is to make the software free from "submarine" claims introduced by contributors. The patent grants cannot, and are not intended to, manage the risk of claims by third-party noncontributors.

Patent grants in open source licenses are narrowly drawn to not extend to downstream modifications. So if you contribute to version X.2 and pass it along to me, and if I create version X.2, then I do not get the benefit of a patent license for any of my own contributions. Only upstream licensors grant rights in an open source license.

### Defensive Termination

In a peripheral way, use of the code or mere redistribution does affect one's patents. If a party ("You") is exercising the license, and if it brings a claim accusing the open source software being provided under the license, then it loses the benefit of the patent licenses granted to it, but it does not lose not the copyright license.

Different open source licenses implement variations on this theme. For example, the Apache defensive termination provision is triggered by a defensive patent counterclaim. If that sounds harsh, keep in mind that the claim must accuse the Apache software in order to trigger the termination. Mozilla Public License has a broader defensive termination provision that also terminates the copyright license.

Appendix C contains a table of the patent license grants and defensive termination provisions of some of the most common open source licenses.

Chapter 14

# Open Source and Patent Litigation Strategy[1]

When Richard Stallman wrote in GPL 2 "Any free program is threatened constant-ly by software patents," he crystallized the ideological battle between open source software and the software patent business. In 1991, when GPL 2 was released, that battle was in its nascent stages. Today, both open source licensing and software pat-enting have come into full flower, though their growth has proceeded on orthogonal axes; most open source software is never accused of patent infringement, and most software patent infringement suits don't accuse open source software. In fact, they so seldom directly interact that the lawyers who practice in these areas do not inter-act much either. This means those defending patent infringement suits may not be thinking about the tactics open source patent licensing offers to patent defendants.

In patent litigation defense, every little bit helps. Today, patent defendants should be paying attention to open source licensing and its possible effect on patent infringement claims. When you are sued for patent infringement by anyone other than a pure nonpracticing entity, your first areas of internal investigation should include the open source position of the plaintiff and, if you are consider-ing retaliatory patent claims, your own open source position as well.

Patent lawyers may be surprised to know that while today, most companies use open source software, most of them also struggle greatly with implementing the internal controls to coordinate their use of open source software with their patent portfolio management. This means it may be quite possible that a company will seek patent protection or seek to enforce patents that read on open source software the company is using or developing—a combination of activities that would often not be considered economically rational.

There have been at least two cases in which defendants have successfully used open source license enforcement as a defensive tactic in a patent lawsuit. The first case is the one most often cited to support the enforceability of open source

[1] This chapter appeared as "OPEN SOURCE—THE LAST PATENT DEFENSE?" Febru-ary 11, 2014, www.outercurve.org/blog/2014/02/11/Open-Source--The-Last-Patent-Defense/.

licenses; most people forget that the case started as a patent claim. In *Jacobsen v. Katzer*, both parties developed and distributed software for controlling model railroads—with Jacobsen making his JMRI software available under an open source license free of charge and Katzer (via his company, Kamind Associates) selling commercial products under proprietary licenses. Jacobsen received a letter inviting him to license patents owned by Kamind, suggesting that the patents were infringed by the JMRI software. Jacobsen filed a declaratory judgment action asking the court to rule that the patents were invalid due to prior art (or failure to disclose prior art, including that of Jacobsen himself) or not infringed. As the patent case progressed, however, Jacobsen discovered that Katzer had copied some of Jacobsen's open source software and used it in Katzer's proprietary product, without the proper attributions and license notices. *Jacobsen v. Katzer* was finally settled in 2010, but only after becoming the seminal US case on open source licensing—not patent infringement—and resulting in a settlement payment by Katzer for violation of the open source license.

In *Twin Peaks Software Inc. v. Red Hat, Inc.*, Twin Peaks Software (TPS), which made proprietary network backup software, sued Red Hat and Red Hat's recently acquired subsidiary Gluster. TPS claimed that the GlusterFS software—a network file system that aggregated multiple storage shares into a single volume—violated TPS's patent covering TPS's Mirror File System (MFS). Red Hat initially responded to the patent infringement suit by denying the infringement and asserting that the patent was invalid, but it later brought a counterclaim alleging the TPS products incorporated open source software from Red Hat's product without complying with GPL. Red Hat sought an injunction against the TPS products. The case ended soon in a settlement, suggesting that TPS thought better of pursuing its patent claims in light of the facts.

In both these cases, the patent plaintiff was using open source software of the defendant and the patent defendant discovered a violation of the applicable open source license that it used to turn the tables on the plaintiff. In this way, open source license enforcement can be a substitute for a more traditional retaliatory patent claim. In each case, the plaintiff and defendant were in similar product markets—a very common context for patent litigation—which made the use of the defendant's open source code by the plaintiff likely. The moral of this story, for a patent plaintiff, is that one should have a robust open source compliance program in place before asserting a patent in a related space.

There are other, more subtle tactics as well. Open source licenses—particularly those written in the last 10 to 15 years—contain two kinds of provisions that bear upon patent litigation strategy. The first and more straightforward provision is the patent license. See for instance the license in Apache 2.0, which says this in Section 3:

**Grant of Patent License**. Subject to the terms and conditions of this License, each Contributor hereby grants to You a perpetual, world-wide, non-exclusive, no-charge, royalty-free, irrevocable (except as stated in this section) patent license to make, have made, use, offer to sell, sell, import, and otherwise transfer the Work, where such license applies only to those patent claims licensable by such Contributor that are necessarily infringed by their Contribution(s) alone or by combination of their Contribution(s) with the Work to which such Contribution(s) was submitted.

This license only applies to contributors, so a mere reuser or redistributor of the software does not grant any rights. However, if a company has contributed to the software under an open source license or under a similar contribution license, then that company may have granted a license that can be used as a defense to an infringement claim.

For example, suppose company P (patent plaintiff) sues company D (defendant) for patent infringement. However, company P has contributed software embodying the claims of the asserted patent to a project covered by this license. The Apache 2.0 license is a permissive license, so it may be easy for D to claim it is using software under this license. Raising this as a license defense can avoid liability—or at least create an unexpected defense that will add significant cost to P's prosecuting the suit.

Now consider the defensive termination provision of Apache 2.0:

If You institute patent litigation against any entity (including a cross-claim or counterclaim in a lawsuit) alleging that the Work or a Contribution incorporated within the Work constitutes direct or contributory patent infringement, then any patent licenses granted to You under this License for that Work shall terminate as of the date such litigation is filed.

This means that by filing the lawsuit, P may have given up any patent licenses it has received from any contributors to the software—which may include D or third parties who may be aligned with D. This provision applies to all licensees, not just contributors. Even if D is not a contributor with patent claims to bring, bringing the claim exposes P to potential liability. Pointing this out may shift the balance in favor of the defense.

It's important to understand that patent defensive termination provisions in different open source licenses have different terms. Some, like Apache 2.0, are triggered by defensive claims, but some are not. Some, like MPL (or the corresponding "liberty or death" provision in GPL 3), also trigger a termination of the copyright license, making them even more powerful defense tools.

So the next time you are sued for patent infringement, you have not done your homework until you know the answers to all of the following questions:

- Is the plaintiff using any open source software of yours (related to the patent or not) in violation of the license?
- Does the asserted claim read on any open source software you are using? If so, would the complaint trigger a defensive termination provision that might apply to the plaintiff?
- Did the plaintiff contribute to any open source project any code under terms that would include a patent license? If so, do you have a defense under that license?

Investigating the last question can be an informational challenge, but it may not be as difficult as you think. Records regarding contributions may be available publicly, or open source projects may be willing to cooperate if it helps them defeat patent claims accusing their code.

The drafters of open source licenses intended to use the terms of those licenses to win a war against software patents, and whether they can do that remains to be seen, but in the meantime, patent litigators should not pass up the opportunity to use the principles of open source licensing to win their own battles as well.

# Trademarks

Open source licenses are copyright and patent licenses, and they say little or nothing about trademarks. Yet trademark is a robust and ubiquitous intellectual property right. Trademarks are cheaper and easier to enforce than patents, trademark law is clearer and better settled than copyright law (at least with respect to software), and unlike either copyright or patent rights, trademarks can last forever. The machinery for enforcing trademarks exists all over the world, and lawsuits for trademark infringement are very common and can yield significant damages. Overall, trademark is one of the strongest tools in a company's intellectual property arsenal.

But trademark law is quite different from patent or copyright law—so different, in fact, that some think it should not be called intellectual property law at all. At least theoretically, trademark law serves primarily to protect the consuming public, rather than the owner of the trademark. Most people think of trademarks as logos, like the Nike swoosh or the McDonald's golden arches. But in fact, a trademark need not be a picture or even stylized writing. Trademarks started as simply the name or sign a tradesman put on his product. A trademark can consist of just a company name, with no logo—whenever it is used to designate the origin of a product.

The United States has a different trademark law from those of other countries: it is a first-to-use system rather than a first-to-file system. One gains rights in a trademark by using it in commerce, and in the United States, one gains rights under the federal trademark laws by using the mark in interstate commerce. In some other countries, filing a trademark registration can make one the owner of a mark even without using it in commerce. So, trademarks are not like copyrights, which arise immediately upon the work's fixation in the tangible medium. Trademarks are also not like patents in that registration is merely evidence of ownership and not ownership itself.

A trademark represents the source of origin of a product, and a service mark represents the source or origin of a service. For purposes of this discussion, we will only discuss trademarks, but service marks work in roughly the same way. Because it represents a source, a trademark also represents the quality of goods associated with the source. If you buy a coffee at a Starbucks coffeehouse in a strange city, you assume the product you buy will be like the coffee you get in a Starbucks coffeehouse in your hometown. If just anyone could use that trademark, you might be fooled into buying something of lower quality or something entirely different from what you expect. Using trademark law, a court can prevent counterfeiters from misusing the trademark so the public will not be misled.

Trademark law imposes more duties on the owner of the intellectual property than does patent or copyright. It is relatively difficult to lose the copyright in a work, other than by expressly dedicating the work to the public domain. It is possible to lose the rights in a patent by not paying maintenance fees to the Patent and Trademark Office (PTO). But trademark law requires that the owner police a trademark to maintain rights in it. If it were otherwise, the trademark would not protect consumers. A trademark owner is expected to maintain quality control over goods that bear the mark, including any goods that are made by others under license. Trademark law is therefore a "use it or lose it" regime. When an owner of a trademark fails to do this, it is called *dilution, genericness,* or *blurring.* Some very famous marks—like aspirin and heroin—have become generic and no longer point to any particular source.

## Trademarks in the Open Source World

Therefore, open source software licensing and trademarks make strange bedfellows. They are inherently opposed schemes; while open source licenses allow anyone to modify code,[1] no trademark owner can allow use of the trademark on that code without controlling the nature of the resulting product.

Early open source licenses dealt obliquely with this issue. For example, early forms of BSD contained this:

> Neither the name of the University nor the names of its contributors may be used to endorse or promote products derived from this software without specific prior written permission.

In substance, this clause states that no trademark license is granted to use the name of the University (of California). Other licenses contain variations of such language. Although their drafting is awkward, they probably mean to say that no express trademark license has been granted.

---

[1] See the open source definition at **www.opensource.org/docs/definition.php**.

Many of the more sophisticated open source projects recognize the potential conflicts between open source licensing and trademark principles. They also recognize that the average open source developer is probably unaware of what is or is not allowed under trademark law. Therefore, many open source projects set written guidelines for trademark use. These trademark guidelines usually describe what is not allowed, what is always allowed, and what is allowed with a license. Most of their content simply maps existing trademark law onto the use of the project's name. A list of example policies appears in Appendix F.

Attorneys who are accustomed to managing trademarks in conventional commerce might find these policies surprising; the conventional way to manage a brand is to allow no use at all, except pursuant to a formal license agreement, and to be aggressive about enforcement. But in the open source world, aggressive enforcement practices, particularly against hapless infringers, can have the effect of alienating the very community the company is trying to promote. So open source projects often allow use of the trademark for purposes such as naming user or developer groups, holding conferences, and creating T-shirts and other promotional items. These are all actions that would not be allowed in conventional brand management.

## What's in a Name?

As a result, open source software licensing is a confused sea of brand management. That is not surprising, nor is it necessarily a problem because it may be unclear whether the names of projects are intended to be used as trademarks at all. Many of them probably are not; every project needs a name, but not all of them are whole products and many of them are only intended as templates for skilled developers to create products. Therefore, such projects might not enjoy the quality control that a finished product might warrant. (For lawyers, think about the forms and models that you get from your colleagues and that are usually provided with the admonition that they need to be adapted for your use.) However, it seems likely that branding fights will become more common in the open source world, as open source software becomes more integral to commercial products.[2]

As a case in point, consider the brand management, or lack thereof, for the most popular and valuable piece of open source software—the Linux kernel. Many people associate Linux with a bowling pin–shaped penguin logo. That pen-

---

[2] For an excellent article on genericness in open source trademarks, see Pamela S. Chestek, 2013, "Who Owns the Project Name?" *International Free and Open Source Software Law Review*, 5(2), 105–120. See **www.ifosslr.org/ifosslr/article/view/87/159**.

guin, nicknamed Tux, is not actually a trademark.[3] The copyright in the original logo is dedicated to the public domain, and variations of it have been used for many Linux distributions. It has sometimes been called a mascot rather than a trademark (and it appears on the cover of this book).

The name *Linux* is based on UNIX and the name of the original author of the kernel, Linus Torvalds. The use of Linux as a trademark is policed—at least nominally—by the Linux Mark Institute (**www.linuxmark.org**). However, at this point, the name *Linux* has been used so broadly and on so many different products that as a trademark, it may be generic and unenforceable.[4] Nevertheless, if a company were to try to sell a Linux product that bore no resemblance to the Linux kernel or that was not licensed under GPL, then even if there were no trademark claims to be made, such a use might give rise to consumer lawsuits claiming the name was misleading. Given the tendency of businesses to try to capitalize on the label "open source" in many areas, such claims seem inevitable.

The moral of this story is that while best practices for brand management for a company running an open source project are fundamentally no different from those for any other product, they may need to be adjusted to suit the business objectives of the project. It's best to clearly distinguish from our other product lines any open source project you may run. This will help you avoid having the brand on your other products become generic. Also, setting branding policy is partly an educational effort, helping the community understand how to avoid infringing the company's trademarks.

But the most important part of trademark management in open source is to think about it in the first place. What you call your project may become very important, and you and your community may very well have an interest in avoiding a war of versions that can confuse potential users and developers.

---

[3] The use of the penguin has provided fodder for plenty of amusement. See the discussion of the meaning and history of Tux at **en.wikipedia.org/wiki/Tux**.

[4] Confusion over what constitutes a "Linux" product is evidenced by the FSF's strophic explanation of the difference between Linux and GNU/Linux. The GNU code base includes a set of tools promulgated by the GNU Project. These tools are usually part of a product distribution that contains the Linux kernel. See Wikipedia's definition of *Linux*: "Strictly, the name Linux refers only to the Linux kernel, but it is commonly used to describe entire Unix-like operating systems (also known as GNU/Linux) that are based on the Linux kernel and libraries and tools from the GNU project." See **en.wikipedia.org/wiki/Linux**.

# Part V

# Contributions and Code Releases

Chapter 16

# Open Source Releases

This chapter is about releasing new software—software a business has written for itself—under an open source software license.

Maybe your company has not yet arrived at the point of wanting to do this. But if you keep using open source software long enough, you will eventually see the value of giving back. Free riding on the work of others may seem like manna from heaven, but cooperative development is usually even more rewarding. Even profit-making companies may decide to release open source code for many reasons. For example, they may want to promote adoption of a certain protocol or method, and making source code available may be the quickest and easiest way to accomplish that goal. Or, they may decide that an existing product is stale, commoditized, or no longer profitable and wide adoption of it might benefit their other business lines.

Sometimes pressure to release code as open source comes from the company's engineering staff. This can create competing interests. In the short term, it's not a responsible use of shareholders' capital to develop software only to give it away. Sometimes, engineers consider releasing open source software to be a résumé enhancement, and they may put the interest of their own reputation ahead of their company's bottom line. But also, many times, the competing interests align when giving away software is good for business.

When companies decide to release open source software they have written, they often ask, "What license should we use?" In a way, the choice of an open source license a choice between many options, each of which is imperfect in some way. Some companies then assume they should write their own license, and this is generally not a good idea. A license often backfires, and even if it is clearer and better drafted than the common alternatives, introducing a unique license will probably substantially hamper the very adoption that the company is trying to achieve with its code release.

Figure 16.1 represents one way to approach selecting a license for an open source code release. Note that realistically, the licenses referenced in the diagram are the only good choices for open source releases. They are all very common and well understood.

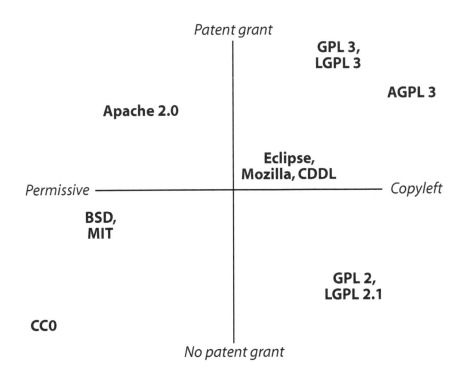

**Figure 16.1** Dimensions of license selection

There are two axes in the diagram, each of which represents a decision. The X (horizontal) axis is copyleft. Here, there is a spectrum of choices. However, the most important factor is your answer to the question "Do I want to use a copyleft or a permissive license?" Most permissive licenses are fungible from a copyright point of view, meaning you could use any of them. Also, CC0 is actually a dedication to the public domain, rather than a license. The difference between CC0 and BSD or MIT is that CC0 does not require any license notice to be retained; CC0 waives all copyrights (but not patent rights) in the code.

The $Y$ (vertical) axis represents your yes-or-no answer to the question "Do I prefer an express patent grant in the license?" Generally, licensors who have valuable patent portfolios to manage prefer licenses with express grants. This is because such licensors are concerned about the scope of implied grants.[1]

---

[1] The law on implied patent licensing is vague—see Chapter 13: Open Source and Patents. However, there is also a school of thought—less popular—that using a license with no express grant means no patent rights have been granted. Some companies also choose to release code under a license with no patent grant—like BSD—and then grant a separate patent license. (See, for example, Google's grant of additional rights for WebM at **www.webmproject.org/license/additional/**).

If you decide on copyleft, you need to choose how strong a copyleft regime you want—from AGPL (the strongest) to Mozilla or CDDL (the weakest). Here, "strong" or "weak" refers to how much the license attempts to govern the delivery of source code for other code that is integrated with the open source code. (Refer back to Chapter 3: Common Open Source Licenses for details.)

One you have made these two choices, the license nearly selects itself. More importantly, "Which license?" is not really the right question. The right question is "What are my goals for releasing this code, and how does releasing it help my business?" Below are some use cases that might help illustrate how to answer that question. Of course, it's fine to release any software under a permissive license if you want to maximize adoption and don't care about others' free riding on your code. But when it comes to copyleft licenses, some of them don't make sense for certain use cases.

- **Development utility.** This kind of program is not usually distributed—it is usually used internally. Therefore, strong copyleft licenses like GPL are fine, but they won't do much to encourage sharing of source code. The source code disclosure conditions of GPL only attach on distribution. Even a license like Affero GPL will probably be of little help in this regard.

- **Content management system.** This kind of application is a good choice for AGPL. Where it is not used internally, it will probably be used to provide services and AGPL will require users to share source code. GPL will not.

- **User application.** This kind of program often gets distributed, and because it is a stand-alone program, GPL makes sense.

- **Code library.** LGPL or one of the weak copyleft licenses is a good choice in this case. If you choose GPL instead, you will reduce adoption because using the library in an application will require the developer to put the entire application under GPL.

- **Non-software.** Don't confuse the world by releasing things like documentation, photos, music, or books under software licenses. Use a Creative Commons license instead. Conversely, don't release software under non-software licenses like CC-BY-SA. It's a good idea to dedicate code with limited copyright protection to the public domain. Don't make the world try to figure out the extent of copyright law to use your release.

If you prefer procedural approaches to diagrams, see the end of this chapter for some "pseudocode" for the license choice, according to the rules that usually make sense in a business context.

Here are some examples of business cases and how they might map onto these license choices.

### Helper Code: CC0

A company sells a wearable personal note-taking device that is wireless enabled and can interface with HTML applications. A small reference code routine can be embedded in the application to implement the device's API. The code is very simple, probably has little copyright protection, and must be built directly into the application. This company chooses CC0 because it wants to increase adoption and does not want to require its developers to provide any attribution or notices on a small device.

### Adoption of Open Standards: Apache 2.0

A company has created a new local area communications protocol. The company wants as many developers and users as possible to start using the new protocol. To facilitate this, it releases some development libraries that can be included in applications to implement the standard. This code offers the ability to encode and decode into standard compliant formats. The company has not sought to protect this standard via patent protection. Instead, its business model seeks to encourage as much widespread adoption as possible while selling applications and products that meet the standard. In other words, this is an open standard. Also, the company would prefer to have a licensing notice on the code to publicize the availability of the code and its company name. The company chooses Apache 2.0 because it is a permissive license that will give developers and users confidence that the company is not seeking to reserve patent rights.

### Dual Licensing

The company's business model seeks to provide an application for personal financial management that can be used to provide online services. The company plans to make a stripped-down version of the software available under an open source license; it also wants to offer a fuller-featured version—which will have the ability to support multiple mirrored servers—for a license fee. The company chooses Affero GPL 3. It also offers an alternative license under proprietary terms.

### Disrupt Competition

The company has been selling, for many years, a spell-checking utility. But recently, the company's sales have dwindled because there are so many competitive products on the market. Maintaining the product has become expensive, and one of the company's competitors still has an edge in sales. However, if the competitor's product becomes a standard, the company will have to engage in significant engineering efforts to make its product compatible with that standard. The company chooses GPL 2. By doing so, it creates a free substitute for its competitor's product while preventing the competitor from privatizing the code in its own products (because the terms of GPL don't allow that).

## Trademark Stewardship

Whenever a company launches a new product, it needs to consider branding and trademarks. Trademarks are among the most important elements of the intellectual property used to insulate a product from competition. Releasing an open source project is no different, but branding in the open source world can be tricky.

There is an inherent tension between open source licensing and trademark licensing. However, the two can coexist if properly stewarded. (For more on trademark law and open source in general, see Chapter 15: Trademarks.) This section focuses on the business strategy for doing a code release and best practices to steward trademark rights in the context of an open source code release. Trademarks protect not only their owners but the open source community as well. Developing conscientious trademark practices will help not only the company running the project but the consumers and developers using the code as well.

### Be Careful How You Mix Marks

Companies that release software under open source licenses should always ensure that the open source software is under a brand that is distinct from their other products. It can be tricky to maintain strong trademark rights in open source code, so if something goes wrong and the rights weaken, the company's other products should not be compromised. For example, lots of companies like to call products "FOOBAR" and "Open FOOBAR" (or "FOOBAR Community Edition"). This works well for dual-licensing initiatives, but not for independent open source projects that will be primarily under community (rather than company) control. Companies releasing software for the purpose of starting a community project should choose a new brand for the project. When the project is no longer under company control, the trademark will no longer represent the company's quality control and will therefore no longer be, strictly speaking, an appropriate product to bear a company mark.

### Transparent Policies

A code release should always include a coherent and transparent trademark policy. Open source licensees rarely understand the distinction between open source licensing and trademark use. Having a policy not only helps the company establish systematic quality control to maintain the rights in the mark, but it helps the user base avoid accidentally infringing those rights. Traditional trademark policies allow users to do almost nothing; open source policies need to be more moderated and walk a fine line between control and freedom. A list of example trademark policies for an open source code release appears in Appendix F.

Here are some things to consider when developing such a policy:

- If a license modifies the code, can it still retain the mark? Most policies say that any modification requires removal of the mark, but some allow minor changes like configuration or default settings to be changed.

- What uses of the project name can be made by user groups or developer groups? A trademark policy will usually require express permission to register domain names that include the project mark or any variation of it. Some policies allow user and developer groups to create merchandise to help raise funds; some do not.

- To avoid mistakes, it's best to remove logos and trademarks from the public source tree. While some companies may make binaries available for download with the logos intact, removing the logos from the source tree may inadvertently cause misuse of the trademark by licensees.

## Open Source Business Models

Many people have asked me, "How can you make money selling open source software?" Most companies don't make money that way exactly—but they use open source as a business tool to make money doing other things.

- **Support and services.** The most obvious business model for open source is providing maintenance and support services or professional services. This is the model of companies like Red Hat. In such a business model, licensing fees are not a substantial source of revenue.

- **Razor and blades.** In the business strategy made famous by King C. Gillette, companies can build consumer bases by selling a product (such as a razor) cheaply and selling disposable accessories for it (such as razor blades) at a profit. Many companies release open source software to boost sales of complementary revenue-producing products like hardware devices (such as specialized computers or consumer electronics) or online services (such as hosting the open source software, for those who don't want to run it on their own).

- **Freemium.** Many companies provide an open source version of their software—sometimes called a *community edition*—and an upsell product with additional features that are licensed on a proprietary basis.

- **Dual licensing.** Some companies offer the same software under an open source license—usually GPL or AGPL—and offer proprietary licenses as an alternative for those licensees who do not want to abide by the conditions of GPL. This model was pioneered by MySQL, with a product now owned by Oracle Corporation. In fact, Oracle is a successful purveyor of dual-licensed products, including MySQL, Sleepycat, InnoDB, and others, as a result of a series of acquisitions in the 2000s. One important thing to keep in mind about dual licensing is that to implement this strategy, the licensor must have the right to bifurcate its outbound licensing terms. This is usually true only when the licensor is the owner of the copyright in the code. For example, if software contains third-party GPL software, it cannot be relicensed under proprietary terms. Many people find the dual-licensing model confusing because they assume that the licensor, as well as the licensee, is bound by the conditions of a copyleft license. However, copyleft conditions only run downstream—so, absent inbound third-party limitations, the licensor can choose the outbound licensing model it prefers.

## Contribution Agreements[2]

Once you have decided what license will govern the rights granted by your project to the world, you should consider what will govern the rights granted by the world to your project. Many open source projects use inbound licenses called *contribution agreements*. The objective of a contribution agreement is to make sure the project has the latitude to change the outbound license it applies to the project. For a project made available under a permissive license, the question of whether to use a contribution agreement is not as crucial or complicated, so here we will only focus on the case of a project under a copyleft license.

Contribution agreements have many variations, but the most common is the Apache Corporate Contribution License Agreement (CLA).[3] Other variations on contribution licenses include assignments rather than licenses and restrictions

---

[2] An earlier version of this section appeared in "Legal Issues: The Contribution Conundrum," *Enterprise Open Source Journal*, July 2006. There are also more comments here: heathermeeker. squarespace.com/news/2014/6/30/contributions-and-the-latest-generation.html.

[3] www.apache.org/licenses/cla-corporate.txt.

on the relicensing of code (such as limiting it to open source licenses). However, these variations are less common than a simple unrestricted license—roughly the equivalent of a permissive open source license, but without the notice requirements. Contribution agreements are not standardized, except to the extent that the Apache CLA is a de facto standard. A project can make whatever bargain with its contributors that it likes. Some projects will accept contributions under different terms from different contributors, and some projects are more transparent about this decision than others.

Of course, the simplest and most transparent way to accept contributions is not to use a CLA at all. This approach is popular among some in the open source community, but it can hamstring and even kill open source projects that decide to change their license terms. If you accept contributions under GPL, for instance, the project can never change to LGPL or Apache without a potentially cumbersome or impossible relicensing effort.[4] Projects that do not use contribution licenses sometimes use a *certificate of originality*, which does not dispose of licensing rights[5] but which requires the contributor to show that the contribution is his original work—therefore providing evidence that contributing it is not an infringement of third-party copyrights.

The Free Software Foundation generally requires that all rights to contributions to FSF projects be assigned to it.[6] The theory is that this approach makes it easier to enforce rights in the outbound open source license because the project owns all the code and therefore has standing to sue for copyright infringement for every portion of the code base. However, most projects do not use this approach—relying instead on a copyright in most of the code, as well as on ownership of the copyright (however thin) of the compilation of all of the various contributions.

Those who object to contribution agreements mainly want the project's practices to be transparent—the mantra being "License in equals license out." They prioritize the contributor's right to know the disposition of his contribution over the freedom of the project to change its licensing policies.[7]

---

[4] It is generally understood, for instance, that changing the license for the Linux kernel from GPL 2 only to anything else is impossible, given the number of contributors and lack of a contribution agreement.

[5] See for example the Developer Certificate of Origin, **elinux.org/Developer_Certificate_Of_Origin**.

[6] **www.gnu.org/licenses/why-assign.html**.

[7] For a good exposition of the view against contribution agreements, see Simon Phipps, "Governance for the GitHub generation," *Infoworld*, June 30, 2014, **www.infoworld.com/article/2608195/open-source-software/governance-for-the-github-generation.html**.

## Relicensing Code

If a project decides to change its outbound license, it almost always changes from a more restrictive license (like GPL) to a less restrictive one (like BSD). This is because the reverse does not make much sense; once code has been released under an open source license, the rights can never be taken back. The project can release the code under a more restrictive license, but the rights granted under the less restrictive license will still be available. Occasionally, relicensing under a more restrictive license can be effectively done with a major update; in that case, the old version will be available under the old license and the new elements will be limited to the more restrictive license.

Of course, the ability to relicense may depend on whether the project has used a contribution agreement. If, for instance, a project starts under GPL and does not use a contribution agreement, all contributions will be covered by GPL and cannot be changed without the contributor's permission.

Therefore, if a project is unsure about which license to use, it is best to start with a more restrictive license and move to a more permissive one if it becomes evident that more permissiveness will serve the project better.

## Corporate Organization

Some companies take the extra step of creating a separate entity to run a new open source project. Doing so can be a good strategy for untangling intellectual property rights in the open source project from the rest of the company's operations. Also, because large open source projects can involve market competitors, the separate entity gives the participants a level and transparent playing field in which to engage in interactions that might otherwise raise antitrust concerns. An entity specially created to run open source projects often takes the form of a not-for-profit entity. However, the last few years have seen many travails for US companies seeking not-for-profit status.[8]

## Just for Fun ... Pseudocode for License Choice

Below is *pseudocode*—instructions written in the procedural style of programming, but not in a programming language—for license choices for code releases, according to the rules that usually make sense in a business context.

---

[8] See Ryan Paul, "IRS Policy that Targeted Political Groups Also Aimed at Open Source Projects," *Ars Technica*, July 2, 2014. For more on the tax decision, see Heather Meeker and Stephanie Petit, "The New Foundations of Open Source," 32 *Santa Clara High Technology Law Journal* (forthcoming 2015).

1. Are you contemplating a dual license program? If so, choose GPL 3. END.

2. Which is more important: broad adoption of the code or thwarting privatization of the code? If broad adoption, go to "PERMISSIVE." If thwarting privatization, go to "COPYLEFT."

3. PERMISSIVE

3.1. Do you want to limit the patent rights you are granting for the software? If yes, go to PERMISSIVE PATENT STEWARD.

3.2. If no, do you want to compel other contributors to your project to grant patent licenses?[9]

    3.2.1. If yes, choose Apache 2.0. END.

    3.2.2. If no, go to PERMISSIVE NO PATENT GRANT.

3.3. PERMISSIVE PATENT STEWARD. Do you want to compel other contributors to your project to grant patent licenses?[10]

    3.3.1. If yes, choose Apache 2.0. END.

    3.3.2. If no, choose CC0. END.

3.4. PERMISSIVE NO PATENT GRANT. Do you want others to retain your licensing notice when they redistribute the code?

    3.4.1. If yes, choose BSD or MIT. END.

    3.4.2. If no, choose CC0. END.

4. COPYLEFT. Do you want to limit the patent rights you are granting for the software?

4.1. If yes, go to COPYLEFT PATENT STEWARD.

4.2. If no, go to COPYLEFT NO PATENT GRANT.

4.3. COPYLEFT NO PATENT GRANT. Is the code a stand-alone program?

    4.3.1. If yes, choose GPLv2. END.

    4.3.2. If no, choose LGPLv2.1. END.

5. COPYLEFT PATENT STEWARD. Is the code a stand-alone program?

5.1. If yes, go to STRONG COPYLEFT PATENT STEWARD.

5.2. If no, go to WEAK COPYLEFT PATENT STEWARD.

5.3. STRONG COPYLEFT PATENT STEWARD.

---

[9] This can also be addressed with a contribution license; this pseudocode assumes there is none.

[10] This can also be addressed with a contribution license; this pseudocode assumes there is none.

5.3.1. Do you want to compel competitors to disclose source code if they use the software for SAAS? If yes, choose AGPL 3. END.

5.3.2. If no, choose GPL 3. This choice will discourage adoption by private business, so if adoption is more important than the comfort of an express patent grant, go to COPYLEFT NO PATENT GRANT.

5.4. WEAK COPYLEFT PATENT STEWARD.

5.4.1. Choose MPL 2. (LGPL 3, CDDL, and Eclipse are also possibilities, but LGPL 3 will weaken adoption and CDDL and Eclipse are less compatible with other licenses.)

You will note that there is no endpoint in this pseudocode for LGPL 3, CDDL, and Eclipse, as well as many other open source licenses. This does not mean they are never the right choices. The approach above is intended to address most cases where a private business wants to release open source software. Also, free software advocates will certainly take issue with the premise that the version 3 licenses—GPL 3 and LGPL 3—will limit adoption. At this time, many companies have internal policies against using code under these licenses. That may change over time, but until these licenses gain broader acceptance, they will discourage adoption. (For a more detailed discussion, see Chapter 10: GPL 3 and Affero GPL 3.)

Generally, permissive licenses will encourage adoption more than will copyleft licenses. Most businesses have few internal policy restrictions on using permissively licensed code. A business may want to choose copyleft for public relations and moral or political reasons, but most private businesses choose copyleft licenses for code releases in order to disrupt competition. Permissive licenses easily enable competitors to privatize code in their own products; copyleft licenses require competitors to make source code available, which substantially reduces any potential free-rider gain by a competitor—at least for distributed software.

And finally, because it's only fair to eat one's own dog food, I hereby dedicate the copyright in the above pseudocode to the public domain. If you use or cite it, please consider the rules of academic practice, rather than copyright, and cite this book where appropriate.

# Part VI

# Additional Topics

Chapter 17

# Mergers & Acquisitions and Other Transactions

The handling of open source issues in transactions has changed radically over the last two decades. Today, almost all software contains some open source elements, so it's clear to almost everyone that asking a vendor or seller to represent that it uses no open source software is archaic and pointless. Today, most transactions focus on disclosure and allocation of risk. One sea change that has occurred is that open source representations are now almost as common in day-to-day procurement or development deals as they are in mergers and acquisitions (M&A) and investments.

Nevertheless, open source representations are almost always poorly written—either too narrow or too broad (or sometimes both) to the point of being nonsensical. In some ways, open source representations are the same as those for other technology and intellectual property; in other ways, they are quite different.

First, consider this representation, which is very common in all sorts of technology transactions:

> The use of the Software will not infringe any third-party intellectual property rights.

If this warranty appears in your deal, you have already covered most of the risk attendant on the use of open source software. Violating open source license conditions causes the license to terminate (or be quickly subject to termination, in the case of the few licenses that allow cure periods for violation of license terms). Therefore, violating open source conditions will trigger a breach of this representation. However, many lawyers erroneously assume that specific additional open source representations are needed to address liability. In fact, they are probably not necessary, although additional terms or representations are useful for due diligence.

Most transactions today require a disclosure of basic open source information so the buyer can conduct its own diligence. Such disclosures in day-to-day transactions usually are limited to self-reporting. Most M&A transactions today use an outside code scanner to do a forensic analysis. (For some of the challenges of conducting due diligence on self-reported open source disclosures, see Chapter 12: Audits and Due Diligence.)

Although such information can certainly be requested separately as a matter of due diligence, it is usually tied to a listing representation, compelling the vendor or seller to disclose the open source software included in a product as a part of an exhibit or disclosure schedule. Drafting and listing representations in such agreements can be more challenging. Many of them ask for too little information and too much information at the same time.

The first step in drafting open source provisions for agreements is to define *open source software*. Here is a sample definition that contains some of the drafting issues that are most common:

> *Public Software* is any software that is used by the Company and made generally publicly available in source code form or under any public source, freeware, community, or open source license approved by the Open Source Initiative, including the Sun Binary Code License, the GNU Public License, and the Netscape Public License.

The above example is fairly awful, with many defects:

- *Public Software* is not a term of art used by the open source community.
- Names licenses that have been deprecated.
- Names licenses that don't exist.
- Assumes all open source licenses are approved by OSI.
- Includes freeware, which is proprietary software.
- Includes all software that is always in source code form (like JavaScript).[1]
- Includes software owned and released by the Company, rather than licensed to the Company by third parties.
- Requires disclosure of all software used by the Company, instead of software in the products.

Here are some sample definitions that I think work better:

> *Open Source License* means any license meeting the Open Source Definition (as promulgated by the Open Source Initiative) or the Free Software Definition (as promulgated by the Free Software Foundation), or any substantially similar license, including but not limited to any license approved by the Open Source Initiative or any

---

[1] For more on this topic, see Chapter 2: A Tutorial on Computer Software.

Creative Commons License. For avoidance of doubt, Open Source Licenses include without limitation Copyleft Licenses.

*Copyleft License* means any license that requires, as a condition of use, modification or distribution of a work of authorship, that such work of authorship or derivative works thereof be made available free of charge under such license, and that, in the case of software, be made available in source code form, or under terms that allow such software to be reverse engineered. Copyleft licenses include without limitation the GNU General Public License, the GNU Lesser General Public License, the Mozilla Public License, the Common Development and Distribution License, the Eclipse Public License, and all Creative Commons "sharealike" licenses.

Creating a separate definition for *Copyleft License* can help one avoid requiring unnecessary disclosure for permissive open source software. The purpose of these representations is to compel the disclosure of enough information to conduct due diligence but not so much information as to flood the seller with make-work and the buyer with unnecessary information that will slow down the diligence process.

*Open Source and Copyleft Materials.* All use and distribution of Company Products by Company, and all use by Company of any materials subject to an Open Source License, is in compliance with all Open Source Licenses applicable thereto, including without limitation all copyright notice and attribution requirements and all requirements to make available source code. Section [_____] of the Disclosure Schedule lists all Open Source Materials (including release number, if any) included the Company Products, and (1) the Open Source License (including version number, if any) under which Company uses such Open Source Materials, (2) the location on the Internet, if any, where the Open Source Materials were most recently accessed by Company, (3) whether the Open Source Materials have been modified by or for Company, (4) whether the Open Source Materials have been distributed by or for Company, (5) the applicable Company Product, and (6) with respect to Copyleft Materials, how such Copyleft Materials are integrated with or interact with the remainder of the applicable Company Product. Without limiting the foregoing, Company has not used Copyleft Materials in a manner that requires the Company Products, any portion thereof, to be subject to any Copyleft License.

Today, most attorneys understand that the open source software elements in a product are of far more concern than any used by the vendor or seller for back-end processing or even product development. Accordingly, the need to compel disclosure has been narrowed to the elements actually used in the product that forms the value basis for the transaction.

## Allocation of Risk

Clients frequently ask me what is reasonable and customary in allocation of open source–related risk in transactions. They are either convinced that a vendor should bear no liability for third-party open source software or that it should bear all liability for it—usually depending on what side of the deal they are on.

Of course, there is no one answer to such a question. Allocation of risk in transactions usually depends on who has the greater bargaining power. Plenty of vendors have agreed to bear risk for open source software over which they have no control, in order to get deals done. But there are rational ways to assess the issue.

Often, those negotiating deals find it hard to allocate risk because they view it as a moral issue. It is not—it is a commercial issue. There are two overarching ways to approach allocation of risk: control and pricing.

One school of thought holds that risk should be borne by the party in a transaction who can best control it. This makes sense from a practical viewpoint, and it also appeals to the need for a moral element of blame for problems. According to this theory, the party that makes a decision to use third-party software should bear the risk. Of course, that is almost always the vendor.

Another school of thought holds that the party who is making the money on the transaction should bear the risk. In accounting terms, the party receiving payments for the product can reserve some portion of the purchase price against future liability or loss. Of course, this is almost always the vendor as well.

Although both of these theories are useful, they do not tell the whole story. Take, for example, a customer who buys a storage device that consists of off-the-shelf hardware, an application for the Linux platform, and a Linux system. Let's assume the application, which provides the most added value in the product, consists primarily of code written by the vendor and is proprietary. Who should bear the risk for the Linux system?

This can be a thorny question to answer. While it is true that the vendor chose the software, it may be unrealistic today to expect a vendor of such products to use anything else. Linux is very popular in embedded systems. Also, at least theoretically, the customer benefits from the royalty-free nature of the Linux platform and therefore pays a lower price. So even though the vendor is receiving payment for the product, the customer is saving money by choosing the open source–based product.

As another example, consider a product that consists of an e-commerce application that runs on a LAMP stack. The vendor may, for convenience, deliver a working instance of the software that includes both the application and the LAMP stack, together. But the customer could just as easily have procured the LAMP stack on its own, or the customer could have chosen an application that runs on a Windows system rather than on a Linux system. In this sense, using Linux is as much the customer's decision as the vendor's.

Because of these nuances, the vendor often does not bear risk for third-party open source.

Keep in mind, as well, that there are different categories of risk—the two main ones being performance warranties and intellectual property warranties. *Performance warranties* say that the product will function as advertised, and *intellectual property warranties* say that the product will not infringe third-party intellectual property rights. Vendors almost always undertake risk for performance warranties. That is because they usually have confidence in the open source software they have selected and their quality control checks are not very dependent on whether the software in the product is open source or not.

Intellectual property warranties are different. For the most part, the vendor has no intellectual property coverage from its own upstream supplier, which may be a noncommercial open source project or a commercial vendor such as Red Hat. Keep in mind that open source licenses are granted as-is, so there is no coverage except by separate contract.

However, there are sometimes nuances to how much liability a vendor undertakes for third-party open source components to its product. The vendor will, more often, undertake liability for libraries or other small open source components that are integrated into the vendor's product. But as open source computing platforms become more popular, the vendor may disclaim liability for infrastructure software such as the LAMP stack, Hadoop, or OpenStack.

Ironically, these popular infrastructure elements are probably the least risky when considering third-party infringement liability. Copyright and trade secret claims accusing open source projects are actually quite rare. The main risk is third-party patent infringement. And more ironically, this is the issue upon which open source and proprietary software differ the least—and upon which the vendor's own code and open source code differ the least. Any of these can be subject to third-party infringement claims, and even proprietary vendors try to avoid liability for third-party patent claims on code they wrote themselves.

Ten or twenty years ago, it was common for purchasers in M&A deals to insist that open source representations were *special representations*—for which liability might be enhanced or even unlimited. In M&A deals, liability is usually quite limited, often to 10 to 15 percent of the purchase price, via an escrow against which the buyer can make claims for breach of representations and warranties. Today, open source representations are unlikely to be treated any differently from other intellectual property representations, and rightly so, because open source intellectual property problems are, generally speaking, no more risky than any other intellectual property problem. The clamor for enhanced remedies probably sprang from the mistaken idea that "viral" licenses caused proprietary code to be automatically subject to those licenses. If that were true, then enhanced remedies would be appropriate, but it has never happened and is not even likely to be possible under law.[2] Once the fear of this catastrophic result subsided, buyer insistence on unlimited remedies for breach of open source representations subsided as well.

## Drafting the Customer Agreement

If you are responsible for preparing customer agreements for proprietary products that include open source software, there are a few rules you should follow.

The most important is that GPL and LGPL do not allow licensing of binaries on different terms. For this reason, it is actually a violation of the license to purport to relicense a product including these elements under other terms. If you plan to include GPL or LGPL components in your product (assuming your plan to do so is compliant—for which see Chapters 8 and 9 on GPL and LGPL compliance), you must carve out the licensing for those products from your customer agreement. This carve-out might look like this:

> Notwithstanding the foregoing [reference license grant], Licensee acknowledges that certain components of the Software may be covered by so-called open source software licenses (*Open Source Components*), which means any software licenses approved as open source licenses by the Open Source Initiative or any substantially similar licenses, including without limitation any license that, as a condition of distribution of the software licensed under such license, requires that the distributor make the software available in source code format. To the extent required by the licenses covering Open Source Components, the terms of such licenses will apply to such Open Source Components in lieu of the terms of this Agreement. To the extent the terms of the licenses applicable to Open Source Components prohibit any of the restrictions in this Agreement with respect to such Open Source Components, such restrictions will not apply to such Open Source Components. To the extent

---

[2] For a discussion of copyleft licenses and their remedies, see Chapter 6: What Is Distribution?

> the terms of the licenses applicable to Open Source Components require Licensor to make an offer to provide source code or related information in connection with the Software, such offer is hereby made. Any request for source code or related information should be directed only to _____. Licensee acknowledges receipt of notices for the Open Source Components for the initial delivery of the Software.

Most of the weak copyleft licenses allow licensing of binaries under other licenses, as long as the source code is made available under the copyleft license. Because this is the simplest approach for a binary distribution, it is the approach most companies take. The provision above says, "To the extent required by the licenses covering Open Source Components, the terms of such licenses will apply to such Open Source Components in lieu of the terms of this Agreement." In such cases, it is not required. The same is true, of course, for permissively licensing open source components.

The provision above is purposely general. It is possible to "hard code" the exceptions into your license, but then you must revise it every time the open source components in the product change. Most companies find it easier to avoid such an approach, which could result in noncompliance.

One element of the provision above is specifically directed to LGPL components. LGPL 2.1 says this in Section 6:

> As an exception to the Sections above, you may also combine or link a "work that uses the Library" with the Library to produce a work containing portions of the Library, and distribute that work under terms of your choice, provided that the terms permit modification of the work for the customer's own use and reverse engineering for debugging such modifications.

End user licenses for proprietary products usually include reverse engineering prohibitions that would conflict with this provision of LGPL.

Keep in mind that the carve-out language above prioritizes compliance with the open source license over potential conflicts in the proprietary EULA. This is based on the assumption that a minor incursion into the EULA's terms—such as making its reverse engineering prohibitions inapplicable to reverse engineering for dubbing modifications of LGPL code—is a small price to pay for ensuring compliance with the open source license and avoiding losing the license to the open source software.

## Development Agreements

Companies that engage developers to create software have long used agreements that assign intellectual property rights to the customer.[3] A typical development agreement might include the following "buckets" of intellectual property:

- Materials developed by the developer prior to or independent of the project. The materials are licensed to the customer, usually without restriction.
- Materials newly developed by the developer for the project. The intellectual property rights in these materials are usually assigned to the customer.

Today, however, a great deal of development either consists of modifications to third-party open source software or requires the integration of third-party open source software into the material being developed. This new development paradigm requires a more nuanced intellectual property structure. Here are some examples:

- Materials developed by the developer prior to or independent of the project. The materials are licensed to the customer, usually without restriction.
- Materials newly developed by the developer for the project. The intellectual property rights in these materials are usually assigned to the customer.
    - These may include modifications to third-party copyleft materials. The intellectual property rights in these modifications are usually assigned to the customer but may be effectively subject to third-party open source license conditions.
- Third-party open source materials. These are provided to the customer by the developer but licensed by the open source licensors.

Also, some developers today are hired specifically to create and release open source materials. In that case, the customer—rather than seeking an assignment of rights in the software—may want the developer to release the resulting development to the public under an open source license. The cautious customer will also receive a separate license to the material to ensure that it cannot be subject to an intellectual property claim for violating the open source license—which would be ironic after it paid for the development. Also, the customer may have an interest in ensuring that the developer seeks no patents on the software being developed.

---

[3] These are sometimes referred to as "work for hire" agreements—though that is a misnomer. The work made for hire doctrine of copyright law generally applies only to employees.

Accordingly, the customer may seek a promise to this effect or an assignment of the patent rights.

Because almost all development projects today are somehow related to open source, companies funding development are well served by paying close attention to the third-party open source that may be used in development projects. Many companies unwittingly violate open source licenses when they engage developers who do not use proper open source compliance processes. A company should apply its open source compliance policies to outside developers just as it does to in-house developers.

It is a good practice to combine open source review and technical review in developer projects. Accordingly, many companies now include open source reviews in their acceptance processes. Exhibit 6 to Appendix A is an example of a developer certification that embodies this process.

Chapter 18

# Government Regulation[1]

Software is a largely unregulated market, so most of the rules of software licensing are a matter of private ordering, both in open source and proprietary models. However, in some tangential areas, government regulation and software licensing can come into conflict. This chapter discusses how to resolve—or at least balance—the rules of open source licensing and government regulation.

## Government Procurement

The open source software movement embraces freedom and transparency. Open source software licenses use the power of copyright law to ensure that all users have the freedom to study, modify, and redistribute software. As the FSF says, "If you use a program to carry out activities in your life, your freedom depends on your having control over the program."[2] Laying open source code for all to see makes backdoors, spyware, or other hidden control mechanisms easy to find and eradicate.

Freedom and transparency also underlie modern theories of government. As Justice Brandeis said, sunshine is the best disinfectant. Today, governments rely on technology to perform many basic functions. When software executes the functions of government, secrecy of source code is a political problem. Today, nearly every interaction between a citizen and the state involves a computer—whether that means citizens dealing with government agencies via websites, governments accessing one's electronic information by fiat, or governments using software and technology to conduct elections. Accordingly, many in and outside the open source movement believe that governments should employ open source software as much as possible to preserve freedom and transparency.

---

[1] Particular thanks to Sabir Ibrahim, Greta Lichtenbaum, and David Ribner for their help with this chapter.

[2] www.gnu.org/philosophy/free-software-even-more-important.html.

A government that buys its tools of operation with taxpayer funds also owes a duty of transparency to its citizens. In the United States, acquisition by governments or their agencies is governed by a web of procurement regulations. Federal procurement is governed by the Federal Acquisition Regulations (FAR), which govern acquisitions by all executive agencies.[3] Defense-related technology procurement is governed by FAR and its defense supplement, the Defense Federal Acquisition Regulation Supplement (DFAR). Acquisitions by states are governed by state procurement regulations, which are not necessarily consistent with the FAR or each other.

Although open source licenses certainly grant broad rights that can be useful to government, they do not always mesh with government procurement processes or requirements. Also, the open source development model may be inconsistent with the requirements of government procurement. For example, many jurisdictions have laws or procurement regulations requiring that goods purchased by the government be wholly or substantially manufactured within the government's territory of jurisdiction. Open source projects often solicit contributions from the general public, and contributors may be based anywhere. Also, the tendency of government to prefer cost-plus development may not mesh well with a project maintained by a group of volunteers.

In some areas, open source licenses either lack appropriate terms or conflict with government technology procurement requirements:

- **Governing law.** Some government procurement regulations require the application of local state law or federal law to the terms and conditions of any contract. Most open source licenses purposely lack law- or venue-selection provisions.

- **Venue.** Many state and federal procurement regulations require that disputes be resolved in particular venues. Most open source licenses have no venue selection terms.

- **March-in rights.** Government funding of technology development under the FARs can entitle the government to compel a supplier to grant broad licenses to the technology.[4] Most open source licenses do not contemplate march-in rights, and such rights may have fewer restrictions than the applicable license.

- **Sovereign immunity.** A state government cannot be the target of a civil suit unless it has expressly waived its immunity. Contracting with state governments often involves a waiver of sovereign immunity to make agree-

---

[3]  www.acquisition.gov/far/reissue/FARvol1ForPaperOnly.pdf.

[4]  35 USC.§ 203: March-in rights.

ments enforceable. In other words, by default law, no copyleft condition could be enforced against a state government unless the state government consents. Keep in mind that copyright law is federal law, and federal courts would not otherwise have jurisdiction over state governments.

Some of these issues could be addressed by supplementing existing open source licenses with side agreements for use when the licensee is a government agency. But this is not possible when the alternative term is a change to the scope or free exercise of the license, as opposed to ancillary agreements. For example, one might think that a government agency wishing to use GPL software could take the software under GPL and enter into an agreement with the licensor stating that the GPL will be interpreted under the law of the government's jurisdiction. GPL prohibits alterations of the license and also prohibits further restrictions on the license. Section 10 of GPL version 3 states, "You may not impose any further restrictions on the exercise of the rights granted or affirmed under this License."[5] Section 7 informs the licensee that if the software "contains a notice stating that it is governed by this License along with a term that is a further restriction," that notice may be ignored.[6]

There is much debate in the open source community as to what constitutes a "further restriction" prohibited by licenses like GPL, and FSF tends to take an expansive view of what this might include. For example, controversies persist over whether the Apple App Store terms (such as terms limiting use of software to a particular device) constitute an additional restriction and whether the patent defensive termination provision of Apache 2 makes it incompatible with GPL 2. Licensors and suppliers to government therefore take the risk of violating licenses like GPL if they agree to restrictions.

Moreover, even if the additional government-specific terms would not be considered additional restrictions or modifications in violation of a license, many government agencies, in practice, will not vary their procurement terms to accommodate open source licensing models.

Accordingly, as things currently stand, there is a fundamental inconsistency between copyleft licenses and government procurement, and it is unclear which side will be the first to blink. Governments continue to express a preference for open source software, but their policy objectives do not always mesh with their procurement rules.

---

[5] www.gnu.org/copyleft/gpl.html.

[6] www.gnu.org/copyleft/gpl.html.

## Exports

In the United States, exports are covered by various regulations. The element of software that is commonly regulated under export law is encryption. Encryption products are regulated by the US Department of Commerce's Bureau of Industry and Security (BIS) through the Export Administration Regulations (EAR), 15 C.F.R. §§ 730–774. Exports of encryption products specifically designed for military applications are regulated by the Department of State's Directorate of Defense Trade Controls (DDTC) through the International Traffic in Arms Regulations (ITAR), 22 C.F.R. §§ 120–130.

Software that is controlled for export is classified under the EAR by Export Control Classification Numbers (ECCNs) listed in the Commerce Control List (CCL), Supplement No. 1 to Part 774 of the EAR. Encryption items fall under CCL Category 5, Part 2 (Information Security), and they are assigned a code based on the kind of product (such as 5D002 - Software).

If you want to export controlled software, you need to classify the item to determine the applicable export controls. Determining the appropriate classification under the EAR can be complex, but encryption software generally falls into three categories:

1. Products that can be self-classified by the exporter and can be exported without submitting anything to BIS

2. Products that can be self-classified but that must be registered with BIS prior to any export

3. Products for which an encryption classification request must be filed with BIS prior to export

Both encryption registrations and encryption classification requests can be filed online through BIS's SNAP-R system (**snapr.bis.doc.gov/snapr/**). Exporters of software requiring an encryption registration must also file an annual self-classification report with BIS.

Encryption software that is correctly classified is usually eligible for export under license exceptions that obviate the need for export licenses. For example, License Exception TSU is available to encryption source code classified under ECCN 5D002 that is made publicly available (15 C.F.R. § 740.13(e)). To take advantage of this license exception, exporters must notify BIS and the ENC

Encryption Request Coordinator by simply emailing the URL of the publicly available encryption source code (15 C.F.R. § 740.13(e)(3)).[7]

Unfortunately, the regulations can be difficult to read and understand. Also, these requirements can and do change from time to time. It is always best to get professional advice about export requirements before relying on an exception or classification.

---

[7] Even in cases where encryption items are eligible for a license exception, additional materials may need to be filed with BIS. For example, for certain encryption items under License Exception ENC, exporters must file semiannual sales reports.

# Chapter 19

# Enforcement and Obstacles to Enforcement[1]

The twenty-first century has seen the first serious enforcement efforts by licensors of open source software, so we are truly at the dawning of the age of enforcement. But open source claims are not like other claims. Understanding the distinctions between open source software claims and other intellectual property claims is key to reacting to open source claims gracefully, effectively, and with a minimum of embarrassment and cost.

A survey of where we stand today demonstrates how the enforcement area has developed. We will be soon nearing the point where including catalogs of open source claims in books like this one will no longer be sensible or useful, but for now, seeing where we have been neatly explains where we are.

The first years of the twenty-first century saw the first written opinion on open source licensing law handed down in the United States. That decision, *Jacobsen v. Katzer*, was generally seen as a victory for open source licensing. It underscored the fact that open source licenses are not prima facie unenforceable, nor are they vulnerable to contract formation claims. Leading up to *Jacobsen* were a variety of claims—mostly settled long before they threatened to create case law—that set the groundwork for enforcement. Below is a list of most of the cases relating to open source licensing.

## I. The Early Years: Pre-Jacobsen

### A. Progress v. NuSphere (2001–2002)

NuSphere and MySQL had a business relationship in which NuSphere marketed several products that included both MySQL software and other proprietary software. Proprietary code (called Gemini) was statically linked to MySQL code in the NuSphere MySQL Advantage product. Although MySQL alleged a breach

---

[1] An earlier version of this chapter appeared as "Open Source and the Age of Enforcement," *Hastings Science & Technology Law Journal*, September 14, 2012.

of its GPL license, the case was decided on trademark grounds, with the court sidestepping the GPL issues.[2]

### B. Drew Technologies Inc. v. Society of Auto Engineers (2003–2005)

This was one of the earliest open source cases, filed in November 2003 and settled in early 2005. *Drew Tech* released certain software under the GNU General Public License (GPL), and that software was posted by an employee of Drew Tech on a message board run by the Society of Auto Engineers. Drew Tech sued to compel removal of the posting, and the case was settled and the posting removed. No reported opinion resulted, but the result suggested the GPL was enforceable.[3]

Although this case received little press and fanfare, it involved a familiar fact pattern, but in mirror image. Drew's employee posted the software without its GPL notices. The more common situation is the opposite. Today's technology companies often employ software engineers who are very enthusiastic about open source software. Those employees may, upon leaving the company or even before, make unauthorized code releases under open source terms that conflict with the proprietary terms offered by their company. This situation sometimes is a result of a misunderstanding regarding who owns the code,[4] but it occasionally results from the actual malfeasance of disgruntled employees. In any case, unauthorized code releases are often resolved via a takedown of the code—as quietly as possible.

### C. Jin v. IChessU (2006–2008)

*Jin v. IChessU* was a case that briefly whetted the appetite of open source lawyers because it squarely concerned the scope and interpretation of GPL—one of the big unresolved issues of open source law. In this case, International Chess University allegedly distributed the plaintiff's GPL software, a chess client called "Jin," and added an audiovisual library to it, taking the position that the GPL

---

[2] *Progress Software Corp. v. MySQL* AB, 195 F. Supp. 2d 328 (D. Mass. 2002). MySQL was historically licensed under the so-called GPL plus "FLOSS" exception, which would make linking proprietary code to it noncompliant. For MySQL's posting about the case, see: **www.mysql. com/news-and-events/generate-article.php?id=75.**

[3] For more detail, here is the *Groklaw* posting about the case: **www.groklaw.net/articlebasic.php? story=20050225223848129.**

[4] Employees often do not fully understand the work-for-hire doctrine under copyright law, and they believe they own rights to open source software created during their employment "on their own time." The misunderstanding usually centers on the complexity of what constitutes the employee's own time and the breadth of assignments of rights in Employee Invention Assignment Agreements.

did not require publication of the source code for the library. The author of Jin claimed it did. The case, which was brought in the courts of Israel, was settled in 2008.[5]

## D. Planetary Motion, Inc. v. Techplosion, Inc. (2001)

This trademark case pointed to the use of GPL licensing notices as evidence of the trademark owner's intent to control the use of its mark.[6] The court said, "Because a GNU General Public License requires licensees who wish to copy, distribute, or modify the software to include a copyright notice, the license itself is evidence of [the licensor's] efforts to control the use of the 'CoolMail' mark in connection with the Software." Since 2001 when this case was decided, understanding of the relationship between open source licensing and trademark husbandry has developed significantly. Companies like Red Hat have pioneered the husbandry of trademark rights parallel to open source licenses, rather than through them. Most commentators today would therefore consider GPL notices not to function as trademark notices. However, the court in this case was looking at the totality of the circumstances to assess whether the plaintiff had intended to use the mark as a trademark, and other facts and circumstances also contributed to the court's decision.

## E. Computer Associates International v. Quest Software, Inc. (2004)

This opinion declares that "Bison is open source code, meaning that it is distributed by the FSF at no cost," that programs under the GPL are "freely released into the public domain," and that "[t]he GPL would prevent plaintiff from attempting to claim copyright in that modified version of Bison."[7] Again, understanding of open source licensing has developed significantly since this 2004 case, and so the court's comments should be viewed with skepticism; they represent an incorrect or, at best, an oversimplified view of open source licensing.[8]

## F. gpl-violations.org (2004–2015)

This set of cases is usually considered the first significant enforcement effort for GPL. They were brought by gpl-violations.org, an organization spearheaded by Harald Welte, a technologist and open source advocate in Germany. That

---

[5] For details, see **www.jinchess.com/ichessu/**.

[6] 261 F.3d 1188,; 2001 US App. LEXIS 18481; 59 USP.Q.2D (BNA) 1894 (11th Cir. 2001).

[7] 333 F. Supp. 2d. 688, 697–98; 2004 US Dist. Lexis 11832 (N.D. Ill. 2004).

[8] My thanks to Terry Ilardi for pointing me to the *CAI* and *Planetary Motion* cases.

these cases preceded actions in the United States is not surprising; the German legal system differs substantially from the US legal system. For instance, German courts allow ex parte actions for injunction—a suit for an injunction brought by the plaintiff where the defendant does not participate and the plaintiff pursues the injunction directly with a court.[9] Some, but not all, of the initial string of cases brought by this organization related to Mr. Welte's own software. The most widely publicized of these cases was against Fortinet UK. A Munich district court granted a preliminary injunction against Fortinet prohibiting distribution of their products absent compliance with the GPL. Welte also claimed that Fortinet was obfuscating the existence of GPL code in its product, a fact Fortinet disputed. Fortinet eventually agreed to make certain source code in its products available under GPL.

Since that time, other authors empowered gpl-violations.org to bring claims on their behalf in a similar fashion, and gpl-violations.org grew in scope to an ad hoc enforcement organization for GPL and other free software, working with FSF Europe.[10]

## II. Formal Enforcement in the United States Bears Fruit

### A. The BusyBox Cases (2007–Present)

Starting in 2007, the Software Freedom Law Center (SFLC) filed a series of lawsuits on behalf of Erik Andersen and Rob Landley, two of the authors of the BusyBox software. BusyBox emulates many standard UNIX tools in a small, efficient executable that's useful for embedded devices. The first suit was filed against Monsoon Multimedia, Inc. That case was settled with the release of source code and an undisclosed settlement payment. SFLC next brought suit against Xterasys and High-Gain Antenna. Both soon settled. Further suits were brought from 2007 to 2009 against Verizon Communications, Bell Microproducts, and Super Micro Computer. All settled quickly.

On December 14, 2009, SFLC filed another lawsuit naming fourteen defendants, including Best Buy, JVC, and Samsung. Some of these are still pending.

One case, against Westinghouse Digital Electronics, resulted in a damages award, but this was because the defendant was in liquidation and defaulted on the litigation by failing to answer discovery requests. The judge awarded statutory

---

[9] Germany is a jurisdiction particularly friendly to the granting of intellectual property injunctions. See **www.managingip.com/?Page=17&ISS=21425&SID=614860**.

[10] The website shut down in early 2015; see **en.wikipedia.org/wiki/Gpl-violations.org**.

damages, attorneys' fees, and injunctive relief.[11] Although the order characterizes the damages as "treble," that was only true in the sense that the court awarded three times the upper limit of statutory damages in the absence of willfulness. The better characterization is enhanced damages—under 17 USC § 504, a court can in its discretion award up to $150,000 per work in statutory damages if the infringement is willful. The court did not make a finding of actual damages because the defendant failed to respond to discovery and thus never presented evidence to support calculation of actual damages. Also, as described in footnote 39 of the order, absent the default, statutory damages might have been unavailable because the plaintiff had failed to register the copyright in a timely fashion. Given that most software authors do not register their copyrights, this could often be a significant limitation on claims enforcing open source licenses. This case's result is interesting mostly because it confirms that injunction and statutory damages are available for open source claims, but the facts were unusual and thus probably difficult to extrapolate to non-default judgments.

In a further development in the same case, a successor entity of Westing-house Digital Electronics met the same fate. On August 8, 2011, the District Court for the Southern District of New York held Westinghouse Digital, LLC ("WD") in contempt for failing to defend its BusyBox case. Westinghouse Digital Electronics, LLC ("WDE"), with the default judgment standing against it, liquidated its assets after severe business distress and told the court it would not defend the litigation. WD purchased the assets of WDE. The court assessed whether there was "a substantial continuity of identity" between WDE and WD, and it found that there was. The court invited evidence on damages and attorneys' fees and ordered forfeiture of all infringing articles.

It is important to note that the BusyBox cases involved only some of the developers of BusyBox and notably did not include Bruce Perens, the original author, and Dave Cinege, the maintainer who had made significant contributions to BusyBox. Perens subsequently released a statement criticizing the current BusyBox developers, saying, "The version 0.60.3 of Busybox upon which Mr. Andersen claims copyright registration in the lawsuits is to a great extent my own work and that of other developers. I am not party to the registration. It is not at all clear that Mr. Andersen holds a majority interest in that work."[12]

Joint ownership is a lurking issue in open source enforcement. While in the case of BusyBox, the primary authors were more or less sequential (the laboring oar having been passed from Perens to Cinege, and so forth), open source projects are often collaborative efforts. The messaging and rhetoric regarding open source

---

[11]  Attorneys' fees were awarded because of the default.

[12]  lists.gnu.org/archive/html/fsf-community-team/2009-12/msg00127.html.

development often emphasizes open source's collaborative nature, and this is ripe fodder for an argument that open source projects are actually joint works. Under US law, joint authors all have an undivided interest in the work and can freely license it.[13] Therefore, defendants facing claims of a single author among many may be in a position to seek a license from a joint author and claim a license defense. Alternatively, defendants may be able to raise procedural arguments that all authors must be joined to the suit for the claim to go forward. US courts sometimes require this and sometimes do not. When they do, the reason given is that if any author could have granted a license, then the claim cannot be resolved until they are all involved. Even if a defendant is not ultimately successful in claiming a license from a nonplaintiff author, it may be able to delay and complicate the suit enough to make enforcement difficult.

The BusyBox cases in many respects comprise the quintessential action of the "Age of Enforcement." They are brought by SFLC, albeit on behalf of private parties. Their settlement tends to be quick, reflecting SFLC's strategy of establishing a track record of enforcement by selecting clear violations to pursue. The press releases announcing the terms of these settlements read like a template and almost always describe the following in some detail: appointment of an open source compliance officer, covenants to bring distribution into compliance (via communication of notices and release of source code), and the payment of damages—though probably less than one would expect from a proprietary software lawsuit. This form of settlement reflects the quintessential concerns of a zealous plaintiff—with a focus on compliance and transparency, rather than substantial damages.

### B. Jacobsen v. Katzer (2006–2010)

In August 2008, the US Court of Appeals for the Federal Circuit issued the most significant decision on open source licensing in the United States to date—and followed the guidance of the open source community.

The case arose from a complicated set of facts. Both parties developed and distributed software for controlling model railroads. Jacobsen made his "Java Model Railroad Interface" (JMRI) software available under an open source license free of charge, and Katzer (via his company Kamind Associates) sold commercial products under proprietary licenses. In particular, Jacobsen made available through the JMRI project software called DecoderPro, which is used by model railroad enthusiasts to program decoder chips in model trains to control lights, sounds, and speed.

---

[13] Subject to certain requirements to account, for instance. See *Oddo v. Ries*, 743 F.2d 630 (9th Cir. 1984).

Jacobsen received a letter inviting him to license patents owned by Kamind, suggesting the patents were infringed by the JMRI software. Jacobsen filed a declaratory judgment action asking the court to rule that the patent was invalid due to prior art (or failure to disclose prior art, including that of Jacobsen himself) or not infringed. Katzer's original claim received a great deal of press in the open source world, feeding fears that the existence of software patents spelled death for open source projects. As the patent case progressed, Jacobsen discovered that Katzer had copied some of Jacobsen's open source software and used it in Katzer's proprietary product. Jacobsen's software was licensed under the Artistic License, which is a relatively rarely used license that was originally written to provide rights to the PERL programming language interpreter. The requirements of the Artistic License are modest; it is generally considered a permissive open source license, similar to the Apache, BSD, or MIT licenses. The Artistic License requires, as a condition to exercise of the license, certain copyright and license notices and identification of changes made to the original author's source code. Because these notices were not preserved by Katzer, Jacobsen made a counterclaim, alleging violation of the license.

In 2007, the District Court for the Northern District of California issued a preliminary ruling in the case, stating that the license violation constituted a breach of contract. However, the court's ruling did not support a claim for copyright infringement. The court reasoned that Katzer was exercising rights in the copyrightable work but was licensed to so do and thus was not liable for infringement. Copyright infringement claims can result from breach of the scope of a license, but the court distinguished violations of license scope and license conditions. This distinction is core to open source law because open source licenses grant all the rights of copyright—and so it is generally not possible to violate the scope of an open source license, only its conditions.

Proponents of free software such as the Free Software Foundation have long taken the position that their licenses are not contracts. Originally, this position may have been a strategic attempt to avoid the contract formation issues that plagued the law of online distribution of the software in the early 1990s, but the position persists notwithstanding the intervening publication of a line of cases supporting enforceability of contracts in the download context.

The issue in this case is sometimes referred to in the open source legal community as the *license or contract* issue. In other words, are open source licenses contracts, or are they merely conditional licenses? (See Chapter 5: Conditional Licensing for an extended discussion of this issue.) The status of an open source license as a license or contract dictates the types of remedies available if a licensee violates the conditions of the license. If the conditions of an open source license are mere contractual covenants, as the district court order stated, then injunctive relief is generally not available. If, however, violating the conditions places the activities of the licensee outside the scope of the license, as the appellate court stated, then the unlicensed activity is copyright infringement and far more likely to garner injunctive relief. Open source advocates also are concerned that the money damages for violation of open source licenses under contract law may be more limited than those available under copyright law, which can include statutory damages as well as actual damages.

The Free Software Foundation has long taken the position that open source licenses are licenses rather than contracts—however, this can be misleading because the two are not mutually exclusive. Most licensing contracts are both conditional licenses and contracts. The *Jacobsen* case holds that violating the conditions of an open source license can constitute copyright infringement but not that open source licenses are not contracts.

The flip side of this question—whether the conditions of a license could be considered covenants whose performance might be ordered by a court—was not at issue. But this is the "bet the company" issue for most corporate free software users. If providing source code were a contractual covenant, then failure to do so would be a breach of contract. However, even if it were a breach, specific performance of covenants is not generally available under contract law. Most companies' biggest fear when dealing with GPL is that they will be compelled to lay open proprietary software. In fact, the likely worst-case scenario is that they will be given a Hobson's choice: to lay it open and comply with GPL, or to replace the GPL code.

On the question of whether the claim could sound in copyright—that is, whether it could be cast in terms of copyright—the appellate court reversed and remanded the case back to the district court to determine whether Jacobsen had established his claim to an injunction. The Federal Circuit opinion was hailed as a victory for open source licensing.

Ironies abounded in this case. This, possibly the most significant decision in open source software licensing to date, relates to the relatively obscure Artistic License—though the court's mention of the GPL in a footnote suggests it intended the same result to hold for other open source licenses. Moreover, the decision was issued by the US Court of Appeals for the Federal Circuit, which is the circuit that primarily adjudicates the enforcement of patents—the villains of the open source world. Finally, the case was only brought because Katzer chose to pursue a patent claim against a party whose code he had apparently copied—a strategy probably best avoided.

On December 10, 2009, on remand, the lower court issued an order granting and denying portions of motions for summary judgment by the parties. The court said, "Although it is undisputed that Plaintiff distributed the copied work on the Internet at no cost, there is also evidence in the record attributing a monetary value for the actual work performed by the contributors to the JMRI product." As a result, the court said that the record "may establish a monetary damages figure." This dispels the notion that no actual damages would be available for open source authors bringing claims of infringement because of the royalty-free nature of open source licensing.

*Jacobsen v. Katzer* was finally settled in 2010, obviating a second appeal. The settlement included an injunction by the district court against further infringing activities, and it was not sealed. Most settlements are confidential, and an actual injunction by the court in a settlement is a bit unusual. But the injunction would have carried more precedential weight if it had been won in court rather than agreed to in settlement. (The District Court had previously declined to issue an injunction.)

It was significant that this case involved the original Artistic License. If a permissive license is enforceable, that lays substantial groundwork for enforceability of copyleft licenses. In *Jacobsen*, the question of actual harm to the copyright owner was squarely at issue. For Jacobsen to prevail, the court had to decide that there was sufficient harm to give rise to a remedy. With a permissive license, the harm is, essentially, failure to deliver notices. For a copyleft license, the conditions are much more significant, and violating them would give rise to greater harm and, in turn, greater opportunities for relief.

### C. FSF v. Linksys (2008–2009)

This suit was notable in that it was the first lawsuit filed for FSF as a plaintiff. Compliance issues regarding GPL software in Linksys consumer wireless routers had existed since Cisco acquired Linksys in 2003. (For details about the informal dispute that took place in the early 2000s, see my 2005 article "The Legend of Linksys" in *Linux Insider*.[14]) This dispute resulted in a fairly quick release of source code, but FSF continued to find compliance issues with the routers and finally filed suit in 2008. The accused software included various GPL and LGPL components.[15] That suit was settled in 2009 with no substantial docket activity, via a settlement that, according to the press release describing it, was very similar to those in the BusyBox cases.[16]

---

[14] www.linuxinsider.com/story/43996.html?wlc=1300413418.

[15] See the complaint and FSF's press release here:
www.fsf.org/blogs/licensing/2008-12-cisco-complaint.

[16] www.fsf.org/news/2009-05-cisco-settlement.html.

## III. Post-Jacobsen and Strategic Plaintiffs

### A. Artifex Cases (2008–Present)

Artifex is the purveyor of the "Ghostscript" line of software, which is primarily used as embedded software in printers. In 2008 and 2009, Artifex filed some of the first lawsuits brought by a private company to enforce GPL. The first plaintiff was Premier Election Solutions, at the time a subsidiary of Diebold. That case was settled quickly and confidentially. In 2009, in an action related to its MuPDF software (a high-performance PDF-rendering engine), it brought claims against Palm, Inc. and various other defendants. The cases have settled.

### B. Twin Peaks Software, Inc. v. Red Hat, Inc. et al. (July 2013)

Twin Peaks Software (TPS), which made proprietary network backup software, sued Red Hat and Red Hat's recently acquired subsidiary Gluster. TPS claimed that the GlusterFS software—a network file system that aggregated multiple storage shares into a single volume—violated TPS's patent covering TPS's Mirror File System (MFS). Red Hat initially responded to the patent infringement suit by denying the infringement and asserting that the patent was invalid, but it later brought a counterclaim alleging the TPS products incorporated open source software from Red Hat's product but failed to comply with GPL. Red Hat sought an injunction against the TPS products. The case ended soon in a settlement, suggesting that TPS thought better of pursuing its patent claims in light of the facts.

### C. US Customs Case (Unfiled)—Fusion Garage

In September 2010, a Linux kernel developer, Matthew Garrett, posted a blog entry[17] threatening to file a US Customs case based on GPL violations. His blog describes failed attempts to get the source code for JooJoo Android tablets. According to this blog, the maker of the tablet, Fusion Garage, has not responded to requests for source code as required by GPL.

This method of enforcement is sometimes called a *337 action* because it is authorized by Section 337 of the Tariff Act of 1930 (19 USC. § 1337). If the US ITC (US International Trade Commission) finds Section 337 has been violated, it may issue an order directing that infringing goods be excluded from import into the United States. The order is executed by Customs and Border Protection (CBP), which may seize the goods at the border. CBP's border enforcement of

---

[17] mjg59.livejournal.com/126865.html.

copyrights is essentially limited to copyrights that have been registered with the US Library of Congress and also recorded with CBP.

A circular published by the US government says this:

> Members of the public may inform CBP of potential intellectual property rights violations via CBP's on-line trade violation reporting mechanism called e-Allegations. The public may access e-Allegations and additional relevant information at **www. cbp.gov/trade/trade-community/e-allegations/e-allegations-faqs/**. CBP also maintains an on-line recordation system, Intellectual Property Rights e-Recordation, which allows rights owners to electronically record their trademarks and copyrights with CBP and facilitates IPR seizures by making IPR recordation information readily available to CBP personnel.

This means that while only the owner of the copyright can bring a claim, anyone can report an infringing import. These 337 actions have long been used as a tactic to enforce intellectual property rights. They are generally faster and cheaper than federal litigation, and for this reason, they are particularly popular with patent plaintiffs. However, the remedies available are different from those in federal court—for example, a quick emergency exclusion order is more likely, but damages are not available. In addition, in a patent action, the complainant must show that the patent is being used in an "existing domestic industry" (19 USC. 1337(a)(1)(B), (a)(2–3)). This may exclude actions by nonpracticing entities (NPEs) or patent trolls.

Since Garrett's blog post, nothing appears to have been filed, but the case is still worth mentioning because it shows another approach to litigation in the open source sphere: using a tactic already popular for patent and other intellectual property claims.

### D. Microsoft's Linux Patent Enforcement Program (2009–Present)

In 2009, Microsoft filed a patent lawsuit against TomTom, makers of consumer GPS devices, accusing code in the Linux kernel of infringing certain patents of Microsoft, including three file management patents. The suit was settled very soon thereafter, with payment of a license fee to Microsoft and a five-year patent cross license between the parties. A joint press release called the settlement "fully compliant with TomTom's obligations under the General Public License Version 2." TomTom also agreed to remove from its products the functionality related to two file management systems patents over a two-year period.[18]

The patent claims asserted in the TomTom case are also the basis of a string of enforcement activities by Microsoft, which has clearly identified Linux as a competitive threat. Virtually all the enforcement has been in the consumer electronics space: I-O DATA, Amazon.com, Novell, Brother International Corp., Fuji Xerox Co. Ltd., Kyocera Document Solutions Corp., LG Electronics, and Samsung Electronics Co. Ltd.

Although these claims are not strictly related to open source licensing—the outbound license of the accused product being irrelevant to the central patent infringement questions of infringement and validity—they bear upon open source licensing in two ways. First, Microsoft's form of settlement was tailored to conform to the defendant's licensing of the accused software under GPL 2 but not GPL 3, which contains provisions that would contradict the terms of most such settlement agreements.[19] Second, Microsoft is probably one of the very few technology product companies that does not distribute Linux—if it did, it might have significant challenges enforcing patents that read on GPL code.[20]

Microsoft's enforcement actions are ongoing.

### E. Oracle America v. Google (2010–Present)

In 2010, Oracle, after having acquired Sun Microsystems (and renaming it Oracle America, Inc.), filed suit alleging that Google's Android mobile platform infringed certain patents of Oracle America, as well as copyrights in Oracle's Java platform. Oracle licenses Java under, among other terms, GPL plus a "Classpath exception."[21] In this suit, Oracle alleged that Google's reimplementation of portions of the Java API infringed copyrights associated with Java. The district court found for Google on all patent and copyright claims. The court ruled, "So long as the specific code used to implement a method is different, anyone is free under the Copyright Act to write his or her own code to carry out exactly the same function or specification of any methods used in the Java API. It does not matter

---

[18] news.microsoft.com/2009/03/30/microsoft-and-tomtom-settle-patent-infringement-cases/.

[19] See the terms of paragraphs 5, 6 and 7 of GPL 3 Section 11—the so-called "anti-Microsoft" and "anti-Novell" provisions.

[20] The topic of what patent rights are licensed under GPL 2 is a subject of controversy—or better said, mystery—but is beyond the scope of this paper. For more information, see Laura Majerus's paper: www.fenwick.com/docstore/publications/ip/potential_defenses.pdf.

[21] The Groklaw site (www.groklaw.net) contains extensive information about the case.

that the declaration or method header lines are identical."[22] Therefore, Google's actions did not require a copyright license from Oracle; under section 102(b) of the Copyright Act, the API was a "system or method of operation" that did not enjoy copyright protection. The case therefore did not, ultimately, turn on whether the GPL had been violated. The case was appealed to the Federal Circuit, which reversed, and as this book goes to press, a petition for certiorari is pending with the US Supreme Court.[23]

### F. Penrose Trademark Dispute (2011)

A complaint was filed against Red Hat in the Northern District of California on May 6, 2011, alleging various claims, including a request to cancel a trademark registration. According to the complaint, Alex Karasulu, founder of the Apache Directory Server Project, set up a domain at **www.safehaus.org** to provide an ecosystem for open source software components related to directory and security infrastructure. Karasulu was approached by Jim Yang about the development of open source virtual directory software, and Karasulu offered to develop the software as a project for Safehaus. Karasulu used the name "Penrose" for the virtual directory software project. The initial version of the Penrose software was released on May 23, 2005. On March 13, 2008, Yang filed an application to register the trademark Penrose for software through a company he owned called Identyx, Inc. Yang subsequently sold Identyx to Red Hat. The complaint alleges that in the trademark application, Yang misrepresented the facts underlying the first use of the mark and failed to acknowledge prior use and ownership by Safehaus, and it also alleges that Red Hat knew statements made in the trademark application by Identyx were false because of information received by Red Hat in the due diligence process for the acquisition. Based on the above allegations, the complaint alleged various claims and asks the court to declare the trademark registration invalid.

### G. Lawsuit by gpl-violations.org Against FANTEC (2013)

Gpl-violations.org filed a successful claim in Germany against FANTEC, a European company selling devices that facilitate streaming of media content.

One of FANTEC's products, the FANTEC 3DFHDL Media Player, included firmware based on the Linux operating system. Linux includes many software components covered by the GNU GPL 2, which requires that any distributor of binaries make the source code available to binary recipients. To comply with the

---

[22]  *Oracle Am., Inc. v. Google Inc.*, 872 F. Supp. 2d 974 (E.D. Cal. 2012).

[23]  For the Electronic Frontier Foundation's current summary, see **www.eff.org/cases/oracle-v-google/**.

GPL, FANTEC made a version of the source code available for download that it had received from its Chinese contract manufacturer. Unfortunately, it was not the right source code for the binaries.

Harald Welte brought the action as one of the authors of iptables, a packet-filtering utility licensed under GPL. FANTEC had previously settled a GPL dispute with Welte in 2010 by agreeing to a cease-and-desist declaration that provided for contractual penalties if FANTEC committed any future GPL violation. At a 2012 "Hacking for Compliance" workshop hosted by the Free Software Foundation, compliance engineers discovered that the firmware object code shipping with the 3DFHDL included iptables and that the source code provided by FANTEC did not. This information was forwarded to Welte, who gave FANTEC notice of the violation and demanded that FANTEC pay the contractual penalty set forth in the cease-and-desist declaration. FANTEC responded that it had been assured by its contract manufacturer that the source code was complete, and it refused Welte's demand. Welte sued FANTEC in the Regional Court of Hamburg, seeking to enforce the cease-and-desist letter.

FANTEC claimed that analyzing the source code would have been a costly process whose results may not have been reliable, and it argued that because only the author could determine with certainty whether the source code was accurate and complete, FANTEC should be permitted to rely on the representations of its contract manufacturer, who provided the firmware. However, the court disagreed and held FANTEC responsible for the error.

This case is a cautionary tale about a very common problem. Like many consumer electronics companies, FANTEC was caught between its customers and its supply chain. In ruling for Welte, the court held that a distributor of software may not rely on assurances made by the supplier of the software that the software does not infringe the rights of any third party. According to the court, FANTEC was "culpably negligent" in distributing incomplete source code. The court held that FANTEC was responsible for determining, "by [its] own assessment or with the help of a qualified third party," that the software did not infringe any third-party rights, even if doing so would have caused FANTEC to incur additional costs.

An open source distributor cannot rely on the culpability of its suppliers to avoid liability. It is best to always make delivery of source code, as well as a demonstration that it corresponds to the binaries, part of the acceptance testing for deliverables from one's supply chain.

### H. Mein Büro (2013)

Adhoc Dataservice GmbH settled with Buhl Data Service GmbH, the developer of the WISO Mein Büro (My Office) enterprise application software.

Buhl agreed to pay €15,000 for violating the LGPL terms under which Adhoc provides its FreeadhocUDF open source library (which includes various functions for UDF). The settlement disposed of a court case that resulted in a January 2011 opinion from a lower court in Bochum, Germany, that the use of the FreeadhocUDF library in WISO Mein Büro 2009 violated the LGPL's licensing terms.[24]

### I. Continuent, Inc. v. Tekelec, Inc. (2013)

In this recent case involving a GPL enforcement claim in the United States, a private company sued to enforce the GPL. The complaint, filed July 2, 2013, in the US District Court for the Southern District of California, alleged that defendant Tekelec copied and distributed Continuent's software without permission and in violation of GPL 2, thus infringing on Continuent's copyright. The case settled and was dismissed.

### J. Versata/Ameriprise/Ximpleware (2014)

A series of cases recently raised issues relating to distribution, the scope of GPL, and remedies for violation of GPL. For a good summary of these cases, see **opensource.com/law/14/7/lawsuit-threatens-break-new-ground-gpl-and-software-licensing-issues**. However, those cases have now settled and been dismissed.

## IV. Other Open Source–Related Cases and Disputes

Several notable cases did not strictly involve open source licensing issues but had an impact on perceptions of intellectual property risk in open source.

### A. SCO v. IBM, Novell, Red Hat, AutoZone & Daimler-Benz (2003–Present)

While this set of related cases was by far the most publicized in the open source world, the SCO cases were primarily breach-of-contract cases and did not seek to enforce any open source license. In fact, IBM raised SCO's breach of the GPL as a counterclaim, but this series of cases was resolved on different facts. A jury verdict in April 2010 determined that SCO did not own the copyright in UNIX, all but killing SCO's claims. The true end will be dismissal of SCO's case against IBM, which was stayed pending the disposition of SCO's bankruptcy, which will in turn depend heavily on the result in the Novell suit. This case, while not exactly over, is in the process of dying a long, slow death.

---

[24] For the German decision, see **www.telemedicus.info/urteile/Urheberrecht/Open-Source/1148-LG-Bochum-Az-I-8-O-29309-Ansprueche-bei-Verletzung-der-LGPL.html**.

### B. MontaVista Software v. Lineo (2000)

MontaVista sued its competitor, Lineo, claiming Lineo was distributing software written by MontaVista with the copyright notices removed.[25] The case was settled. The issue in this case—the stripping of notice—was not particular to open source.

### C. Monotype v. Red Hat (2003)

Monotype sued Red Hat claiming copyright and trademark infringements. The suit was settled, and in December 2003, the parties entered into a license agreement that provided Red Hat the right to distribute certain Monotype commercial fonts over a five-year period. The license cost Red Hat $500,000. This was not a suit to enforce any open source license; it was an infringement suit regarding proprietary software.[26]

### D. MDY v. Blizzard (2010)

This case did not involve open source software, but it is notable for its possible tension with *Jacobsen v. Katzer*. This case involved the creation by MDY of Glider, a "leveling bot" for use in Blizzard's *World of Warcraft*. MDY sold copies of this bot to users, causing concerns for Blizzard. Blizzard added a provision to its terms of use for *WoW*, prohibiting the use of bots. This case was an action for declaratory judgment by MDY, claiming that its exploitation of the bot did not infringe Blizzard's copyright in the *WoW* software. The lower court awarded damages for contributory copyright infringement, based on MDY's customers' use of the bot. The Ninth Circuit reversed, stating that the violation of the bot prohibition did not have a sufficient nexus to copyright to support a claim for infringement. In so ruling, it interpreted the prohibition as a covenant rather than a condition, citing relevant state law. (In contrast, the Federal Circuit in *Jacobsen* did not defer to state law, viewing the case as an intellectual property claim.)

### E. SAS Institute Inc. v. World Programming Ltd. (2010)

This case is not strictly about open source software, but it addresses the issue of whether APIs are copyrightable. The Royal Court of Justice issued an opinion

---

[25] Steven Shankland, "Linux Companies Settle Copyright Suit," *C/Net News.com*, October 13, 2003, news.cnet.com/Linux-companies-settle-copyright-suit/2100-7344_3-5090704.html.

[26] See Red Hat's 10-K dated February 29, 2004, www.secinfo.com/d14D5a.12Mg6.htm.

on July 23, 2010.[27] SAS Institute Inc. is a developer of the SAS system, which allows users to write scripts to manipulate and analyze statistical information. World Programming Ltd. created a product called World Programming System, which was designed to emulate much of the functionality of the SAS system as closely as possible via the same programmatic interface. WPL had no access to the source code of the SAS system. SAS alleged that World Programming had infringed the copyright in the interface and documentation. The court referred questions of protectability of programmatic interfaces under copyright law to the European Court of Justice, noting that "national courts must interpret both European and domestic legislation as far as possible in the light of the wording and purpose of relevant international agreements to which the EU is a party, such as TRIPS and the WIPO Copyright Treaty."

The copyrightability of APIs is a potentially significant issue to open source licensing, because the Free Software Foundation's position—that linking of new software to GPL software creates a derivative work of the original GPL software—depends on the ability of an author, under GPL, to protect the interface to software based on copyright law. Also, many open source software projects (such as Linux) are reimplementations of proprietary software that have been reverse engineered from their APIs.

### F. FFmpeg Trademark Dispute

The FFmpeg project—a very popular open source implementation of MPEG codecs—posted a note about a legal threat that concerned the logo for the project.[28] FFmpeg says the threat comes from "a previous root admin of FFmpeg, who now is root admin of the Libav fork of FFmpeg." The threat claimed a copyright on the diagonal-line logo. FFmpeg replaced it with a new version that represented the same shape with different shading and contours. FFmpeg posted an email suggesting that the claimant did not come up with the original shape, only a particular rendering of it. This is a garden variety trademark dispute, unrelated to the open source nature of the project.

### G. Novell/CPTN/Attachmate Antitrust Issues

In November 2010, Novell announced its acquisition by Attachmate for $2.2 billion. Novell's press release[29] stated that it would continue to be the owner of its copyrights to UNIX following the merger. Novell separately sold 882 pat-

---

[27] www.bailii.org/ew/cases/EWHC/Ch/2010/1829.html#para29.

[28] Originally at www.ffmpeg.org/%EF%BB%BF. The posting has since been taken down.

[29] www.novell.com/company/ir/message.html.

ents to CPTN Holdings, a technology consortium led by Microsoft, for $450 million. The deal caused consternation over whether the sale of the patents was a threat to Linux.

However, Novell's patents were apparently already encumbered in favor of Linux at the time of the sale. Novell was a founding member of the Open Invention Network (OIN), which would have made its patents subject to OIN's patent policies. OIN is essentially a patent commons for Linux; members agree to enter into cross-licenses of their patents to cover Linux, as defined broadly by OIN. OIN's current license agreement generally provides that any patent licenses survive a change of control—which is to be expected for such a license.[30] (Novell, however, probably agreed to an earlier version.)

In addition, Novell had previously made a public Novell patent pledge:

> Novell will use its patent portfolio to protect itself against claims made against the Linux kernel or open source programs included in Novell's offerings, as dictated by the actions of others. ... In the event of a patent claim against a Novell open source product, Novell would respond using the same measures generally used to defend proprietary software products accused of patent infringement. Among other things, Novell would seek to address the claim by identifying prior art that could invalidate the patent; demonstrating that the product does not infringe the patent; redesigning the product to avoid infringement; or pursuing a license with the patent owner.[31]

This was couched as a covenant rather than a license. Thus, it was not clear whether the pledge would inure to Attachmate, and if so, whether Attachmate could withdraw it. Because the ownership of the patents and company diverged, it was unclear whether the patents remained in Novell's patent portfolio. Also, it was unclear whether the pledge would continue to encumber the rights of CPTN, as a license would have, or evaporate with the transfer, as a covenant might.

The DOJ reviewed the transaction and later issued a press release[32] about the modification of the Novell sale. The DOJ required Microsoft to "sell back to Attachmate all of the Novell patents that Microsoft would have otherwise acquired," leaving Microsoft only with a license. The DOJ also unwound the sale to EMC of 33 patents and patent applications related to virtualization. The DOJ's press release said, "All of the Novell patents will be acquired subject to the GNU General

Public License, Version 2 … and the Open Invention Network (OIN) License." It is unclear exactly what the release meant by the GPL reference, given that GPL 2 has no express patent grant (perhaps referring to an implied license), but the statement clarifies that the patents will remain subject to OIN license terms. The DOJ also said, "CPTN does not have the right to limit which of the patents, if any, are available under the OIN license," suggesting that the limiting elections possible under the OIN license cannot be made in the short term by CPTN. The full documents were not made public but may be available when the settlement is filed with the court as a part of the Tunney Act approval process. The Tunney Act is a US antitrust law that, among other things, requires that the government and an antitrust defendant disclose communications related to the settlement process.

## H. Distribution (2010)

On November 17, 2010, the English High Court ruled in *Football Dataco Limited, et al. v Sportradar GmbH, et al.* that the act of making material available to the public by online transmission occurs where the transmission takes place, and not where it is received, for the purposes of copyright.

Plaintiffs alleged copyright infringement of their live streams of data (such as goals scored, goal scorers, penalties, yellow and red cards, and substitutions) for soccer matches in a package called "Football Live." The defendants were in the business of assembling similar data from public sources. The defendants' data were stored on web servers in Germany and Austria but could be accessed via links from other locations, including the UK.

The defendants argued that there was no jurisdiction for the English Court because no acts of infringement had occurred in the UK. The court held that Sportradar had not done any act of reproduction (in respect of copyright) or extraction (in respect of database rights) in the UK.

Database rights are governed by Article 7(2)(b) of the Database Directive: "Any form of **making available** to the public all or a substantial part of the contents of a database by the distribution of copies by renting, by on-line or other forms of transmission" [emphasis added]. The court stated that the question of where the act of "making available" occurred under this Directive was related to where "making available" occurred for the purpose of s.20 Copyright Designs and Patents Act 1988. The court analogized to the precedent of where a "broadcast" occurred under the Directive on Satellite Broadcasting and Cable Re-transmission for broadcasts originating within the EU; under that directive, the act of broadcast occurs where the signals are introduced under the control of the person making the broadcast into an uninterrupted chain of communication (which is referred to as *emission theory*).

The court stated, "[T]he act of making available to the public by online transmission is committed … only where the transmission takes place. It is true that the placing of data on a server in one state can make the data available to the public of another state but that does not mean that the party who has made the data available has committed the act of making available by transmission in the State of reception."

This decision tangentially effects the interpretation of copyleft obligations of open source licenses. The effect turns on the extent to which copyleft obligations are triggered by "making available" software as opposed to "distribution" of software. It has long been a source of speculation in open source licensing whether "distribution" in a license like GPL 2 could be interpreted to include "making available"—the former being primarily a US legal concept and the latter common in Europe and the UK. There is not settled law on whether SAAS use of software constitutes "making available"—though it would not constitute distribution in the US. Those who make code available but do not distribute it (such as via a SAAS product) have puzzled over whether they could inadvertently trip copyleft obligations if the software were accessed in Europe and the UK. Now, at least in the UK, there seems to be some comfort on the issue.

### I. Patent Trolls.

There have been a number of suits by nonpracticing entities that accuse open source software. These include, for instance, *IP Innovation LLC v. Red Hat Inc.* (filed October 9, 2007, E.D. Texas), *Software Tree LLC v. Red Hat Inc.* (filed March 3, 2009, E.D. Texas), and *Bedrock Computer Technologies, LLC v. Softlayer Technologies, Inc.,* (filed June 16, 2009, E.D. Texas). This is by no means an exhaustive list; these cases are not unique to the open source context, as software patent troll cases abound in the Eastern District.

## V. The Cast of Characters

Open source claims are not like other intellectual property claims. They must be addressed differently. Treating them like ordinary intellectual property claims may lead an accused party to do exactly the wrong thing on a strategic level.

The object lesson of the cases described above is that we are in a time of transition. Open source claimants today come in two varieties: the advocates and the strategists. Of course, free software has always had its zealous advocates—it is, after all, a movement started for the greater good, based on the idea that access to software source code should be a techno-political right. The first claims brought in the area of open source enforcement were claims brought by advocates.

Those efforts bore the clear fingerprints of advocacy and focused on embarrassing the miscreants and demanding their compliance. This strategy meant that filing a lawsuit was a last resort. Most compliance disputes were resolved informally and without resort to legal process. Once legal process was filed, the threat of bad press was gone, so few claims resulted in lawsuits. The main goals were compliance and transparency. Although the early enforcement actions of the SFLC sometimes included monetary settlements, these were often characterized as a contribution to offset the cost of litigation—and rightly so, as compared to the average intellectual property dispute, the amounts involved were minimal. Settlements were announced publicly in greater detail than is customary in intellectual property disputes.

Here are examples of this type of claimant:

- **Free Software Foundation (FSF)**. The FSF stewards the GPL and runs the GNU project. Although it was originally involved in enforcement of GPL violations, most of its enforcement activities have now been taken over by SFLC.
- **Software Freedom Law Center (SFLC)**. This is a legal advocacy organization that represents pro bono clients, including FSF, in GPL enforcement and other free software law matters.
- **gpl-violations.org**. As described above, this organization has brought various enforcement actions in Europe.
- **Software Freedom Conservancy**. This organization has not yet filed any lawsuits, but it has conducted informal enforcement claims. It represents projects like BusyBox and SAMBA.
- Individual authors acting via any of the above.

As we move into the "teens," we are seeing the emergence of a new kind of claimant—the strategic claimant—who has most of the same goals as other intellectual property claimants and who sometimes is both a copyright and a patent claimant. Strategic claimants are building on the foundation of *Jacobsen v. Katzer* to enforce their rights in open source software via intellectual property disputes. And like other intellectual property disputes prosecuted by strategic plaintiffs, such disputes tend to be the battles of titans. This kind of plaintiff wants to gain a strategic edge, whether via delaying a competing product's release, embarrassing a competitor, or extracting money to defund a competitor's development plans. Notably, however, this kind of claimant wants damages or remedies for past infringement and not merely compliance going forward. Settlements tend to be slower and more confidential.

In between the advocates and the strategists are individual authors who are not affiliated with an advocacy organization. Many are academics who use open source licenses because of university policy or hobbyists who write open source software as a résumé item. They often are not represented by counsel at all—eschewing the pure political motivation of the advocates and therefore not sharing their goals. These authors seldom make formal claims and often demand modest license fees to grant an alternative license that would obviate the need to comply with open source requirements. (Advocates, on the other hand, would usually refuse to agree to other licenses.) Obviously, the claims of these individuals are best handled via a quick and confidential settlement. Attorneys handling such claims must be mindful of ethical issues relating to interaction with unrepresented parties[33] and are best advised to keep the discussion straightforward and the documents short. Adding complex releases, indemnities, and patent grants will usually backfire.

The possibility still exists that such authors will become "copyright trolls." As open source software becomes ever more pervasive and some companies still have inadequate controls to avoid unintended use of open source, it is quite possible that a popular bit of code could become the subject of "submarine" copyright claims.

## VI. Running the Numbers

Since copyleft enforcement began in the late 1980s,[34] there has been a steady increase in compliance actions. Because most enforcement starts as an informal dialogue,[35] statistics on the number of enforcement actions can be hard to verify.

According to the Executive Director of the Software Freedom Conservancy (SFC), Bradley Kuhn, the SFC logged 100 GPL violations as of 2007, and as of 2012, it was pursuing (or planned to pursue) over 300 violations, with new reports coming in each week.[36] Because copyleft advocacy groups focus mostly

---

[33] Of course, the ethical rule concerns represented parties. (See ABA Model Rule 4.2.) However, unrepresented parties can easily engage representation, and the client may not be aware of the effect of the rule. In other words, if you are negotiating a license with someone and he engages counsel to review the license agreement you have proposed, you can no longer talk to him directly—and if he calls you, you must tell him so.

[34] See Bradley Kuhn, "13 Years of Copyleft License Compliance: A Historical Perspective," October 12, 2012, **www.ebb.org/bkuhn/talks/Open-World-Forum-2012/Compliance-History/compliance.html**.

[35] Bradley Kuhn mentioned that "99.999% of GPL enforcement matters get resolved without a lawsuit," February 1, 2012, **sfconservancy.org/blog/?tag=gpl**.

[36] See Bradley Kuhn, "13 Years of Copyleft License Compliance: A Historical Perspective," October 12, 2012, **www.ebb.org/bkuhn/talks/Open-World-Forum-2012/Compliance-History/compliance.html**.

on compliance and only request monetary compensation for legal work and related expenses, the "damages" paid for these actions are not terribly significant: $204,750 for fiscal year 2010 (with $82,404 of enforcement-related expenses paid to SFLC) and $128,136 for fiscal year 2011 (with $98,813 of enforcement-related expenses paid to SFLC). In comparison, SFLC's enforcement-related revenue dropped every year in the most recently reported four-year period: $223,854 for fiscal year 2008; $164,400 for fiscal year 2009; $124,122 for fiscal year 2010; and $45,246 for fiscal year 2011. However, this may reflect that SFC has taken over some of the activity previously handled by SFLC.

Harald Welte and the gpl-violations.org project did not publish such numbers (only keeping track of reported GPL violations in the project's internal request-tracking system), but their legal archive contained discussion threads that listed at least a few publicly discussed potential violations each month. After its start in 2003, the project "hit the magic '100 cases finished' mark in June 2006, at an exciting '100% legal success' mark." In 2008, the project reported, "In the past 30 months, gpl-violations.org has helped uncover and negotiate more than 100 GPL violations and has obtained numerous out-of-court settlement agreements." In addition to information about court cases pursued in Germany and France, gpl-violations.org claims that in virtually every instance where a violation has been found and action taken, the enforcement has been successful—including out-of-court settlements with a number of large vendors, such as Fujitsu-Siemens. The project published a separate Frequently Asked Questions (FAQ) page aimed specifically at source code releases, which was "compiled as a result of more than sixty successful GPL enforcements."[37]

Many potential open source users ask about the likelihood that a disclosure of proprietary code will be forced due to the "viral" effect of GPL.[38] Because most enforcement has focused on failure to include licensing notices or source code offers for third-party GPL code, the question of the GPL's scope—and the concomitant question of the necessity to release derivative works containing proprietary code—has not been the subject of most enforcement actions so far. (For an exception, see the *Jin v. IChessU* case discussed in I.C above).

The most widely publicized release of source code as the result of a claimed GPL violation was the one made by Cisco in connection with the early days of the Linksys dispute (discussed in II.C above). Bradley Kuhn cites the NeXT Ob-

---

[37] Unfortunately, the website for gpl-violations.org is no longer available; however, these facts were taken from that site in 2011, when it was still online.

[38] In fact, this generally represents a misunderstanding of the nature of open source enforcement and the available remedies for violation of licenses. For more discussion, see Heather Meeker, "Open Source and the Eradication of Viruses," March 19, 2013, *Open Source Delivers*, **osdelivers. blackducksoftware.com/2013/03/19/open-source-and-the-eradication-of-viruses/**.

jective C compiler as the first GPL violation, in 1989. As a result, NeXT released its source code for the compiler.[39] Asus recently released changes to the Linux kernel in response to demands from the open source community.[40] In August 2013, Samsung made a code release after an anonymous hacker (a 19-year-old college student based in Europe) posted to GITHUB what she claimed were snippets of Linux code being used by Samsung in its Android exFAT functionality.[41] Although the hacker clearly had no right to post the code, Samsung worked proactively with SFC to make a source code release.[42] These are only examples, and necessarily anecdotal. Releases of formerly proprietary source code tend to be done with a minimum of fanfare and are likely to go unremarked unless the release is made after a copyleft violation has been widely publicized. Many enterprises make regular and automatic releases for their products' open source components, so a source code release seldom appears unusual or remarkable.

Some distributors of third-party code have decided to pull noncompliant products from their virtual shelves in answer to third-party GPL violation complaints, as Apple did in 2010 with GNU Go[43] or in 2011 with VLC Media Player.[44] This represents a kind of "hidden enforcement" that does not reflect a dialogue between author and infringer at all, taking place via the DMCA notice and takedown of a third party. If the alleged infringer is a small company, the removal of its product from an important reseller store may be the end of its business. As with any DMCA takedown request, the reseller has no legal obligation to resolve the dispute on its merits, and so it is up to the reseller how much investigation and analysis to pursue.

[39] www.ebb.org/bkuhn/talks/Open-World-Forum-2012/Compliance-History/compliance.html.

[40] Ryan Paul, "Asus Resolves Eee GPL Violation, Releases asus_acpi code changes," arstechnica.com/information-technology/2007/11/asus-resolves-eee-gpl-violation-releases-asus-acpi-code-changes/.

[41] See "Busted for Dodging Linux License, Samsung Makes Nice with Free Code," August 20, 2013, www.wired.com/wiredenterprise/2013/08/samsung_exfat/.

[42] sfconservancy.org/news/2013/aug/16/exfat-samsung/.

[43] See, for example, Brett Smith, "GPL Enforcement in Apple's App Store," May 25, 2010, www.fsf.org/news/2010-05-app-store-compliance/.

[44] For details on this and the controversy over GPL versus App store terms, see heathermeeker.squarespace.com/news/2011/1/9/gpl-apps-pulled-from-iphone-store.html.

## VII. What to Do If You Receive a Claim

Best practices include, immediately and foremost, an assessment of the type of claimant facing you. Advocates primarily want compliance and tend to be tolerant of foot faults.[45] A sincere, timely, and robust compliance program will often meet their demands. But strategic plaintiffs can draw you into a world of complex and unsettled open source law, in addition to the typically painful process of intellectual property litigation.

If you receive an open source claim, it is crucial to act on it quickly. That may sound simple, but it can be unexpectedly difficult because not all open source claims are made through formal channels. Companies should train their technical employees to recognize complaints and take them seriously. Complaints often come in the form of emails sent to technical employees who, typically, represent the company's face to the software development community. Claimants may not be aware that there are accepted formal means of making claims, such as service of process. In contrast, a traditional intellectual property complaint will often come to a legal or management representative, who will easily recognize it as a legal claim, or via a formal complaint. In addition, technical employees should be trained to react immediately to any request for source code made pursuant to a copyleft license like GPL. If that request is not answered on a timely basis, or if the company demands fees to fulfill it, a formal open source claim is likely to follow quickly. Of course, only a downstream recipient has the right to make such a request, and only the upstream author has the right to make a legal claim.[46] So in truth, these are not infringement claims. However, recipients whose demands for source code are unmet often complain to SFLC or the authors, who do have the right to bring a claim.

Because at this time advocates make up most claimants, quick action to remedy compliance issues or answer questions can often avoid legal process entirely. SFLC is usually not quick to file lawsuits and first attempts to gain compliance via informal actions. The SFLC also is often not involved until the author has unsuccessfully tried to seek compliance, sometimes repeatedly, without result.

In truth, claims from advocates are the easiest to handle. The goals and actions of advocates are predictable. The emphasis is on compliance and attribution, and only secondarily on damages. Injunctive action is usually not on the table at all. Contrast this approach with that of strategists, who would generally prefer

---

[45] Brad Kuhn, often considered the informal czar of GPL compliance, discusses this here: **www.ebb.org/bkuhn/blog/2009/11/08/gpl-enforcement.html.**

[46] The conditions in a license like GPL run downstream only. Recipients are not third-party beneficiaries of the GPL; those who take the position that the GPL is not a contract would say that there can be no third-party beneficiary under a conditional license.

injunction and damages over compliance because such rulings serve their goal to disrupt the market for a competitive product.

Strategic plaintiffs may also make multiple claims, only one of which will be copyright infringement. Those who receive such claims should consider the special legal issues that arise in open source claims. As a baseline, any lawsuit that involves open source licensing is likely to touch upon novel issues of law, as well as draw significant attention from the press and the free software community.

## VIII. Best Practices

In summary, here are the points to remember about open source litigation and disputes.

- Take open source claims seriously, even if they are made informally or by unrepresented parties. Train your technical staff to recognize claims.
- If you receive a claim, act in a timely fashion. Ignoring open source advocates who complain about your practices, formally or informally, is not an effective strategy.
- Don't treat open source claims like other IP claims. The path to resolution is different. Open source disputes can be resolved more quickly and economically than other intellectual property disputes, if you understand the landscape.

## Obstacles to Enforcement[47]

Before GPL was ever enforced in court, various commentators postulated many barriers to enforcement, most of which have been discredited. In its lawsuit against IBM, SCO claimed that the GPL violated the US Constitution.[48] A later suit claimed that the GPL violated antitrust law.[49] Many said the license was unenforceable because it had never been tested in court—a solipsistic and uninformed argument that, fortunately, is seldom heard anymore; those making it probably did not consider how deeply it would contradict fundamental legal principles to require that a court hold a contract enforceable in advance—a requirement that

---

[47] For an excellent article on the topic, see Jason Wacha, "Taking the Case: Is the GPL Enforceable?" reprinted at **digitalcommons.law.scu.edu/chtlj/vol21/iss2/5/**. Wacha's article discusses the enforcement challenges typically cited in the 2000s.

[48] "Open Letter on Copyrights," Daryl McBride, The SCO Group Inc., December 4, 2003, **www.sco.com/copyright/**.

[49] Order dismissing *Wallace v. Free Software Foundation, Inc.* (S. Dist. Ind., October 28, 2005).

would wipe out freedom of contract in a single blow. Contract formation defenses may linger, but they are strategically unattractive to a potential licensee who has no other way to exercise distribution rights (see Chapter 6: What Is Distribution?). Unsurprisingly, none of these arguments has been remotely successful in an actual lawsuit.

However, there are some obstacles to enforcement worth considering. This is not to imply that one should not enforce open source licenses; in fact, it can be quick and effective to enforce them. But before you make the choice to send a demand letter or file a lawsuit, you should make sure you have not missed one of these potential defenses.

### Don't Commit Intellectual Property Suicide

If you are going to throw the stones of noncompliance at open source licenses, be sure you are not living in a glass house. Before you bring a claim, you should be sure your own open source compliance is in order, at least to the extent that you have not infringed the rights of the party you are about to sue. This advice also holds true for claims of software patent infringement and violations of software licenses.

Counterexamples to this rule of thumb include *Jacobsen v. Katzer* (discussed in Chapter 14: Open Source and Patent Litigation Strategy) and the Versata/Ameriprise/Ximpleware cases (now settled and dismissed).

### Joint Authorship, Standing, and Joinder

Open source is a collaborative development model. Many open source projects emphasize that they aim to create a single, cohesive work of authorship from the work of many contributors. But then, who is the author of the copyrightable work that consists of the software?

In the United States, authors who collaborate on a work can be considered joint authors. Joint authors need not be conjoined in time or geography.[50] The copyright law states that a joint work arises when both authors intended, at the time the work was created, "that their contributions be merged into inseparable or interdependent parts of a unitary whole." The Second Circuit has stated that "Parts of a unitary whole are 'inseparable' when they have little or no independent meaning standing alone. ... By contrast, parts of a unitary whole are 'interdependent' when they have some meaning standing alone but achieve their primary significance because of their combined effect."[51] Whether a work is a joint work

---

[50] See for example, *Edward B. Marks Music Corp. v. Jerry Vogel Music Co.*, 140 F.2d 267 (2d Cir. 1944).

[51] *Childress v. Taylor*, 945 F.2d 500, 505 (2nd Cir. 1991).

may turn on the intent of the authors. Nimmer observes, "The distinction lies in the intent of each contributing author at the time his contribution is written. If his work is written 'with the intention that [his] contribution ... be merged into inseparable or interdependent parts of a unitary whole,' then the merger of his contribution with that of others creates a joint work. If such intention occurs only after the work has been written, then the merger results in a derivative or collective work."[52] Opinion is split on whether the individual authors need contribute copyrightable expression or whether contribution of ideas alone will suffice.[53] Contributors to an open source project may find it difficult to argue that their work is not a joint work.

The default rule for a jointly owned work is that each author has the right to use the work without limitation, subject to default law obligations to account to other authors.[54] Clearly, such rules—which were developed to apply to works like books, music, and audiovisual works—were never intended to address the kind of massive collaboration that arises from modern technology like GITHUB, Wikis, and the like.

Because all authors can grant any nonexclusive licenses they like, if one author sues for copyright infringement, courts often require all authors to be joined as parties to the suit. Under 17 USC Section 501(b), a court "may require the joinder, and shall permit the intervention, of any person having or claiming an interest in the copyright." Otherwise, the defendant would be able to claim it had a legitimate license from one of the authors who was not a party.

Moreover, under US law, only the author or copyright owner has standing to bring a lawsuit for infringement. Although any author could sue for infringement of his own portion of the project that was considered its own work of authorship, a court would require, if equity demands it, that the principal owners of the infringed material be joined to any case meant to enforce rights in the work. The court has discretion to require combined or separate lawsuits.[55]

---

[52] Nimmer on Copyright Section 6.05 (2005).

[53] *Ashton-Tate Corp. v. Ross*, 916 F.2d 516 (9th Cir. 1990).

[54] *Oddo v. Ries*, 743 F.2d 630 (9th Cir. 1984).

[55] *Edward B. Marks Music Corp. v. Jerry Vogel Music Co.*, 140 F.2d 268 (2d Cir. 1944) held that co-owners were not indispensable parties; for the opposite view, see *Key West Hand Fabrics v. Serbin, Inc.*, 244 F. Supp. 287 (S.D.Fla. 1965). Case law on the subject is scant.

Chapter 20

# Open Standards and Open Source

Much has been written about open standards, which are sometimes confused with open source software licensing. Open source licensing is a paradigm specific to software; *open standards* is a more general term with no single accepted definition. However, open standards mostly refer to standards that are developed with no known patent claims or with an understanding that any patent claims will be licensed on a royalty-free and nondiscriminatory basis.

## *What Is a Standard?*

Standards are specifications that many in an industry agree to use in order to maximize the interoperability of products and promote commerce. Consider the quintessential example of nuts and bolts. Hundreds of years ago, every nut and bolt pair had its own thread pattern. As time went on, nuts and bolts were mass-produced and standardized so that any nut and bolt would be made for particular thread configuration[1] and one could buy nuts and bolts with those specifications and know they would work together.

Particularly in the United States, standardization takes place mostly by consensus. So it is possible that an industry can lack critical mass for standardization. Also, there can arise competing standards—as in the VHS and Betamax wars. Lack of standardization makes consumers and producers cautious about buying products, which decreases economic activity.

Standards-setting organizations (SSOs), such as IEEE and W3C, promote the orderly development of standards. If industry players decide to work on a standard, they usually create a *working group* under the aegis of an SSO. Participants in the working group discuss the content of the standard. They don't always agree, but when they do, the standard is adopted and published. To clarify what patents cover the standard, SSOs usually have intellectual property policies that participants must agree to prior to joining a working group. Obviously, it is pos-

---

[1] For a great explanation of threading standardization, see the Wikipedia article **en.wikipedia.org/wiki/Screw_thread.**

sible that not all patent holders might participate in the working group, and if that happens, the standard may be created and adopted but may be thwarted by third-party patent claims. In the optimal case, all of the important patent holders participate in the working group and agree to license their patents to those who want to practice the standard.

Beyond this, the rules can vary a great deal. Some standards are royalty bearing but licensed on *reasonable and nondiscriminatory* (RAND) terms. Some are licensed on RAND terms with no royalties, sometimes called *RAND-z*. Sometimes, the standard is intended to be patent-free, and that is sometimes accomplished by the working group's taking care to avoid including portions in the specification that are likely to be subject to patent claims.

One reason for the popularity of RAND licensing is that it deflects antitrust liability. RAND means no one can be excluded from practicing the standards, and licenses must be offered to everyone—though royalties can be adjusted for volume, use case, and so forth.[2] When standards are mandated by government regulation, RAND can be obligatory, but this is more common in Europe than in the United States.

Each SSO has its own rules for licensing of standards-essential patents. For instance, IEEE requires RAND,[3] W3C has requires RAND-z licenses,[4] and IETF requires RAND.[5]

## Standards and Open Source

Open source software can be a great vehicle for standards adoption. It brings down the licensing barriers for the use and adaptation of reference software, and particularly if it is offered under a permissive license, it promotes widespread adoption. But clearly, if open source software implements a royalty-bearing or *non-free* standard, notwithstanding the royalty-free grant of copyright under the open source license, users would be at risk of patent infringement claims when using the software.

---

[2] The Department of Justice Guidelines generally consider intellectual property licensing to be pro-competitive. See Antitrust Guidelines for the Licensing of Intellectual Property, April 6, 1995, Department of Justice, **www.usdoj.gov/atr/public/guidelines/0558.htm**. However, license arrangements can stray into the prohibited area of horizontal output restraints or price fixing. Famously, Rambus Inc. was subjected to a protracted legal battle over the failure to disclose intellectual property related to a standard in the course of a standards development process; see **www.ftc.gov/os/adjpro/d9302/060802commissionopinion.pdf**.

[3] standards.ieee.org/faqs/copyrightFAQ.html.

[4] www.w3.org/Consortium/Patent-Policy-20040205.

[5] ftp.rfc-editor.org/in-notes/bcp/bcp79.txt.

While open source licenses grant patent rights, they only grant rights in patents owned by the author of the software. It is possible—in fact, common—that software can practice inventions claimed by patents owned by third parties. When practicing a standard, this is almost surely the case.

For example, FFMPEG is a very popular open source audiovisual codec, which encodes and decodes data files stored in the various standard formats. FFMPEG is licensed under open source licenses, but the patents covering certain MPEG standards are owned by others. Anyone seeking to use the FFMPEG software must consider not only the need to comply with the open source licenses that govern its use but also the need to get a separate patent license—or of course, take a risk of patent infringement claims. This is an example of how open source software licensing and non-free standards can clash.

## Different Rules

Standards licensing has been around for a long time, and although it can be complex, it is settled and familiar territory to those who deal with patent issues outside of the open source context. So in a way, it is easier for many companies to become comfortable with standards licensing than open source licensing. When the two interact, it can result in a clash of cultures and skills sets. Standards licensing is mostly the purview of patent lawyers, and open source licensing is more familiar to corporate lawyers and businesspeople.

In some ways, they are similar. Open source licenses create a patent *commons* to practice the copyright in the software, and standards licensing also creates a patent commons to practice a standard. But beyond that, the two are very different.[6]

First, they have different boundaries. A standard is usually expressed in a copyrightable document called a specification, but generally, the copyright is not the valuable part of the document. The more important rights are the patent rights that cover the standards. These are sometimes called *standards essential patents* (SEPs), and the claims of those patents are often called *necessary claims*. The claims that are licensed are those necessary to practice the standard.

Open source licenses, in contrast, are bounded by the software they cover. When they include patent license grants, they often use similar terminology such as "essential patent claims." But it is easier to tell if open source software practices a patent than to determine whether a patent is necessary to practice a standard. That is because the standard describes a technological solution but does

---

[6] For in-depth information on standards and the implementation of the intellectual property rules of standards bodies, see Jorge L. Contreras (Ed.), *Technical Standards Patent Policy Manual*, American Bar Association Publishing (2007).

not instantiate or implement it. A single standard can have many implementations; software is a single work.

The rules are also quite different. Standards licenses often extend only to those who practice the standard exactly as adopted and that practice it fully. Open source licensing places no limits on modification of the subject matter it licenses. But it is worth noting that the patent licenses in neither paradigm extend to downstream modification. The difference is that while open source licensing encourages divergence, standards licensing encourages uniformity.

Also, open source licenses do not require licensees to grant back rights in their own patents or agree to a variety of other terms that sometimes attend standards licensing. There is no one set of standard terms for a standards license, and in RAND or RANDz schemes, each licensor may offer its own set of terms. Sometimes, licensors band together for "one-stop shopping" in RAND patent licenses, such as in the case of MPEG-LA—but that is the exception, not the rule.

Chapter 21

# Open Hardware and Data

As the idea of "open" has matured, there have been attempts to expand the model of copyleft outside the software context. Some have fared well: Creative Commons has ably applied copyleft (or, in the Creative Commons lingo, "sharealike") licensing to non-software copyrightable works such as music, text, and audiovisual works. However, attempts to apply copyleft licensing outside of the context of copyrightable works have been mostly disappointing. This is not the fault of those who have attempted it; moving beyond copyright removes one of the pillars of copyleft, and without it, licenses are set adrift in an intellectual property limbo.

For copyrightable works, the threshold for protection is very low compared to the degree of creativity and expression usually embodied in a work. For example, any software program with more than a few lines of code probably qualifies for copyright protection. Other intellectual property subject matter, such as patentable inventions and rights in data, do not enjoy this level of protection. When applying copyleft to hardware, there is a threshold question of what is the quid pro quo for the copyleft conditions of the license. For software, the price of exercising the rights of copyright is adhering to the copyleft conditions. Any licensee trying to avoid the copyleft conditions is between a rock and a hard place. If one wishes to distribute software, one needs a copyright license to do so; no license means no rights.

Translating this to hardware is difficult in at least two ways: (1) establishing a threshold level of rights to enforce the copyleft conditions and (2) determining the materials necessary to enable reproduction of the design.

Most hardware designs are embodied in a specification or design document. Those making hardware are not particularly interested in distributing copies of product specifications. Merely "using" a specification, in the sense of reading it and following its instructions, is not an activity regulated by copyright. Even if a manufacturer violated the copyright in the specification by reproducing or distributing it, the damages for doing so would likely be trivial. Ideas are not protectable under copyright. The damages for exercising the copyright interest in the specification would have to accrue from the value of the work of authorship consisting of the specification, not the value of making the products. Moreover, the copyright protection of a specification may be thin to nonexistent. Copyright does not protect facts. Specifications consisting of tables of numbers, for example, might not be protected at all. Therefore, if a license says, "I will grant you the right to practice the copyright in this specification as long as you share your changes to it," the licensee might very well conclude there is nothing to be granted, refuse to adhere to the condition, and take a calculated risk that the licensor has no means to enforce the conditions.

Moreover, there is the question of what copyleft requires the licensee to disclose. The main copyleft condition in a license like GPL is making available the source code for the software. GPL 3 defines the source code for a program as "the preferred form of the work for making modifications to it." Although reasonable people might differ as to what *source code* means, fundamentally, it is the code that, when run through the correct compiler and builder, produces the object code being distributed. But what is the "source code" for hardware? To know how to make hardware, at a minimum, one needs a product design or specification. But this "source code" may be technology specific. That which is necessary to make a semiconductor is not the same as that which is necessary to make a television, a mobile phone, or a server blade. Using a general definition like "the designs necessary to make the product" is too broad and vague—it could require process technology that is expensive and not part of the product or commodity parts that no product manufacturer would even need to make for itself.

Finally, determining what is a "derivative" or modification that is subject to the copyleft terms of the license is hard enough for software; for hardware, it is even more difficult. The notion of a derivative work is confined to copyrightable works of authorship. Modifications to products by downstream licensees might correspond to changes in a specification, or not. They might be separately protectable under copyright law as changes to the specification or under patent law as new inventions. If they are new inventions, they may be changes to the original design or additional features, and the line of distinction is difficult to draw. A downstream licensee who makes a change may or may not have any rights in such a modification to license to others.

For these reasons, structuring hardware licensing by hanging one's hat on the practice of a copyright is risky. And of course, fundamentally, it is the power of patent, and not copyright, that protects hardware. What "open hardware" truly requires is a compulsion to license patents. Some licenses condition the practice of the rights in the specification on a requirement to license patents. But even this notion is vulnerable to a claim that the specification is not protectable in the first place, either because the specification is not protectable under copyright or because the creators of the specification have no patent rights to grant.

There is a time-honored way of creating a patent commons for hardware, but it is standards licensing rather than open source licensing. Standards licensing, however, is not usually an "open" model, and it is certainly not the kind of self-executing paradigm of cooperative development that is copyleft licensing; it is top-down licensing, with rights flowing in one direction from the specification's authors down to those practicing the specification. It does not account for licensing of downstream changes to the specification because traditional standards licensing is intended to discourage changes to the standard. In fact, in standards licensing, any modification of the standard is usually not licensed at all; some standards licenses require licensees to promise not to make alterations to products that make them inconsistent with the standard.

Therefore, open hardware licenses seem destined to walk the precarious line between standards licensing and open source licensing. Although no copyleft hardware license has yet gained significant traction, it is early days, and this model may very well be developed and refined over time.

## Open Data

Copyleft open data licensing has fared no better. The Open Data Commons Open Database License (OdBL) is a case in point. OdBL applies to Open Street Maps, a very popular database of mapping information, and licensees find it difficult to distinguish a "Derivative Database" from a new and separate database or a Collective Database. This kind of problem is endemic to any copyleft license, but it is particularly difficult for licenses without broad adoption. Unlike GPL, for which industry practice as to its scope was ironed out over many years, the OdBL is not widely used.

But part of the difficulty lies in the lack of clarity of the underlying law. In the United States, databases enjoy only very thin protection under copyright law. After the seminal *Feist* case,[1] that protection has been considered easy to avoid absent a wholesale copying of the data. The European Union has a more specific law on database protection—Directive 96/9/EC of the European Parliament and of the Council of 11 March 1996 on the legal protection of databases—but that law has been subject to little interpretation in the courts. Neither legal regime provides much useful guidance on what kind of changes or additions to a database might be derivative works, rather than new works.

---

[1] *Feist Pubs., Inc. v. Rural Tel. Svc. Co., Inc.* 499 US 340 (1991).

## Permissive Licensing

The conundrum of applying copyleft to hardware and data licensing does not, of course, apply in the same way to permissive licensing. Even permissive licensing faces the quid pro quo problem because the requirement to apply licensing or attribution notices depends on the granting of a right. Even so, there is much to be said for simply placing databases and hardware specifications in the public domain and promoting cooperation and sharing by means other than licensing. An attribution requirement may seem innocuous until a single database or specification requires scores or hundreds of them.[2]

## Examples

The following licenses have attempted to tackle the implementation of copyleft in non-software areas, but none has become widely adopted.

- CERN Open Hardware License. **www.ohwr.org/projects/cernohl/wiki**
- TAPR Open Hardware License. **www.tapr.org/ohl.html**
- Open Compute Project Hardware License. **www.opencompute.org/blog/request-for-comment-ocp-hardware-license-agreement/**
- Tidepool Open Access to Health Data Software License. **developer.tidepool.io/tidepool-license/**
- Open Data Commons Open Database License (ODbL). **opendatacommons.org/licenses/odbl/**

---

[2] For an excellent real-world example, see **peterdesmet.com/posts/illegal-bullfrogs.html**. Thanks to Luis Villa for pointing out this rather priceless example of attribution run amok.

# **Appendices**

Appendix A

# Company Open Source Policy

## Introduction and Contents

This policy is intended to be short and easy to follow, to enable our decision makers (including technical, business, and legal managers) to leverage open source software while protecting our intellectual property assets and mitigating risk.

The policy includes the following components:

1. Guidelines for use by employees considering use of open source within the company

2. Guidelines for acceptance of code written by contractors

3. Guidelines for contribution of code by employees to outside projects

4. Guidelines for voluntary release of company code under open source licenses

5. [OPTIONAL] Guidelines and model language for handling open source during transactions, including contracting, M&A, and customer-facing EULAs

The following paragraph is not strictly necessary. However, parties enforcing open source licenses have often requested that compliance officers be appointed. Some companies instead convene an open source committee that includes technical, legal, and business resources. We recommend that some person or task force within the organization have ownership of the policy, including availability to answer questions about it and serve as champions of company strategy on open source.

Our company has appointed an open source compliance officer to oversee implementation of this policy. If you have questions about this policy, they should be directed to Legal or to that officer.

## Part 1: Use of Open Source Software in Our Operations and Products

The following steps must be taken before using, or beginning development that uses, open source software.

This process will be driven by engineering staff. Because it will also involve legal and business analysis, it should be started early in the development cycle.

This policy should be considered in light of our other policies on software, including security policies. Approval of use of open source software does not supersede the requirements of other policies we may have for use of software or third-party software.

### Step 1: Identify and Evaluate the Open Source Software

Once you have identified open source software that meets a specific engineering need, the next step is to assess the software and any alternatives. This should include an analysis of

- the quality of the software;
- its price (including total cost of ownership);
- availability and ease of support (including strength of supporting companies or communities);
- risk of infringing others' intellectual property rights;
- the effect on our own intellectual property assets (e.g., does the license require sharing of other source code?); and
- reputational issues, because our customers will want to know (and often must be informed) about what open source software we are using in our products.

If you identify open source software to use, you should be prepared to explain how you took these factors into account in selecting the software. Remember, our decision to use third-party software should be driven by the goal of creating excellent products that serve our customer needs. We should not choose open source or proprietary software just because of the type of license covering it.

### Step 2: Identify the Use Case

Our process for accepting or rejecting open source software requires identification of how the software will be used. In particular, the engineering team must identify (1) whether the open source software will be used internally, accessible to customers via online services, provided to our corporate affiliates, or distributed to customers and (2) how the open source software will integrate with other software components (e.g., by static or dynamic linking, or by communication through standard protocols). Engineers should also identify and flag any situations that may change over time, such as tools that are currently intended only for internal use but that are related to the company's overall business and therefore may over time be productized and distributed.

This analysis is required because the risks and rewards attendant on using open source software depend on the type of use we intend to make of the software. For instance, embedding open source software in a distributed product is riskier than using open source software as a development tool, to provide SAAS offerings, or to run internal nonproduction business systems.

### Step 3: Identify Proprietary Alternatives

To be sure we have made the right decision, before we use open source software, we should consider proprietary alternatives, if any. We need to compare the support we would receive, our ability to drive features and functionality, and price—including not only license fees but also implementation and ongoing costs (such as support) that may accrue over the life cycle of the product.

### Step 4: Identify the Open Source License

After completing Steps 1–3, to make the right decision, we need to verify the open source licensing terms that would apply to the software we want to use. Some open source projects are better than others at being clear about the licensing terms that apply to their software. Some usual places to look for open source licenses are (1) the project's website and associated online documentation; (2) in a text file contained in the distribution called LICENSE or COPYING; or (3) notices at the top of individual source files (sometimes called headers).

When you are looking for the license that applies, keep in mind that there can be different licenses for different parts of a given piece of software. Sometimes those layers of licenses are compatible, and sometimes they are not. To perform the complete analysis, these layered terms need to be identified so that we can not only be sure to comply with all the licenses (not just the first that comes up) but also be sure there are not license incompatibilities that will make it impossible to comply with all of them at once.

Similarly, sometimes several licenses can apply to the same item of code. That is sometimes called "dual licensing." Sometimes, dual licensing can include multiple open source licenses or a choice between proprietary and open source licenses. When multiple terms are available, we want to be sure we use the terms that allow us the greatest flexibility and compatibility with our other obligations.

### Step 5: Consult the Open Source Stop/Go/Caution List

After you have determined how you will use the software and which open source license(s) apply to it, select the appropriate category using the Open Source Stop/Go/Caution List (attached as Exhibit 1).

If your license and intended use falls in the "Go" category, you may use the open source software only for your intended use. You must still follow the other requirements of this policy (starting with Step 7, "Track Your Use"). If you later change the intended use or add a new use (such as in a new product), you need to again consult the list and ensure that the new use is acceptable. Just because a piece of software has been used by someone, somewhere in the company, does not mean that you can use it again in a new way and new place without reviewing it again.

If the Stop/Go/Caution List indicates that you must obtain approval from Legal, if your license is not listed, or if there are multiple layers of licenses that may interact with each other, you must obtain approval from Legal as described in the next step.

### Step 6: Obtain Necessary Approvals

If the Stop/Go/Caution List indicates "Caution," which means that you must obtain Legal approval prior to using the open source software, then you can seek the necessary approval by submitting to Legal a request in the form attached as Exhibit 2. You may also request approval for something on the "Stop" list, but you should understand we will be unlikely to approve it, so you should begin serious investigation of alternatives immediately before waiting for a response.

Requests should be made before you start developing the software. This avoids last-minute delays caused by any additional research Legal must conduct, or worse, forcing you to abandon development that has already been done because for some reason the use of the software cannot be approved.

The following model language includes some detail about the approval process. The exact process varies among companies. Some companies allow non-legal personnel to approve certain use cases or licenses. Some require approval on a project-by-project basis, rather than based on license. Many have formed a committee for internal review staffed by members of the legal, business, and engineering teams.

[For items on the "GO" list, the engineering lead on your project has authority to approve use of the code without seeking Legal's approval.]

[Even for licenses on the "GO" list, we need to consider whether there are any known third-party patent claims on similar technology. Although we will not investigate patent issues for every element of open source code, we should leverage our institutional knowledge of patent claims. For instance, some open source projects post licensing FAQs that discuss known patent issues. You should include this information in your open source request. (An example would be the FFMPEG project FAQ, which details known patent issues arising from various MPEG formats.) If you are aware of such information, pass it on to Legal but please do not investigate potential patent infringement issues in detail (such as reading the patents) unless instructed to do so by a lawyer and no one else—not even your manager.]

[For items on the "Caution" list, you and your engineering lead should submit the request to Legal.]

Legal will review the open source usage request and respond to you in a timely manner. You should be prepared to make yourself available to answer questions and provide additional information to Legal during the review process. For software licensed under licenses like GPL or LGPL, you may need to provide structural diagrams or other graphical explanations that show how the open source software interacts with other software.

All usage requests will be tracked as bugs in our [describe bug tracking system]. All licensing bugs should be classified as Priority I and must be resolved prior to product release.

### Step 7: Track Your Use of Open Source Software

This step is highly company specific. This section should describe how open source software is tracked internally. This tracking could take place using source code repository tools, business process tools, or third-party mechanisms like Black Duck or Palamida. The following are examples only and should be conformed to actual and expected practice. The goal of these processes is to have on hand, at all times, sufficient information about the company's open source usage to provide disclosures that may be required by business partners, and to apply company policy as described in this section.

[Our company uses the Black Duck "Protex" software tool to monitor inclusion of open source in our products. This tool tracks the "bill of materials" of our software. When we add third-party open source software components to our code base, this tool tracks that addition and helps us identify the licensing terms for that software. Because of the time and resources required to make regular and systematic use of this tool, we use this tool only on distributed products. The lead engineer for the product is responsible for ensuring that all potential issues identified by the tool are resolved in accordance with this policy. The lead engineer's sign-off is necessary to complete internal protocols for product release. ]

[Our company relies on self-declaration to track open source usage. The lead engineer on each project is responsible for ensuring that all engineers developing code for the product have identified all third-party software, including open source software, to be included in a product. The lead engineer is also responsible for collecting sufficient information to prepare necessary notice files as described in Step 8. We may require a third-party scan for open source or third-party software prior to public release of a product. Engineers are expected to keep open source information up-to-date at all times. This information should be stored in the _____ database. The information provided should include all the information referenced in Exhibit 3.]

## Step 8: Comply with the Open Source License and Company Policy

You must comply strictly with the requirements of the applicable open source license. These requirements are summarized in the Open Source License Matrix (attached as Exhibit 4). They may include requirements to provide notices to customers or to set up procedures to handle requests for source code. Different licenses have different requirements, and it can be challenging to harmonize all of the notice requirements, so you may need to consult with Legal or Operations to ensure that notices are properly delivered. If a notice file must be created, you will be expected to do so, with help from Legal. Similarly, if a license requires the production of source code, engineering will be responsible for producing the source code, with guidance from Legal.

Compliance may also require Legal to put certain contractual clauses in customer or other agreements. Those responsible for negotiating contracts must ensure that Legal has been notified and take appropriate steps to update those agreements:

- **Contents of Notices**
  - If you are distributing source code along with the product, the open source notices should be embedded in the source code and you need take no further action. This is the easiest way to comply with notice requirements.
  - If you are distributing binaries only, you need to copy the notice from the source code into a text file. The text file need not be formatted—plain text is fine. You can put all the notices into one file or leave them in their individual original files (in which case you should group them in a directory or folder).
  - If you create a single text file for all your notices, you need only include each license once. For example, if you have 10 GPL components, you need to include the GPL only once or you can include it 10 times.
- **Delivery of Notices**
  - The notices must be in the product distribution. It is not compliant to place them on the Web, except in limited circumstances described below.
  - If the product is delivered only in electronic form via the Web (i.e., there is no physical product), you may put the notices on the Web on a notice page. The page must be accessible directly from the software download site. In this case, it is highly recommended that you include the source code with the notices embedded.
  - If the product is a physical product, you should not rely on web notices only. You should include the notices in an About box, on a CD, or otherwise in the product distribution package.
  - The notices do not need to be in a particular place, such as an About box. You do not need a click-to-accept mechanism for open source notices. But they cannot be hidden in a directory where the user cannot easily access them. If your product has a user interface, putting a link on a splash screen to "licensing" or "legal notices" is fine, but the text file that the link points to should reside on the same device.
- **Delivery of Source Code**
  - Remember that while not all open source licenses require you to make available source code, all of them allow you to. For permissive licenses (which do not require you to deliver source code), be sure you are clear on whether you want to make the source code available.

- For code under GPL and LGPL, you must make available not only the source code but also all associated build and installation scripts. These scripts should run without errors in a standard compilation environment. If you have used special tools for compilation, call your Legal department.
- Source code can be made available over the Web, in a physical distribution, or in any reasonable way, but it must be in electronic form.
- Do not charge fees for source code delivery if the delivery is required under the open source license.
- The source code must be the exact source code you used to create your binaries.

> The following paragraph is a strategic choice because open source licenses almost always give you the choice to release binaries with an offer to provide source code. However, simultaneous source code releases have emerged as a best practice over time because they help ensure that a company can actually execute upon its open source requirements for its binary distributions.

It is our preference to release source code for all our open source elements that require source code delivery or offers (under GPL, LGPL, and other copyleft licenses) at the time of our binary product release. If this is not possible, you should advise Legal so we can make the appropriate notices or source code offers in our product. You should always check the particular requirements of the open source licenses that apply to the software you are using.

### Step 9: Respond to Requests Based on Licenses

We have set up an open source request email address where recipients of our products can request source code that we are required to provide. This address should be monitored at all times by (1) one person in Legal and (2) the open source coordinator. This address should be monitored at all times, with coverage provided for vacations or absences.

If you receive a request for source code, installation instructions, or other materials, based on the requirements of an open source license, you must contact Legal immediately. Even if you do not think the request is appropriate or warranted, it is important that we respond correctly and promptly—additional delay, even when well intended, can cause additional liability. Also, if you read or overhear complaints about our company's use of open source code, you should contact Legal immediately and provide the details. Both of these are important to maintain our reputation and protect our company's assets.

## Part 2: Open Source Software in Contractor Development

Any deliverables that are provided to the company by a third-party contractor who has not signed the standard Employee Assignment contract must be certified by the contractor to comply with Part 1 of this policy. Each update must also be certified. We will reject deliverables that are not certified or do not comply. We may require the developer or vendor to provide us with a full disclosure in the form of Exhibit 5 and a certification in the form of Exhibit 6.

If you are engaging a contractor to make changes to open source code listed in the Stop/Go/Caution List under Stop or Caution, you must first seek approval from Legal.

Include the following if Part 5 is included below.

Specific provisions may be required in the contracting agreement, such as those described in Part 5 of this policy.

## Part 3: Contributing Code to Third-Party Open Source Projects

You may not make any contributions on behalf of our company to an open source project without obtaining approval from Legal. This is because we must carefully consider and ensure that such contributions will not have an unintended impact on the value of our intellectual property assets.

For example, before submitting contributions to an open source project, the project may require you to sign a contribution agreement, which usually requires you to license or assign ownership of the intellectual property rights in the contribution to the project. Alternately, if you are not required to sign a contribution agreement, the rights granted by making the contribution may be unclear. In either case, the company's intellectual property may be affected, so legal review and approval are necessary before making any contributions to open source projects.

Approval by Legal may be on a project-by-project basis or for particular contributions, or it may be required for each contribution. This will be determined primarily based on the likely effect on our intellectual property assets.

The requirement to consult with Legal before contributing applies only to code that you develop in the course of your employment or engagement with us, or that is related to our business. It does not apply to code that you develop on your own time that is not related to your work for us. However, the place in which you did the development work, or the computer equipment you used, may not be the deciding factor. If you have questions about what is covered, please ask Legal. Releasing code that is owned by our company, if you do not have the authority to do so, is likely to be a serious violation of your employment or consulting agreement. We want to help you avoid problems for all of us.

If you do decide to participate in an open source project independent of your employment or engagement with us, that participation must not

- interfere with your performance of company duties;
- involve the use or misuse of our intellectual property, facilities, influence, or other resources;
- disclose our confidential technology or business plans; or
- compete with us in our present or future business activities.

> The following paragraph is a strategic choice and should not be included except after due consideration. Factors to consider include whether or not the company wishes to be associated with the project and what patents may be implicated by a direct contribution under the project's contributor agreement (if any).

In certain instances, we may allow you to work on open source projects or act as a committer on open source projects on company time. You may be asked to contribute your contributions in your own name rather than ours. If we take this approach, all of the following will apply:

- The copyright in the contribution will be assigned to you.
- You will contribute under your own name.
- You should not send the contribution from a company email account.
- Any contribution agreement will be signed by you, in your own name.
- Your own copyright notice, and not the company's, will appear on the contribution.

If we ask you to contribute in your own name, we will ask you to sign Appendix G, an addendum to your Employee Invention Assignment Agreement that covers this situation.

## Part 4: Releasing Our Code Under an Open Source License

### Background

This Part applies to the decision to voluntarily publish software we have developed under an open source license when we are not required to do so. Such a decision can help reach company goals (such as reducing infrastructure costs or improving recruiting) but must be made with costs, as well as benefits, in mind.

Violation of this policy will be considered a severe misuse of our company's resources, because it could devalue our intellectual property assets and could be considered a basis for termination for cause. We must therefore choose the applicable open source license carefully to ensure that

- the license is consistent with our business objectives (which may vary from avoiding the use of our release in proprietary product to maximizing adoption of the released code);
- there are no unintended consequences for our patent, trade secret, trademark, or other intellectual property assets; and
- the open source license under which we will release code is compatible with the licenses of any third-party open source components that may be included in the release so we do not create liability for violation of open source licenses or other licenses for us or for our customers.

### Process

You must consult your manager and Legal before releasing any code developed by us under an open source license. To publish code, you will first need to write a request and provide the information specified in Exhibit 3.

The decision to release open source code is a serious one that should be made cautiously. Our shareholders expect us to use our human resources and capital to protect and grow our company. Where release of code furthers our business objectives, even indirectly, without compromising our intellectual property, doing so may be a good decision. But it is not the primary objective of our business.

## Part 5: Open Source in Transactions

> The following section is often omitted from shorter policies. It is primarily directed to legal rather than technical personnel, and the company may prefer to address transactions on an ad hoc basis. If omitted from materials distributed to employees, however, it may still be of use to Legal and other management.

This section is primarily for Legal and contract negotiators. If you are not experienced in drafting contracts, or if you are concerned about any of the issues described in this section, please seek help from Legal and do not try to do this on your own.

## Introduction

If you are negotiating a transaction that may involve open source software, the guidelines below explain our requirements for various sorts of agreements and provide standard language that can be used in such agreements. Because, in most cases, complying with the policy will involve modifying or supplementing contract language, you should not use these guidelines without consulting with Legal.

We cannot accept any open source software in products provided to us by third-party vendors or by acquisitions without understanding its impact on our intellectual property position. Accordingly, all agreements we enter into for the acquisition of technology goods or services (including software license agreements, hardware purchase agreements, independent contractor agreements, and M&A agreements) must have appropriate representations, warranties, and indemnities regarding open source software.

In particular, we expect all suppliers to represent and warrant that (1) they have disclosed to us all open source software they have used in their products, along with the license terms that apply to it and (2) that they are providing the product to us in compliance with the licenses that apply to that open source software. This information helps us to comply with the licenses ourselves by placing burdens on those most able to respond to them—the developers who assembled the software.

Similarly, certain outbound customer agreements may also require modifications in order to comply with the requirements of open source licenses. These are further discussed below.

## Contractor or Developer Agreements

We expect any outside developers to follow the same general policies we set for internal development teams. Therefore, you should advise potential contractors of the expectations we have for use of open source in our company. We prefer to integrate our open source requirements into the acceptance process for development. If a developer provides us with software that does not meet our policy, we will view this is a bug that needs to be fixed. The following clauses can be used to implement these requirements in a contractor or developer agreement:

> **"Open Source Materials"** means any software or content subject to an Open Source License.
>
> **"Open Source License"** means any license meeting the Open Source Definition (as promulgated by the Open Source Initiative) or the Free Software Definition (as promulgated by the Free Software Foundation), or any substantially similar li-

cense, including but not limited to any license approved by the Open Source Initiative, or any Creative Commons License.

**Open Source Materials.** Consultant hereby represents and warrants that: (i) The delivery to Company of the Deliverables is in full compliance with all Open Source Licenses applicable thereto, including without limitation all copyright notice and attribution requirements. (ii) Without limiting the foregoing, Consultant has provided full notices suitable for further compliant redistribution of the Open Source Materials in binary form. (iii) Exhibit _____ lists all Open Source Materials included in the Deliverables.

Besides these contractual terms, the engineers handling the transaction must ensure that we receive all source code, object code, and build instructions, as well as any other background information necessary for us to fulfill any notice requirements, for all open source code delivered to us. If you fail to get the source code for software developed by a contractor, our company could find itself with no way to comply with open source license requirements.

## Vendor Agreements

We expect our vendors to act responsibly with respect to open source software. For any software that will be delivered to us, we expect the vendor to agree, in substance, with the following:

I. **Open Source Disclosures.** Vendor has provided to Company [or: Schedule _____ contains] a true and complete list of all Open Source Components included in the Software, or upon which the Software has programmatic dependencies. Such list (a) states the name of the Open Source Component, the license applicable thereto (including the version of such license and describing any alternate or "dual" licensing terms), URL for download of the Open Source Component, URL showing the license therefor (if any), the version of the Open Source Component, whether such Open Source Component has been modified by or for Vendor; and (b) for any Copyleft Component, describes the interfaces between such Copyleft Component and the remainder of the Software (or any other software with programming dependencies on the Copyleft Component), such as dynamic or static linking, forking, command line invocation, or communications protocol interfaces, and lists the names of any published operating systems or language APIs via which such dependencies exist.

In addition, Vendor shall provide Company with full notices that are required by such Open Source Component license (1) in a single text file, (2) with no duplicates. For all Copyleft Components, Vendor shall deliver the complete and corresponding source code (including build and installation instructions) in electronic format along with the Software. Vendor acknowledges that the purpose of Vendor's obligations hereunder is to enable Company to redistribute the Open Source Components of the Software in a compliant manner. Vendor hereby represents and warrants that such information will be accurate and complete at all times. Any updates to the information required to be provided by Vendor regarding Open Source Components hereunder must be provided prior to delivery of the applicable Software update, and any material change to such information must be approved in advance in writing by Company, or Company will have no obligation to accept or use the updated Software and Vendor shall continue to maintain and suppose Company's last accepted version of the Software for as long as Vendor is required hereunder to maintain and support the Update that was rejected.

2. **Remediation.** For Open Source Component that is included in the Software, Vendor shall notify Company immediately of any claim of infringement, noncompliance with Open Source Component licensing terms, license incompatibility, or similar issue of which Vendor knows or becomes aware. In the event Vendor or Company believes such a claim is likely, Vendor shall as soon as possible (i) appropriately modify the Open Source Component or substitute other non-infringing software, so long as such modification or substitution does not materially alter the functionality of the Software; or (ii) obtain a license with respect to the applicable third-party intellectual property rights. Vendor shall indemnify and hold harmless Company and all of its affiliates, employees, agents, customers, distributors, licensees, and end users for any breach of Section 1. Vendor shall cooperate fully with Company, at Vendor's expense, in Company's resolution of any claim arising from any allegation that, if true, would constitute a breach. Vendor acknowledges that Company will maintain full and complete control over the handling of such claims.

3. **Definitions.** "**Open Source Component**" means any software that is generally available to the public in source code form under licenses meeting the Open Source Definition as promulgated by the Open Source Initiative ("OSI"), including without limitation any license approved by the Open Source Initiative and listed at **www.opensource.org/licenses/**, which licenses include without limitation the GNU General Public License, the

GNU Lesser General Public License, the Berkeley Software Distribution (BSD) License, and the Apache License. "**Copyleft Component**" means any Open Source Component made available under a license that requires, as a condition of being distributed or otherwise made available, that the source code for the Open Source Component or any derivative works thereof be made available to recipients, including without limitation any software licensed under the GNU General Public License, the GNU Lesser General Public License, the Mozilla Public License, the Common Public License, or the Affero General Public License.

## Acquisitions

> The following section does not include model language, because many companies do not handle acquisitions in-house or do not want terms and conditions for M&A to be disseminated. Please contact us for model representations.

During company acquisitions, we expect any acquisition target to make full open source representations and disclosures. Attached as Exhibit 5 is a model open source disclosure. Those representations will be presented to the target by Legal along with other deal contracts. Engineers or businesspeople meeting with a potential target should inform them that (1) we reserve the right to perform a code scan prior to signing any commitment to acquire a company; (2) we may require the target to pay the expenses associated with remediation of open source problems, prior to closing the transaction; and (3) we will require detailed disclosures and diligence on open source matters. Please contact Legal for our latest form of open source disclosure request.

## Customer Agreements

If we include code under a copyleft license like GPL or LGPL in one of our products, we need to clarify the licensing of the product to our customers. Our standard EULA does not comply with the terms of GPL, because it restricts the customer's rights to modify the software. As a result, if there are GPL elements in our products, we need to "carve out" the GPL rights from our basic license grant. The following provision does this and also addresses certain notices and source code delivery requirements in licenses like GPL.

> Notwithstanding the foregoing license grant, Customer acknowledges that certain components of the Product may be subject to "open source" software licenses, which means any

software licenses approved as open source licenses by the Open Source Initiative or any substantially similar licenses, including without limitation any license that, as a condition of distribution of the software licensed under such license, requires that the distributor make the software available in source code format (such components, the "Open Source Components"). Licensor shall provide a list of Open Source Components for a particular version of the Product upon Customer's request. Customer hereby acknowledges having received licensing notices for the Open Source Components with respect to the initial delivery of the Product. To the extent required by the licenses covering Open Source Components, the terms of such licenses will apply in lieu of the terms of this Agreement. To the extent the terms of the licenses applicable to Open Source Components prohibit any of the restrictions in this Agreement with respect to such Open Source Component, such restrictions will not apply to such Open Source Component. To the extent the terms of the licenses applicable to Open Source Components require Licensor to make an offer to provide source code in connection with the Product, such offer is hereby made, and you may exercise it by contacting [_____].

### Our Liability in Customer and Distributor Agreements

We do not take responsibility for third-party open source components, and so in any agreement where we deliver software to others, we require the following disclaimer of liability:

Customer acknowledges that the Product may contain or be accompanied by certain third-party software that is developed and made generally publicly available free of charge by third parties ("Third-Party Components"). Notwithstanding anything to the contrary in Section [_____] (Warranties and Indemnities), Licensor will have no liability with respect to claims of infringement or misappropriation of third-party intellectual property arising from such Third-Party Components.

### Our Representations to Customers in Customer and Distributor Agreements

When we negotiate agreements with customers, the customers may ask us to make representations about what open source materials are in the products we distribute to customers. Where open source licenses require us to give notice to recipients of the software, we should agree to provide those notices. We prefer to provide any notices or lists of open source components separately from our contract, so we can update the lists as necessary without amending the contract. We are also willing to represent that our providing the product to the customer is consistent with third-party open source license terms, because it is our company policy to comply with those terms. However, where our customers are able to change our software or integrate it with other technology, we cannot control or guarantee that their redistribution will comply with the requirements of open source licenses.

The following is a sample representation that we are willing to provide. *Any changes to this representation are outside of policy and must be approved by Legal on a case-by-case basis:*

"Open Source Software" means any software licensed to Company under an Open Source License, which means a license approved by the Open Source Initiative; or any substantially similar license, including without limitation the GNU General Public License, the Apache Software License, and the BSD license. The provision of Products by Company to Customer hereunder, in the form provided hereunder, does not violate any Open Source Licenses applicable to software included in the Products. Customer acknowledges that Company has provided a list of all Open Source Software included in the Products and the licenses applicable thereto.

## More Information

If you have any questions regarding this open source policy, please feel free to contact Legal.

Appendix A
Exhibit 1

# Open Source License Stop/Go/Caution List

If your license does not appear on the list, or if the use you intend (i.e., internal vs. distribution) is not listed for that license, then the use will be considered a "Stop." If you are unsure as to the identification of the license, please contact Legal.

## *Go*

You do not need Legal approval to use code licensed under these licenses for all use cases.

- Public Domain
- BSD
- MIT
- Apache 1.1 or 2.0 (not 1.0)
- Artistic License
- PHP License
- Python Software Foundation License
- zlib/libpng License
- Boost Software License
- OpenSSL/SSLeay License
- WTFPL
- CC0 (public domain dedication)
- Creative Commons Attribution-Only ("CC BY")
- Unlicense
- Any software licensed under a *choice* of multiple licenses that include any of the above.

## Caution

You must obtain Legal approval to *distribute*[3] code licensed under these licenses.

You do *not* need Legal approval to use code licensed under these licenses *internally.*[4]

- GPL 2.0 (only when a stand-alone process)
- LGPL 2.1 (only when dynamically linked)
- Mozilla Public License 1.1 or 2.0 (MPL)
- CDDL
- CPL or IBM
- Eclipse Public License
- GPL 2.0 + plus exception (such as linking, Classpath, or FOSS exception)
- Apache 1.0

## Stop

You must obtain Legal approval to use *any* code licensed under these licenses.

- GPL 3.0
- LGPL 3.0
- Affero GPL v1 or v3
- Sleepycat
- GNU Documentation License
- Creative Commons ShareAlike ("CC BY-SA")
- Open Software License
- Academic Free License

---

[3] *Distribution* means including open source code in (a) Distributed Products (including any client software or mobile application) or (b) Web Services (although use in web services may not constitute distribution, our policy is to assume that software used in our web services should be cleared for distribution).

[4] *Internal use* means using the open source code as a development tool or as part of building and running any of our products or services. Please note that all code libraries in a development tool that must be used in a distributed product at run-time (such as those included in SDKs or APIs) are not considered internal use and must be analyzed as distribution.

Appendix A
Exhibit 2

# Open Source Code Use Request Form

This is an example of a form to be filled out by engineers submitting a request
to use open source software in a corporate development project.

To use this form, fill it out and return it to [CONTACT INFORMATION]. You may
also find it useful to refer to the company's open source policy, available at
[DOWNLOAD LOCATION].

Submitter's Name and Title: _____

Date: _____

## I. Identify the Software

Name of free or open source software ("OSS"): URL where you downloaded the
OSS (or describe how else you obtained it):_____

*Note:* Please name the package rather than the directory or file. If the OSS is a platform or system such as Linux, Hadoop, or Eclipse, you only need to submit
one form for the entire package.

Are you aware of any intellectual property issues (patents, disputed ownership)
or any disputes involving the OSS (Y/N)? ____ *If yes,* please contact legal to
discuss. Please do not investigate potential patent infringement issues without
first discussing with legal.

## II. OSS License Background

Which open source license(s) apply to the OSS? (Please include version numbers
if applicable—e.g., Apache License 2.0—and whether the license allows election of use under later versions—e.g. GPL version 2 or any later version).

*Note:* If you list more than one license, explain whether the license is at the recipient's choice, or whether some portions of the package are covered by different
licenses. If so, identify which licenses cover the OSS you want to use. If the

OSS is available under a proprietary license as an alternative, include that information.

If the license is not listed as an approved OSS license at **www.opensource.org**, attach a copy of the license.

### III. Use of OSS

**What does this OSS do?** (Please explain in plain language) _____

_____

_____

**How will the OSS be used?** Check all that apply.

[ ] **Company Internal Tool**: Tools used in development by the Company, such as compilers, converters, debuggers, or parsers. If this is a development tool, please indicate whether it inserts any run-time OSS into developed products (such as standard language routines or classes).

[ ] **Company Internal Use**: Software applications or services used by the Company for internal purposes, such as intranet web server software.

[ ] **ASP/SAAS Use**: Used as part of a service, including websites, that will be accessible outside of the Company.

[ ] **Product Use**: Used in a product that will be distributed outside of the Company. "Distribution" does not include ASP/SAAS use unless the OSS is delivered to a client-side process for execution (such as Javascript or HTML). If the OSS will be used in a Product, please list the Product's name below:

_____

[ ] **Other:** _____

**Do you plan to modify the OSS?** (Configuration or data parameter changes do not count, only source code modifications.) (Y/N)? ____

**All further questions depend on the OSS license.** Please see the STOP/GO/CAUTION chart in our OSS policy. If your license is a "GO," you are done with this form. If you need a copy of our policy, contact: [CONTACT INFO]

**You only need to answer this question if the OSS license is Mozilla, Eclipse, CPL, CDDL, or a variation of those licenses.** If you plan to modify the OSS, describe your modifications: _____

_____

**You only need to answer this question if the OSS license is GPL, LGPL, or a variation of those licenses.** Will the OSS be linked (dynamically or statically) to any other code? (Y/N) ____

*Note:* If the OSS is not in a language that supports linking, please answer "Y" if the OSS will be integrated into the same process as other code. Note that communication through standard O/S or language APIs, pipes, sockets, and command-line arguments is not considered linking.

If "Y," please provide more detail about how the OSS is integrated with other code (such as "as a dynamically linked library" or "as a plug-in"):____

**If the license is GPL or LGPL**, please acknowledge that you will archive and have available for delivery the source code and full build and installation instructions for the OSS. Acknowledged: _____

# Open Source Code Release Request Form

## Introduction

To use this form, fill it out and return it to [CONTACT INFORMATION]. You may also find it useful to refer to the company's open source policy, available at [DOWNLOAD LOCATION].

## I. Identify the Software

A. Name of open source software ("OSS") project to which you wish to contribute: _____

B. Where is the project maintained?_____

C. Please provide URL: _____

D. Name of entity or persons who are stewarding the project: _____
_____

## II. Licensing

A. Which open source license applies to the OSS? (Please include version numbers if applicable; e.g., Apache License 2.0, and whether the license allows election of use under later versions, e.g., "GPL version 2 or any later version")

B. Is the OSS also available under a commercial license (sometimes called a "dual license") (Y/N)? ____ *If yes*, please explain which license will be used (commercial or open source) and explain why: _____
_____

C. Does the project use a contribution agreement? (**yes/no**) If yes, please provide a copy or link: _____

_____

D. Where did you find the licensing information that you used to answer these questions? _____

_____

E. Once the code is contributed, what copyright notice will appear on the Company's contribution? _____

_____

## III. Business Case

Describe why it will benefit the Company to contribute software to this project. For instance, you may describe:

A. Will contributing to the project save the Company maintenance costs? _

_____

B. Will contributing to the project standardize the version Company is using?

_____

C. Will contributing to the project help with engineer recruiting? _____

_____

D. Will contributing to the project help enhance the Company's reputation? _____

_____

E. Will contributing to the project discourage use of the products of competitors? _____

## IV. Intellectual Property

Please have your manager sign off on the following:

[ ] We have determined that the Company has no business interest in keeping the contribution confidential.

[ ] We have determined that the Company has no business interest in enforcing the copyright in the contribution.

[ ] The contribution does not contain material (including source code, images, or data) of third parties.

[ ] The contribution does not contain any of Company's brands or logos.

[ ] The contribution does not contain material of third parties.

[ ] The contribution does not embody any invention on which the Company has sought or received patent protection.

[ ] The contribution does not contain any strong encryption.

[ ] The contribution does not contain any inappropriate comments.

Appendix A
Exhibit 4

# Open Source License Matrix

## *Modifications May Be Distributed Without Source*

### *Public Domain*

Notice Requirement for Redistribution
- None

Compliance Notes, Comments
- Make sure that there are no copyright notices in code. There must be a clear, reliable statement from the author(s) dedicating the code to the public domain.

### *BSD*

Notice Requirement for Redistribution
- Source code: Must retain copyright notice.
- Binary code: Copyright notice must be in documentation or other materials provided with distribution.

Compliance Notes, Comments
- Many variants in use.
- Identify by this language: "Redistribution and use in source and binary forms, with or without modification, are permitted provided that the following conditions are met ..."

## *MIT*

### Notice Requirement for Redistribution
- Copyright notice must be included in software and associated documentation files.

### Compliance Notes, Comments
- Many variants in use.
- Identify by this language: "Permission is hereby granted, free of charge, to any person obtaining a copy of this software and associated documentation files (the "Software"), to deal in the Software ..."

## *Apache 1.0*

### Notice Requirement for Redistribution
- Source code: Must contain copyright notice.
- Binary code: Copyright notice must be in documentation or other materials provided with distribution.

### Compliance Notes, Comments
- Advertising materials must display following acknowledgment: "This product includes software developed by the Apache Group for use in the Apache HTTP server project (www.apache.org)."
- Redistribution in any form must contain the following acknowledgment: "This product includes software developed by the Apache Group for use in the Apache HTTP server project (www.apache.org)."
- Version 1.0 has additional notice requirements and has mostly been abandoned. Check to see if this module is available under Apache 1.1.

## *Apache 1.1*

### Notice Requirement for Redistribution
- Source code: Must contain copyright notice.
- Binary code: Copyright notice must be in documentation or other materials provided with distribution.

### Compliance Notes, Comments
- End user documentation must include the following acknowledgment: "This product includes software developed by the Apache Group for use in the Apache HTTP server project (www.apache.org)."

### Apache 2.0

#### Notice Requirement for Redistribution
- Modified files must include notices that you changed the files.
- Must retain, in source form of any derivative work you distribute, all copyright, patent, trademark, and attribution notices from the source form of the work.
- If there is a NOTICE text file as part of distribution, you must include attribution notices within such NOTICE file.

#### Compliance Notes, Comments
- Note express patent license.

### Artistic License

#### Notice Requirement for Redistribution
- If distributing modified, binary-only version under this license, must give nonstandard executables nonstandard names, clearly document the differences in manual pages (or equivalent), and give instructions on where to get the standard version.

#### Compliance Notes, Comments
- If the component is modified, additional notice requirements apply.
- Some versions of an artistic license contain a Section 8 stating that aggregation of the package with a commercial distribution is permitted if "the use of this Package is embedded; that is, when no overt attempt is made to make this Package's interfaces visible to the end user of the commercial distribution."
- Artistic code is often available under other licenses as well, such as GPL.

### PHP License

#### Notice Requirement for Redistribution
- Source code: Must contain copyright notice.
- Binary code: Copyright notice must be in documentation or other materials provided with distribution.
- Redistribution in any form must retain the following acknowledgment: "This product includes PHP, freely available from <www.php.net>."

## Python Software Foundation License

### Notice Requirement for Redistribution
- Copyright notice and license are retained in any distribution, whether modified or not.
- For distributing derivative works, must include a brief summary of changes made to the original.

## zlib/libpng License

### Notice Requirement for Redistribution
- Copyright notice may not be removed.
- Altered source versions must be plainly marked as such.

## Open LDAP

### Notice Requirement for Redistribution
- Source code: Must contain copyright notice.
- Binary code: Copyright notice must be in documentation or other materials provided with distribution.
- Redistribution must contain verbatim copy of the license.

## Boost Software License

### Notice Requirement for Redistribution
- Source code: Must contain copyright notice.
- Binary code: Copyright notice must be in documentation or other materials provided with distribution.
- If only distributing binaries with no documentation, then no need to include copyright notices.

### Compliance Notes, Comments
- Used with the Boost project. *Be sure* to check the exact files you have downloaded, as not all Boost files are covered by this license.

## OpenSSL

### Notice Requirement for Redistribution
- Source code: Must contain copyright notice.

- Binary code: Copyright notice must be in documentation or other materials provided with distribution.
- Advertising materials mentioning features or use of this software must display the following acknowledgment: "This product includes software developed by the OpenSSL Project for use in the OpenSSL Toolkit (www.openssl.org)."
- Redistribution in any form must retain the following acknowledgment: "This product includes software developed by the OpenSSL Project for use in the OpenSSL Toolkit (www.openssl.org)."

**Compliance Notes, Comments**
- Conjunction of two licenses, OpenSSL and SSLeay.

### SSLeay

**Notice Requirement for Redistribution**
- Source code: Must contain copyright notice.
- Binary code: Copyright notice must be in documentation or other materials provided with distribution.
- Advertising materials mentioning features or use of this software must display following acknowledgment: "This product includes cryptographic software written by Eric Young (eay@cryptsoft.com)."
- If you include Windows-specific code (or a derivative thereof) from the apps directory, you must include an acknowledgment: "This product includes software written by Tim Hudson (tjh@cryptsoft.com)."

**Compliance Notes, Comments**
- Conjunction of two licenses, OpenSSL and SSLeay.

## Modifications May Not Be Distributed Without Source

### Mozilla (MPL) 1.0

**Notice Requirement for Redistribution**
- If you distribute modifications, you must include a file documenting changes you made to the code and the date of any change.
- Must duplicate notice in Exhibit A of the license in each file of the source code.

- If you distribute executables only, you must include a notice stating that the source code and covered code are available under this license, including description of how to obtain the source code.

### Compliance Notes, Comments

- Component must be placed in a different source file from any code covered by other licenses. If the component is modified, additional notice obligations apply.
- This license contains broad patent license termination provisions.
- Allows relicensing on binary terms if source code also available under this license.

## Mozilla (MPL) 1.1

### Notice Requirement for Redistribution

- If you distribute modifications, you must include a file documenting changes you made to the code and the date of any change.
- Must duplicate notice in Exhibit A in each file of the source code.
- Must duplicate this license in any documentation for the source code in which you describe the recipients' rights of ownership relating to the covered code.
- If you distribute executables only, you must include a notice stating that the source code and covered code are available under this license, including description of how to obtain the source code.

### Compliance Notes, Comments

- Component must be placed in a different source file from any code covered by other licenses. If the component is modified, additional notice obligations apply.
- This license contains broad patent license termination provisions.
- Allows relicensing on binary terms if source code also available under this license.

## Mozilla (MPL) 2.0

### Notice Requirement for Redistribution

- Must duplicate notice in Exhibit A in each file of the source code, or (if necessary) "in a location where a recipient would be likely to look for such a notice."

- Must inform recipients how they can obtain a copy of the license.
- If you distribute executables only, you must include a notice informing recipients how they can obtain the source code available under the license.

### Compliance Notes, Comments

- Component must be placed in a different source file from any code covered by other licenses. If the component is modified, additional notice obligations apply.
- This license contains broad patent license termination provisions (similar to but different from MPL 1.1 provisions).
- Allows relicensing on binary terms if source code also available under this license.

## CDDL

### Notice Requirement for Redistribution

- Must include notice in each of your modifications that identifies you as the contributor of the modification.
- Must not remove or alter any copyright, patent, or trademark notices or any attribution text.

### Compliance Notes, Comments

- Component must be placed in a different source file from any code covered by other licenses. If the component is modified, additional notice obligations apply.
- This license contains broad patent license termination provisions.
- Replaces some Sun binary or open source licenses.

## CPL or IBM

### Notice Requirement for Redistribution

- May not remove or alter any copyright notices contained within program.
- Each contributor must identify itself as the originator of its contribution.
- If distributing under own license that is compatible with CPL, must disclaim warranties and conditions and liability of all contributors, state that any provisions that differ from CPL are offered by contributor alone, and state that the source code is available from contributor and how to obtain it.

- For the IBM license, each contributor must include the following in a conspicuous location in the program: "Copyright (C) 1996, 1999 International Business Machines Corporation and others. All Rights Reserved."

### Compliance Notes, Comments

- Object code may be licensed under an EULA, but source code must be made available under CPL.
- Any modules that link to CPL code should be contained in separate source files and should not contain any CPL code. If you have modified this code, seek legal review.
- CPL has largely replaced the IBM Public License.

### Eclipse Public License (EPL)

### Notice Requirement for Redistribution

- May not remove or alter any copyright notices contained within program.
- Each contributor must identify itself as the originator of its contribution.
- If distributing under own license that is compatible with CPL, must disclaim warranties and conditions and liability of all contributors, state that any provisions that differ from CPL are offered by contributor alone, and state that the source code is available from contributor and how to obtain it.

### Compliance Notes, Comments

- Object code may be licensed under an EULA, but source code must be made available under EPL.
- Any modules that link to EPL code should be contained in separate source files and should not contain any EPL code. If you have modified this code, seek legal review.

### GPL 2.0 + runtime exception

### Notice Requirement for Redistribution

- Must include copyright notice and copy of license.
- Modified files must carry prominent notices that you changed the files and the date of any change.

### Compliance Notes, Comments

- This component may be dynamically or statically linked or compiled with proprietary or third-party software (or it may communicate through fork/exec commands, IP protocols, or pipes). This is allowed by the so-called "special exception": "if other files instantiate templates or use macros or inline functions from this file, or you compile this file and link it with other works to produce a work based on this file, this file does not by itself cause the resulting work to be covered by the GNU General Public License."

### GPL 2.0 plus FLOSS (or OSS) exception

#### Notice Requirement for Redistribution
- Notice requirements same as for GPL component.
- Apply notice requirement of each individual FLOSS (or FOSS) licensed component.

#### Compliance Notes, Comments
- This component may be dynamically or statically linked or compiled with software covered by major open source licenses. (See the license for details.)
- Used for MySQL.

### Sleepycat

#### Notice Requirement for Redistribution
- Source code: Must contain copyright notice, list of conditions, and disclaimer.
- Binary code: Copyright notice, list of conditions, and disclaimer must be in documentation or other materials provided with distribution.

#### Compliance Notes, Comments
- Redistributions in any form must be accompanied by information on how to obtain complete source code for the DB software and any accompanying software that uses the DB software. The source code must either be included in the distribution or be available for no more than the cost of distribution plus a nominal fee, and it must be freely redistributable under reasonable conditions.
- The copyleft effect of this license is strong, affecting any software that "uses" the DB software; however, Sleepycat generally permits you to distribute your software under any open source license.

## LGPL 2.1

**Notice Requirement for Redistribution**
- Must include copyright notice and copy of license.
- Modified files must carry prominent notices that you changed the files and the date of any change.
- Consult with Legal if distributing.

**Compliance Notes, Comments**
- If using with proprietary code, only dynamically link to LGPL code.

## LGPL 3.0

**Notice Requirement for Redistribution**
- Consult with Legal.

## GPL 2.0

**Notice Requirement for Redistribution**
- Consult with Legal.

## GPL 3.0

**Notice Requirement for Redistribution**
- Consult with Legal.

## Affero GPL v1 or v3

**Notice Requirement for Redistribution**
- Consult with Legal.

Appendix A
Exhibit 5

# Sample Open Source Disclosure Form

In the form on the following page, list all open source components used in your company project.

| Name | Version | Website | License | Comments | How Integrated |
|------|---------|---------|---------|----------|----------------|
| [Name of module] | [Module version number] | [Open source project's website] | [Name of license(s) and version number of license(s)] [Link to the project's website or revision control system confirming the license if available] | [Comments, such as whether the module has been modified, whether it is being distributed, etc.] | [Is the module statically or dynamically linked?] [Is code from the module incorporated into proprietary code?] [Is proprietary code included in the module?] |
|  |  |  |  |  |  |
|  |  |  |  |  |  |
|  |  |  |  |  |  |
|  |  |  |  |  |  |
|  |  |  |  |  |  |
|  |  |  |  |  |  |
|  |  |  |  |  |  |
|  |  |  |  |  |  |
|  |  |  |  |  |  |
|  |  |  |  |  |  |
|  |  |  |  |  |  |
|  |  |  |  |  |  |
|  |  |  |  |  |  |
|  |  |  |  |  |  |
|  |  |  |  |  |  |
|  |  |  |  |  |  |

Appendix A
Exhibit 6

# Developer Certification for Open Source Software

This certification applies to all software deliverables provided under that certain _____Agreement (the "Developer Agreement") between _____ ("Developer") and _____ ("Customer") dated _____ providing for the development and delivery of certain software or other materials ("Deliverables") by Developer to Customer (the "Development Agreement"). This Certification will not vitiate any obligations of Developer to Customer under the Development Agreement. Developer acknowledges that it is providing this Certification as an inducement for Customer to accept the Deliverables as required in the Development Agreement.

I.  **Open Source Disclosures**. Developer shall not incorporate any Open Source Software into the Deliverables, nor provide any Deliverables with programming dependencies on Open Source Software not included in the Deliverables, without Customer's prior written approval. For Open Source Software that is approved for inclusion in Deliverables, Developer shall provide, no later than delivery of the Deliverables, a complete and accurate list of all such Open Source Software that (a) states the name of the Open Source Software package, the license applicable thereto (including the version of such license and describing any alternate or "dual" licensing terms), URL for download of the Open Source Software, URL showing the license therefor (if any), the version of the Open Source Software, whether such Open Source Software has been modified by or for Developer, and whether such Open Source Software has been previously distributed by Developer; and (b) for any Copyleft Software, describes the interfaces between such Copyleft Software and the remainder of the Deliverables (or any other software with programming dependencies on the Copyleft Software), such as dynamic or static linking, forking, command line invocation, or communications protocol interfaces, and lists the names of any published operating systems or language APIs via which such dependencies exist. In addition, Developer shall provide Customer with full notices that are required by such Open Source Software license (1) in a single text file (2) with no duplicates. For all Copyleft Software, Developer shall deliver the complete and corresponding source code (including without limitation the build and installation instructions used to create any applicable object code files) in electronic format along with the Deliverables. Developer hereby represents and warrants that such information will be accurate and complete at all times. Any updates to the information required to be provided by Developer regarding Open Source Software hereunder must be provided prior to delivery of the applicable Deliverable update, and any material change to such information must be approved in advance in writing by Customer, or Customer will have no obligation to accept or use the updated Deliverable.

2.  **Remediation.** For Open Source Software that is included in the Deliverables, Developer shall notify Customer immediately of any claim of infringement, non-compliance with Open Source Software licensing terms, license incompatibility, or similar issue of which Developer knows or becomes aware. In the event Developer or Customer believes such a claim is likely, Developer shall as soon as possible (i) appropriately modify the Open Source Software, or substitute other non-infringing software, so long as such modification or substitution does not materially alter the functionality of the Deliverables; or (ii) obtain a license with respect to the applicable third-party intellectual property rights. Without limiting the foregoing, Developer shall provide any and all source code, build and installation instructions that may be required to resolve such claim. Developer shall indemnify and hold harmless Customer and all of its affiliates, employees, agents, customers, distributors, licensees and end users for any breach of the warranty contained in Section 1. Developer shall cooperate fully with Customer, at Developer's expense, in Customer's resolution of any claim arising from any allegation that, if true, would constitute a breach. Developer acknowledges that Customer will maintain full and complete control over the handling of such claims.

3.  **Definitions.** "**Open Source Software**" means any software that is generally available to the public in source code form under licenses meeting the Open Source Definition as promulgated by the Open Source Initiative ("OSI"), including without limitation any license approved by the Open Source Initiative and listed at **www.opensource.org/licenses/**, which licenses include without limitation the GNU General Public License, the GNU Lesser Public License, the Berkeley Science Division (BSD) Li-

cense, and the Apache License. **"Copyleft Software"** means any Open Source Software made available under a license that requires, as condition of being distributed or otherwise made available, that the source code for the Open Source Software or any derivative works thereof be made available to recipients, including without limitation any software licensed under the GNU General Public License, the GNU Lesser General Public License, the Mozilla Public License, the Common Public License, or the Affero General Public License.

Agreed and acknowledged:
[DEVELOPER]
By: _____
Print Name: _____

_____
Title: _____
Date: _____

# Addendum to Employee Invention Assignment Agreement

This language can be added to an Employee Invention Assignment Agreement when an employee is asked to contribute to an open source project in their own name.

"Approved Open Source Contributions" means contributions of software code, documentation or other materials, prepared by you, to a third-party open source project, that are approved in advance in writing in accordance with Company policy. Notwithstanding Section _____ of this Agreement [**This should refer to the section containing the assignment of rights**], Company acknowledges that I retain all rights in any Approved Open Source Contributions, and that Approved Open Source Contributions will not be deemed a work made for hire as defined under United States copyright law. I agree to the following:

- "Open Source" shall mean any software or source code licensed under an open source license as defined by the Open Source Initiative (**www.opensource.org**), or any substantially similar license.
- Prior to contributing any software source code or documentation to an Open Source project, even if such materials were created on my own time, I will advise Company in writing of my intent to do so, and if requested to do so by Company, submit my source code to the Company for approval of such contribution.
- I acknowledge that the foregoing does not obligate me to grant any rights to Company that I am not otherwise obligated to grant under this Agreement or under applicable law; however, providing such notice and source code to Company is necessary to assist Company to determine whether it claims an interest therein.

- I will advise Company if I know or have reason to believe that that any Approved Open Source Contribution (1) discloses Company trade secrets; (2) embodies any invention on which Company has expressed an intention to file a patent application; or (3) contains any third-party intellectual property.

- I will not make such contribution to any Open Source project unless the contribution is an Approved Open Source Contribution, or consists entirely of material that that I have no obligation to assign to Company pursuant to California Labor Code § 2870.

- I acknowledge that I have no authority to contribute, release, or make publicly available any Open Source software on behalf of Company.

- When contributing, releasing, or making publicly available any Approved Open Source Contributions, I will use my own copyright notice, and not any notice of Company, and I will not name Company as the source or origin of the Approved Open Source Contributions.

- When contributing any Approved Open Source Contributions to an Open Source project, any contribution agreement will be executed only in my name and not in Company's name.

- For avoidance of doubt, the foregoing will not apply to contributions Company elects to make directly to Open Source projects, even where such contributions are authored or whose contribution is facilitated by me. Any contribution agreement necessary for Company to contribute to such Open Source project will be directly between the Company and the applicable Open Source Project.

# Open Source Licenses

This list does not include all licenses but only those that are more common, approved by OSI, or otherwise of note.

*Note:* Some licenses have license stewards that promulgate new versions that can be chosen by licensees. Some licenses are promulgated by authors or projects that claim copyright in them but have no formal system for stewardship. Others are dedicated to the public domain.

## *Mozilla Public License 1.1*

**Licensed Patents (Originator)**

1.10.1. any patent claim(s), now owned or hereafter acquired, in any patent Licensable by grantor

2.1(b) infringed by the making, using or selling of Original Code

**Licensed Patents (Contributor)**

1.10.1. any patent claim(s), now owned or hereafter acquired, in any patent Licensable by grantor

2.2(b) infringed by the making, using, or selling of Modifications made by that Contributor either alone and/or in combination with its Contributor Version

**Patent Grant (Originator)**

2.1(b) to make, have made, use, practice, sell, and offer for sale, and/or otherwise dispose of the Original Code.

2.1(d) no patent license is granted: 1) for code that You delete from the Original Code; 2) separate from the Original Code; or 3) for infringements caused by: i) the modification of the Original Code or ii) the combination of the Original Code with other software or devices.

**Patent Grant (Contributor)**

2.2(b) to make, use, sell, offer for sale, have made, and/or otherwise dispose of: 1) Modifications made by that Contributor; and 2) the combination of Modifications made by that Contributor with its Contributor Version.

(d) No patent license is granted: 1) for any code that Contributor has deleted from the Contributor Version; 2) separate from the Contributor Version; 3) for infringements caused by: i) third party modifications of Contributor Version or ii) the combination of Modifications made by that Contributor with other software or other devices; or 4) under Patent Claims infringed by Covered Code in the absence of Modifications made by that Contributor.

## Mozilla Public License 2.0

### Licensed Patents (Originator or Contributor)

1.11. "Patent Claims" of a Contributor means any patent claim(s), including without limitation, method, process, and apparatus claims, in any patent Licensable by such Contributor that would be infringed, but for the grant of the License, by the making, using, selling, offering for sale, having made, import, or transfer of either its Contributions or its Contributor Version.

### Patent Grant (Originator or Contributor)

2.1 Each Contributor hereby grants You a world-wide, royalty-free, non-exclusive license: ... (b) under Patent Claims of such Contributor to make, use, sell, offer for sale, have made, import, and otherwise transfer either its Contributions or its Contributor Version.

## Apple PSL 2.0

### Licensed Patents (Originator)

.Originator is Apple. 1.1. "Licensed Patents" are claims of patents that are now or hereafter acquired, owned by or assigned to Apple and that cover subject matter contained in the Original Code, but only to the extent necessary to use, reproduce and/or distribute the Original Code.

### Licensed Patents (Contributor)

1.1 claims of patents that are now or hereafter acquired, owned by or assigned to You and that cover subject matter in Your Modifications, taken alone or in combination with Original Code.

### Patent Grant (Originator)

2. Apple hereby grants You ... a world-wide, royalty-free, non-exclusive license, to:
2.1 use, reproduce, display, perform, internally distribute within Your organization, and Externally Deploy verbatim, unmodified copies of the Original Code
2.2 modify Covered Code and use, reproduce, display, perform, internally distribute within Your organization, and Externally Deploy Your Modifications and Covered Code.

**Patent Grant (Contributor)**

3. You grant to any entity receiving or distributing Covered Code a non-exclusive, royalty-free, perpetual, irrevocable license, under Your Applicable Patent Rights ... to use, reproduce, display, perform, modify, sublicense, distribute and Externally Deploy Your Modifications.

## CDDL

**Licensed Patents (Originator)**

1.11. any patent claim(s), now owned or hereafter acquired, in any patent licensable by grantor

2.1 (b) infringed by the making, using or selling of Original Software

**Licensed Patents (Contributor)**

1.11. any patent claim(s), now owned or hereafter acquired, in any patent licensable by grantor ...

2.2 (b) infringed by the making, using, or selling of Modifications made by that Contributor either alone and/or in combination with its Contributor Version (or portions of such combination).

**Patent Grant (Originator)**

2.1 (b) to make, have made, use, practice, sell, and offer for sale, and/or otherwise dispose of the Original Software.

2.1 (d) no patent license is granted: (1) for code that You delete from the Original Software, or (2) for infringements caused by: (i) the modification of the Original Software, or (ii) the combination of the Original Software with other software or devices.

**Patent Grant (Contributor)**

2.2 (b) to make, use, sell, offer for sale, have made, and/or otherwise dispose of: (1) Modifications made by that Contributor (or portions thereof); and (2) the combination of Modifications made by that Contributor with its Contributor Version (or portions of such combination).

2.2 (d) no patent license is granted: (1) for any code that Contributor has deleted from the Contributor Version; (2) for infringements caused by: (i) third party modifications of Contributor Version, or (ii) the combination of Modifications made by that Contributor with other software (except as part of the Contributor Version) or other devices; or (3) under Patent Claims infringed by Covered Software in the absence of Modifications made by that Contributor.

## GPL 3 (and LGPL 3)

**Licensed Patents (Originator or Contributor)**
A contributor's "essential patent claims" are all patent claims owned or controlled by the contributor, whether already acquired or hereafter acquired, that would be infringed by some manner, permitted by this License, of making, using, or selling its contributor version, but do not include claims that would be infringed only as a consequence of further modification of the contributor version. For purposes of this definition, "control" includes the right to grant patent sublicenses in a manner consistent with the requirements of this License.

**Patent Grant (Originator or Contributor)**
Each contributor grants you a non-exclusive, worldwide, royalty-free patent license under the contributor's essential patent claims, to make, use, sell, offer for sale, import and otherwise run, modify and propagate the contents of its contributor version.

## Apache 2.0

**Licensed Patents (Originator or Contributor)**
3. Patent claims licensable by such Contributor that are necessarily infringed by their Contribution(s) alone or by combination of their Contribution(s) with the Work to which such Contribution(s) was submitted.

**Patent Grant (Originator or Contributor)**
3. Grant of Patent License. Subject to the terms and conditions of this License, each Contributor hereby grants to You a perpetual, worldwide, non-exclusive, no-charge, royalty-free, irrevocable (except as stated in this section) patent license to make, have made, use, offer to sell, sell, import, and otherwise transfer the Work.

## CPL

**Licensed Patents (Originator or Contributor)**
Patent claims licensable by a Contributor which are necessarily infringed by the use or sale of its Contribution alone or when combined with the Program.

**Patent Grant (Originator or Contributor)**
2(b). A non-exclusive, worldwide, royalty-free patent license under Licensed Patents to make, use, sell, offer to sell, import and otherwise transfer the Contribution of such Contributor. This patent license shall apply to the combi-

nation of the Contribution and the Program if, at the time the Contribution is added by the Contributor, such addition of the Contribution causes such combination to be covered by the Licensed Patents. The patent license shall not apply to any other combinations which include the Contribution.

## Eclipse Public License

### Licensed Patents (Originator or Contributor)
Patent claims licensable by a Contributor which are necessarily infringed by the use or sale of its Contribution alone or when combined with the Program.

### Patent Grant (Originator)
2(b) A non-exclusive, worldwide, royalty-free patent license to make, use, sell, offer to sell, import and otherwise transfer the Contribution of such Contributor. This patent license shall apply to the combination of the Contribution and the Program if, at the time the Contribution is added by the Contributor, such addition of the Contribution causes such combination to be covered by the Licensed Patents. The patent license shall not apply to any other combinations which include the Contribution.

### Patent Grant (Originator or Contributor)
Same as above.

| License | Copyleft? | Comments |
|---|---|---|
| Academic Free License | No | |
| Affero GPL (1.0) | Yes | Superseded by version 3; seldom used. |
| Affero GPL (3.0) | Yes | "Ultra-strong" copyleft license that applies copyleft requirements to network (SAAS) use. |
| Apache Software License (1.1) | No | Apache 1.0 is largely no longer in use; version 1.1 removed the "advertising" clause. |
| Apache License, 2.0 | No | Permissive license, but more detailed terms than BSD or MIT, or Apache 1.0 or 1.1 |
| Apple Public Source License | | Weak copyleft, similar to MPL, many provisions specific to Apple |
| Artistic license (original version has been superseded) | No (though the point has been debated[4]) | Not copyleft, but more restrictions than most permissive licenses. Many projects under this license are dual licensed under GPL. |
| Attribution Assurance Licenses | No | Based on BSD, with expanded attribution provisions |
| Boost License | No | Mainly used for Boost project. |

| License | Copyleft? | Comments |
|---------|-----------|----------|
| BSD license | No | Template license—many variants in use. Major variants are the "3-clause" and "2-clause" variants. Earlier versions contained an advertising clause. |
| CeCILL License | Yes | Very loosely based on GPL for use by French government agencies |
| Common Development and Distribution License (CDDL) | Yes | Based on MPL. Successor to Sun Public License. |
| Common Public Attribution License (CPAL) | Yes | "Badgeware" license. Infrequently used. |
| Common Public License 1.0 | Yes | Successor to IBM Public License. See also Eclipse license. |
| Creative Commons Zero (CC0) | No. | Public domain dedication. |
| Eclipse Public License | Yes | Variant of CPL. |
| GNU General Public License (GPL) | Yes | Most commonly used license. Versions 2 and 3 are in common use. |
| "GPL plus Classpath exception" | Yes | Variant of GPL that allows linking (dynamic or static) to proprietary code. This can be hard to distinguish from GPL—look for the "exception" notice, usually at the end of the license text file that identifies the code as covered by GPL. |
| GNU Library or "Lesser" General Public License (LGPL) | Yes | Variant of GPL that allows dynamic linking to proprietary code. Versions 2.1 and 3.0 in common use. |
| IBM Public License | Yes | Similar to GPL generally, but drafted conventionally. Uses derivative works scope calculus similar to that of GPL. Largely superseded by CPL and Eclipse. |
| Intel Open Source License | No | BSD with an export provision. Intel has disavowed its use. |
| Microsoft Limited Public License | Yes | Does not meet open source definition due to limitation to run on Windows platforms. |
| Microsoft Public License 2.0 | No | Source code distribution must be under the same license, but binary only distribution is allowed. |
| Microsoft Reciprocal License | Yes | |
| MIT license | No | Most popular permissive license, after BSD. Also called X or X11 license. |

| License | Copyleft? | Comments |
|---------|-----------|----------|
| Mozilla Public License 1.1 (MPL) | Yes | For major differences between version 1.0 and 1.1, see the chapters below on patent licensing and patent license termination provisions. |
| Mozilla Public License 2.0 (MPL) | Yes | Latest version of MPL, mostly used for Firefox and related code. This version is compatible with GPL 3. |
| GPL + FLOSS Exception | Yes | Like GPL, but allows linking to open source code. Mostly used on MySQL; several variations of the exception have been promulgated over the years, by successive owners MySQL, Sun, and Oracle. |
| Netscape Public License | | Original basis of Mozilla Public License. Not an open source approved license. Contains specific rights for Netscape. |
| Open Font License | Yes | Specifically created for software font implementations. |
| Open Software License | Yes | Copyleft requirements are triggered by online use. Contains limited warranties regarding originality of code. |
| OpenSSL | No | Last paragraph of SSLeay license (which accompanies OpenSSL) contains a language anomaly that appears to be hereditary but is not. Also contains advertising requirement. |
| PHP License | No | |
| Python Software Foundation License | No | Permissive license drafted in a more conventional style than BSD or MIT. Earlier versions of this license contained a governing law provision. There is a good explanation of the change here: **www.python.org/download/ releases/2.4.2/license/**. |
| Qt Public License (QPL) | Yes | GPL variant. Now seldom used because the software ownership changed hands. |
| Reciprocal Public License | Yes | Stronger restrictions than GPL. |
| Ruby License | No | Based roughly on Artistic—see Artistic for copyleft analysis. Most code under this license is available under BSD of GPL. |
| Sleepycat License | Yes | Similar in form and style to BSD, but contains strong distribution restrictions. Sleepycat's products are dual licensed under commercial terms. |
| Sun Industry Standards Source License (SISSL) | Yes | Deprecated; now largely superseded by CDDL. For more information see **www.openoffice.org/ FAQs/license-change.html**. |

| License | Copyleft? | Comments |
|---|---|---|
| Sun Public License | Yes | Now largely superseded by CDDL. |
| University of Illinois/NCSA Open Source License | No | Combination of BSD and MIT licenses |
| WTF License | No | Permissive. |
| W3C License | No | Permissive. Note that W3C is a standards organization; this license covers copyrightable material, and standards can cover other types of intellectual property. |
| zlib/libpng license | No | Permissive. |
| Zope Public License | Yes | |

# Patent Peace (Termination) Provisions in Open Source Licenses and Open Source Patent Pledges

## *Open Source Licenses with Patent Grants*

### *Apache 2.0*

**Termination Trigger:** 3. (Grant of Patent License.) ... If You institute patent litigation against any entity (including a cross-claim or counterclaim in a lawsuit) alleging that the Work or a Contribution incorporated within the Work constitutes direct or contributory patent infringement.

**Rights Terminated:** 3. Any patent licenses granted to You under this License for that Work shall terminate as of the date such litigation is filed.

**Comments:** The approach of Apache 2.0 is now probably the most common approach in open source licensing. Applies to claims accusing the work, and only patent licenses terminate.

### *Microsoft Reciprocal License (MS-RL)*

**Termination Trigger:** 3(C). (Conditions and Limitations) If you bring a patent claim against any contributor over patents that you claim are infringed by the software.

**Rights Terminated:** 3(C). Your patent license from such contributor to the software ends automatically.

**Comments:** This approach is similar to one of the termination provisions of MPL 1.1 in that it terminates licenses from a particular contributor.

### *Mozilla 1.1*

**Termination Trigger:** 8.2. You initiate a patent litigation infringement claim (excluding declaratory judgment actions) against Participant alleging: (a) Contributor Version infringes any patent or (b) any software, hardware, or device, other than such Participant's Contributor Version, directly or indirectly infringes any patent.

**Rights Terminated:** 8.2(a): All rights granted by Participant to You under copyright or patent licenses terminate prospectively.

8.2(b): Any rights granted to You by Participant under patent grants are revoked effective retroactively.

**Comments:** Only license with retroactive termination. Broad patent peace provision terminates all rights if a claim is brought related to the project.

### Mozilla 2.0

**Termination Trigger:** 5.2. If You initiate litigation against any entity by asserting a patent infringement claim (excluding declaratory judgment actions, counter-claims, and cross-claims) alleging that a Contributor Version directly or indirectly infringes any patent.

**Rights Terminated:** 5.2. The rights granted to You by any and all Contributors for the Covered Software under Section 2.1 of this License shall terminate.

**Comments:** Unlike in MPL 1.1, termination is not retroactive and only extends to claims accusing the licensed work. However, copyright license also terminates, as in MPL 1.1. Similar to CDDL.

### CDDL

**Termination Trigger:** 6.2. If You assert a patent infringement claim (excluding declaratory judgment actions) against Initial Developer or a Contributor alleging that entity's contributed software directly or indirectly infringes any patent.

**Rights Terminated:** 6.2 All rights granted to You by all Contributors terminate prospectively.

**Comments:** Broad patent peace provision terminates all rights, copyright and patent, but only for claims relating to the project

### CPL

**Termination Trigger:** 7. If Recipient institutes patent litigation against a Contributor with respect to a patent applicable to any software (including a cross-claim or counterclaim in a lawsuit).

If Recipient institutes patent litigation against any entity (including a cross-claim or counterclaim in a lawsuit) alleging that the Program itself (excluding combinations of the Program with other software or hardware) infringes such Recipient's patents.

**Rights Terminated:** Any patent licenses granted by that Contributor to such Recipient terminate prospectively. Recipient's rights under patent license from any Contributor terminate prospectively.

**Comments:** Patent peace provision terminates patent rights only.

### Eclipse

**Termination Trigger:** 7. If Recipient institutes patent litigation against any entity (including a cross-claim or counterclaim in a lawsuit) alleging that the Program itself (excluding combinations of the Program with other software or hardware) infringes such Recipient's patent(s).

**Rights Terminated:** Such Recipient's patent rights granted under Section 2(b) terminate prospectively.

**Comments:** Same as CPL except narrower patent peace provision.

### GPL 3

**Termination Trigger:** 10. You may not impose any further restrictions on the exercise of the rights granted or affirmed under this License. For example, you may … initiate litigation (including a cross-claim or counterclaim in a lawsuit) alleging that any patent claim is infringed by making, using, selling, offering for sale, or importing the Program or any portion of it.

**Rights Terminated:** All rights can be terminated. (See general termination provision in 8.)

**Comments:** Note this is structured differently from the other licenses. Applies to all recipients ("you") regardless of whether "you" are a contributor.

### WebM Patent Grant

**Termination Trigger:** If you or your agent or exclusive licensee institute or order or agree to the institution of patent litigation against any entity (including a cross-claim or counterclaim in a lawsuit) alleging that this implementation of VP8 or any code incorporated within this implementation of VP8 constitutes direct or contributory patent infringement, or inducement of patent infringement.

**Rights Terminated:** Any patent rights granted to you under this License for this implementation of VP8 shall terminate as of the date such litigation is filed.

**Comments:** Patent and copyright grants are in separate documents. **www.webmproject.org/license/additional/**

## Open Source Patent Pledges

This list is not exhaustive. For more information, see Jorge Contreras's excellent list at **www.pijip.org/non-sdo-patent-commitments/**.

### Twitter (2012)

**Link:** github.com/twitter/innovators-patent-agreement

**Licensed Patents:** Specific patent named and to be assigned.

**Patent Grant or Non-Assert:** Company, on behalf of itself and its successors, agrees not to assert any claims of any Patents ... unless asserted for a Defensive Purpose.

**Termination Trigger:** If Assignee asserts any of the Patent claims against any entity in a manner that breaks the promises of [the non-assert],

**Rights Terminated:** The Inventors, individually or jointly, may grant a patent sublicense to the entity under the Patents.

**Comments:** Blog says, "It is a commitment from a company to its employees that patents can only be used for defensive purposes."

### Microsoft Interoperability Patent Pledge

**Link:** www.microsoft.com/openspecifications/en/us/programs/interop/ interoperability-principles-patent-pledges/default.aspx

**Licensed Patents:** "Microsoft Necessary Claims" are those claims of Microsoft-owned or Microsoft-controlled patents that are necessary to implement the [Open Specifications].

"Open Specifications" (as published at **msdn.microsoft.com/en-us/library/ dd208104(v=prot.10).aspx** or its successor site) for the protocols implemented in the current and future versions of Windows Vista including the .NET Framework, Windows Server 2008, SQL Server 2008, Office 2007, Exchange 2007, and Office SharePoint Server 2007, that are used by any other Microsoft product to connect with these products.

**Patent Grant or Non-Assert:** Microsoft ... promises not to assert any Microsoft Necessary Claims against you as an open source software developer ("You") for making, using, importing, or distributing any implementation of a Covered Specification.

**Termination Trigger and Rights Terminated:** N/A

**Comments:** Does not apply to "commercial" activities. "An "open source project" is a software development project the resulting source code of which is freely distributed, modified, or copied pursuant to an open source license."

### Microsoft Open Specification Promise (Sept. 12, 2006)

**Link:**  www.patent-commons.org/commons/pledgesearch.php?displaypledge =56&titlecopy=&type%5B%5D=12&type%5B%5D=13&type% 5B%5D=14&type%5B%5D=15

**Licensed Patents:** To clarify, "Microsoft Necessary Claims" are those claims of Microsoft-owned or Microsoft-controlled patents that are necessary to implement only the required portions of the Covered Specification that are described in detail and not merely referenced in such Specification. "Covered Specifications" are listed below.

**Patent Grant or Non-Assert:** Microsoft irrevocably promises not to assert any Microsoft Necessary Claims against you for making, using, selling, offering for sale, importing or distributing any implementation to the extent it conforms to a Covered Specification ("Covered Implementation"), subject to the following. This is a personal promise directly from Microsoft to you, and you acknowledge as a condition of benefiting from it that no Microsoft rights are received from suppliers, distributors, or otherwise in connection with this promise. ... No other rights except those expressly stated in this promise shall be deemed granted, waived or received by implication, exhaustion, estoppel, or otherwise.

**Termination Trigger:** If you file, maintain or voluntarily participate in a patent infringement lawsuit ... against a Microsoft implementation of such Covered Specification, ...

**Rights Terminated:** ... then this personal promise does not apply with respect to any Covered Implementation of the same Covered Specification made or used by you.

### Blackboard (Feb. 8, 2007)

**Link:** www-personal.umich.edu/~csev/sakai/blackboard/Blackboard-Patent-Pledge.pdf

**Licensed Patents:** Specific patents relating to Internet Based Support System and Methods and related patent applications .

**Patent Grant or Non-Assert:** Blackboard hereby commits not to assert any of the U.S. patents listed below, as well as all counterparts of these patents issued in other countries, against the development, use or distribution of Open Source Software or Home-Grown Systems to the extent that such Open Source Software and Home-Grown Systems are not Bundled with proprietary software.

**Termination Trigger:** Any party who files a lawsuit asserting patents or other intellectual property rights against Blackboard or its parent or subsidiaries.

**Rights Terminated:** Blackboard [Blackboard] reserves the right to terminate this patent pledge.

### Sun OpenDocument Patent Statement (Sept. 29, 2005)

Link: www.patent-commons.org/commons/pledgesearch.php?displaypledge
=30&titlecopy=&type%5B0%5D=12&type%5B1%5D=13&type%
5B2%5D=14&type%5B3%5D=15&searchSubmit=Find&page=2

**Patent Grant or Non-Assert:** Sun irrevocably covenants that, subject solely to the reciprocity requirement described below, it will not seek to enforce any of its enforceable U.S. or foreign patents against any implementation of the Open Document Format for Office Applications (OpenDocument) v1.0 Specification, or of any subsequent version thereof ("OpenDocument Implementation") in which development Sun participates to the point of incurring an obligation, as defined by the rules of OASIS, to grant (or commit to grant) patent licenses or make equivalent non-assertion covenants.

**Termination Trigger:** Notwithstanding the commitment above, Sun's covenant shall not apply and Sun makes no assurance, covenant or commitment not to assert or enforce any or all of its patent rights against any individual, corporation or other entity that asserts, threatens or seeks at any time to enforce its own or another party's U.S. or foreign patents or patent rights against any OpenDocument Implementation.

**Rights Terminated:** All

### Sun SAML (July 20, 2006)

Link: www.patent-commons.org/commons/pledgesearch.php?displaypledge
=54&titlecopy=&type%5B0%5D=12&type%5B1%5D=13&type%
5B2%5D=14&type%5B3%5D=15&searchSubmit=Find&page=2

**Patent Grant or Non-Assert:** Sun Microsystems irrevocably covenants that, subject solely to the reciprocity requirement described below, it will not seek to enforce any of its enforceable U.S. or foreign patents against that portion of a product that implements the Security Assertion Markup Language (SAML) V2.0 specification or any subsequent version of that specification in whose development Sun participates to the point where Sun would be obligated by the rules of OASIS to grant (or commit to grant) patent licenses or make equivalent non-assertion covenants ("SAML Implementation").

### Sun Microsystems OASIS pledge (Sept. 29, 2005)

Link: www.oasis-open.org/committees/office/ipr.php

**Patent Grant or Non-Assert:** Sun … covenants that, … it will not seek to enforce any of its enforceable U.S. or foreign patents against any implementation of the Open Document Format for Office Applications (OpenDocument) v1.0

Specification ... in which development Sun participates to the point of incurring an obligation, as defined by the rules of OASIS, to grant (or commit to grant) patent licenses or make equivalent non-assertion covenants.

**Termination Trigger:** Sun's covenant shall not apply [for] any individual, corporation or other entity that asserts, threatens or seeks at any time to enforce its own or another party's U.S. or foreign patents or patent rights against any Open Document Implementation.

### Computer Associates Legally Binding Commitment Not to Assert the 14 Named Patents Against OSS (Sept. 7, 2005)

Link: www.patent-commons.org/commons/pledgesearch.php?displaypledge =24&titlecopy=&type%5B%5D=12&type%5B%5D=13&type% 5B%5D=14&type%5B%5D=15&searchSubmit=Find

**Licensed Patents:** 14 listed patents

**Patent Grant or Non-Assert:** The pledge will benefit any Open Source Software. Open Source Software is any computer software program whose source code is published and available for inspection and use by anyone, and is made available under a license agreement that permits recipients to copy, modify and distribute the program's source code without payment of fees or royalties. All licenses certified by opensource.org and listed on their website as of August 1, 2005 are Open Source Software licenses for the purpose of this pledge. Computer Associates hereby commits not to assert any of the 14 U.S. patents listed below, as well as all counterparts of these patents issued in other countries, against the development, use or distribution of Open Source Software.

**Termination Trigger:** Computer Associates reserves the right to terminate this patent pledge and commitment only with regard to any party who files a lawsuit asserting patents or other intellectual property rights against Open Source Software.

### Google Open Pledge (see patent dates)

Link: www.google.com/patents/opnpledge/pledge/

**Licensed Patents:** Specific named Pledged Patents: see **www.google.com/patents/ opnpledge/patents/**

**Patent Grant or Non-Assert:** Google will not bring a lawsuit ...against a Pledge Recipient for patent infringement under any Pledged Patents based on the Pledge Recipient's (i) development, manufacture, use, sale, offer for sale, lease, license, exportation, importation or distribution of any Free or Open Source Software, or (ii) internal-only use of Free or Open Software.

**Termination Trigger:** Any Pledge Recipient (or affiliate) who files a lawsuit or other legal proceeding for patent infringement or who has a direct financial interest in such lawsuit or other legal proceeding (an "Asserting Party") against Google or any entity controlled by Google or against any third party based in whole or in part on any product or service developed by or on behalf of Google or any entity controlled by Google.

**Rights Terminated:** Google reserves the right to terminate the Pledge, to the extent Google deems necessary to protect itself, its affiliates, or its products and services ("Defensive Termination"). Any Defensive Termination by Google with respect to an Asserting Party shall have the same effect as if Our Pledge was never extended to such Asserting Party in the first instance.

## IBM

**Link:** www.ibm.com/ibm/licensing/patents/pledgedpatents.pdf

**Licensed Patents:** 500 U.S. patents listed and their foreign counterparts.

**Patent Grant or Non-Assert:** IBM hereby commits not to assert any of the patents against the development, use or distribution of Open Source Software.

**Termination Trigger:** Any party who files a lawsuit asserting patents or other intellectual property rights against Open Source Software.

**Rights Terminated:** IBM reserves the right to terminate this patent pledge.

**Comments:** Open Source Software is any computer software program whose source code is published and available for inspection and use by anyone, and is made available under a license agreement that permits recipients to copy, modify, and distribute the program's source code without payment of fees or royalties. All licenses certified by **opensource.org** and listed on their website as of January 11, 2005, are Open Source Software licenses for the purpose of this pledge.

## Red Hat

**Link:** www.redhat.com/legal/patent_policy.html

**Licensed Patents:** Any patent held by Red Hat Inc.

**Patent Grant or Non-Assert:** To the extent any party exercises a Patent Right with respect to Open Source/Free Software ... Red Hat agrees to refrain from enforcing the infringed patent against such party for such exercise ("Our Promise").

**Rights Terminated:** Our Promise does not extend to any party who institutes patent litigation against Red Hat with respect to a patent applicable to software (including a cross-claim or counterclaim to a lawsuit).

**Comments:** *Approved License* means any of the following licenses: GNU General Public License v2.0 and v3.0; GNU Lesser General Public License v2.I and v3.0, IBM Public License vI.0; Common Public License vI.0; Q Public License vI.0; Open Software License v3.0; and any open source license granted by Red Hat. Red Hat may add to this list in its sole discretion by publication on this page.

*Open Source/Free Software* means any software which is licensed under an Approved License.

### Google WebM (2010)

**Link:** www.webmproject.org/license/additional/

**Licensed Patents:** License ... applies only to those patent claims, both currently owned by Google and acquired in the future, licensable by Google that are necessarily infringed by this implementation of VP8.

**Patent Grant or Non-Assert:** Google hereby grants to you a perpetual, worldwide, non-exclusive, no-charge, royalty-free, irrevocable (except as stated in this section) patent license to make, have made, use, offer to sell, sell, import, transfer, and otherwise run, modify and propagate the contents of this implementation of VP8.

**Termination Trigger:** If you or your agent or exclusive licensee institute or order or agree to the institution of patent litigation against any entity (including a cross-claim or counterclaim in a lawsuit) alleging that this implementation of VP8 or any code incorporated within this implementation of VP8 constitutes direct or contributory patent infringement, or inducement of patent infringement.

**Rights Terminated:** Any patent rights granted to you under this License for this implementation of VP8 shall terminate as of the date such litigation is filed.

**Comments:** Patent and copyright grants are in separate documents: www.webmproject.org/license/additional/.

### Open Web Foundation CLA

**Link:** www.openwebfoundation.org/legal/the-owf-I-0-agreements/ owf-contributor-license-agreement-I-0---copyright-and-patent

**Licensed Patents:** "Granted Claims" are those patent claims that I own or control, including those patent claims I acquire or control after the Date below, that are infringed by Permitted Uses. Granted Claims include only those patent claims that are infringed by the implementation of any portions of the Specification where the Specification describes the functionality causing the infringement in detail and does not merely reference the functionality causing the infringement. Granted Claims under this CLA exclude those patent claims that would be infringed by an implementation of the Specification if my Contribution to that Specification were removed.

**Patent Grant or Non-Assert:** 3.1.1. The Promise. I, on behalf of myself and my successors in interest and assigns, irrevocably promise not to assert my Granted Claims against you for your Permitted Uses, subject to the terms and conditions of Section 3.1. This is a personal promise directly from me to you, and you acknowledge as a condition of benefiting from it that no rights from me are received from suppliers, distributors, or otherwise in connection with this promise. This promise also applies to your Permitted Uses of any other specifications incorporating all required portions of the Specification.

**Termination Trigger:** 3.1.2.1. ... if you file, maintain, or voluntarily participate in a lawsuit against me or any person or entity asserting that its Permitted Uses infringe any Granted Claims you would have had the right to enforce had you signed this CLA, unless that suit was in response to a corresponding suit first brought against you.

**Rights Terminated:** 3.1.2.1. As a Result of Claims by You. All rights, grants, and promises made by me to you under this CLA are terminated

**Comments:** Termination includes copyright grant.


### Open Invention Network (OIN)

**Link:** www.openinventionnetwork.com/joining-oin/oin-license-agreement/

**Licensed Patents:** Any patent held by OIBN: www.openinventionnetwork.com/pat_owned.php

**Patent Grant or Non-Assert:** 1.2 ... You, on behalf of yourself and your Affiliates, (a) grant to each Licensee and its subsidiaries ... a royalty-free, worldwide, nonexclusive, non-transferable license under Your Patents for making, having made, using, importing, and Distributing any Linux System.

**Termination Trigger:** 3.3 If a Licensee or its Affiliate files one or more Claims against You or Your Subsidiaries based on products that perform substantially the same function as the Linux System, and are Distributed by You or Your Subsidiaries.

**Rights Terminated:** You may suspend the license granted under Section 1.2 to such Licensee and its Subsidiaries.

**Comments:** Section 1.1—OIN to member grant; section 1.2—member to member grant.
*Linux System* is defined broadly and can be updated over time. See www.openinventionnetwork.com/joining-oin/linux-system/.

## LOT (License on Transfer)

**Link:** www.lotnet.com/userfiles/files/LOT%20Agreement%20(vI_3-7_7_14).pdf

**Licensed Patents:** Extensive definition of patents covered: essentially all patents owned by the participating entity.

**Patent Grant or Non-Assert:** A worldwide, royalty-free, non-exclusive, non-sub-licensable, non-transferable license under such Licensor's Subject Patent(s), to make, have made (subject to the provisions of Section 1.1(b) below), operate, have operated (subject to the provisions of Section 1.1(b) below), use, sell, offer for sale, import, or otherwise distribute Licensed Products and Services, provided that such license shall become effective only: (1) immediately prior to an applicable Triggering Event, (2) for the benefit of LOT Users (and their respective Affiliates including their AfterAcquired Affiliates, if any) that are Licensees for the applicable Triggering Event, and (3) with respect to Subject Patents that are Triggered Patents of the applicable Triggering Event.

**Termination Trigger:** In the event that a Licensee initiates or prosecutes an Offensive Patent Proceeding (as the case may be) against a Non-Assertion Entity to which one or more Triggered Patents have been Transferred (whether or not such Non-Assertion Entity is a LOT User). ...

6.42. "Offensive Patent Proceeding" means a claim, action or proceeding for Patent Infringement asserted or instituted by a second Entity in a judicial, administrative, or other governmental body, including but not limited to a court (in any country) or the U.S. International Trade Commission, against a first Entity or its Affiliate, which is not in response to a previous Patent Assertion first made less than two (2) years prior by the first Entity or its Affiliate against the second Entity or its Affiliate or against another Entity based upon alleged Infringement by any of the second Entity's or its Affiliate's Products and Services. For the avoidance of doubt, the following shall not be considered an Offensive Patent Proceeding by an Entity: (i) assertion of a claim or counterclaim or institution of an action or proceeding by such Entity, in each case to establish the invalidity, non-Infringement or unenforceability of a Patent, including but not limited to a declaratory judgment action, in response to a Patent Assertion of such Patent against such Entity, and (ii) institution of a reexamination proceeding or other post-grant challenge of a Patent in a patent office, whether or not in response to a Patent Assertion of such Patent against such Entity.

**Rights Terminated:** Such Non-Assertion Entity shall, subject to the provisions of clause (ii) below, have the option to terminate the License granted to such Licensee ... with respect to the Triggered Patents that have been Transferred to such Non-Assertion Entity.

**Comments:** Detailed definitions of patent assertion and Offensive Patent Proceeding.

# Checklist for Releasing Code to an Open Source Project

These are the recommended steps to take for release of code (the "Software") by Company under an open source license (the "License"). The date the Software is first made available under the License will be referred to as the "Release Date."

1. **Select the License.** Please let us know if you have questions about this. Selection of the license can be time-consuming because it often requires significant internal discussion. This document assumes you will select an existing, standard License such as GPL 2, Apache 2.0, or BSD.

2. **Confirm Ownership of Software.** Company should first confirm that it owns all the code that it intends to release under the License, or otherwise has sufficient rights in it (such as an unrestricted, perpetual, irrevocable license). If necessary, Company should obtain the requisite assignments or licenses for code that it intends release under the License. Assignments are the safest approach. Company may wish to engage a code scanner to scan the code prior to release to identify third-party code, but code scanners usually only look for open source code, and the highest risk will be accidental inclusion of third-party proprietary code.

3. **IP Review—Code.** Ensure that a business decision has been made at a management level that release of the code under the License is consistent with Company's business objectives. Keep in mind that enforcement of copyright in code licensed under open source licenses can be difficult and expensive, and might involve unsettled areas of law. Also keep in mind that open source licenses do not restrict the field of use, and thus any competitors of Company will have the right to use the code for any purpose; if the License is permissive, that will include use in competing proprietary products.

   a. Ensure the software does not contain any trade secret information that the company may not want to release to the public (including in comments or headers). Avoid the exposure of non-public APIs.

b.  Ensure that the source code comments do not contain employee names or personally identifying information, product code names, roadmaps, future product descriptions, or disparaging comments.

c.  As a best practice policy, remove any unused or obsolete code from the software code base. (The community to which the code will be released will appreciate and be more likely to contribute to clean code.)

4.  **IP Review—Patents.** This is the most important IP review aspect for your company. Be sure the code does not practice inventions that you intend to protect via patents. Although release of the open source code will not necessarily eliminate your effective patent interests in the code, it may substantially reduce your ability to procure or enforce the patents, even outside the scope of open source use. Releasing code that practices an invention for which you have not yet filed a patent application may be considered public disclosure of that invention. Public disclosure of an unpatented invention precludes the filing of a patent application in many foreign jurisdictions and begins the one-year period after which the filing of a patent application is precluded in the United States. Be sure that the code does not practice inventions that you have claimed in any pending, unpublished patent applications. Please contact us if you wish to discuss this.

a.  Ensure the software does not require the practice of any proprietary standard. (If so, you will need to develop a policy about use of the software by those who do not have rights to the standard.)

b.  Confirm that there are no known patent claims threatened or likely to be threatened against the software. You may not wish to conduct a deep review, but a basic understanding is a good idea. Software that is likely to be subject to patent claims is not generally a good candidate for release under an open source license.

5.  **IP Review—Branding.** Branding and trademark interests can be difficult to control in the open source area. We do not recommend using the same brand, or a variant of a brand, that Company uses for a proprietary product. For instance if your product is Foobar, do not use Open Foobar.

a.  Develop a trademark policy and FAQ for the name of the project, if you wish to control the use of the project name. For instance, should anyone, such as distributors, user groups, or developers, be able to register domain names that include the name of the project? If so, who will own the domain name? Will the project operate any certification programs to allow the mark to be used for modified products? Open source licenses do not grant trademark rights, but many developers do not understand trademark law and will misuse your marks unless you educate them about your expectations.

b. Ensure that the project name you have chosen is not likely to infringe third-party trademarks. You should perform basic trademark searches on the name.

c. Remove all company logos and trademarks from the public source tree. Code that generates company logos and trademarks should also be removed.

6. **License Terms.** You should be clear and transparent about licensing terms for the release.

a. Company should clearly designate the License (including version) on the project information page, FAQ, and download page.

b. Do not rely on links to other sites (such as OSI or FSF); copy the entire text of the license to your page, as those links may change.

c. The license terms should also be included in a "LICENSE" text file in the download package.

d. Be sure to include your own copyright notices as appropriate for the License.

e. Consider any other proprietary notices (such as patent or trademark notices or disclaimers) that are appropriate. Please contact us if you have questions.

7. **Third-Party Components.** Prior to the Release Date, Company should confirm all known third-party open source components to be provided with the Software.

a. Company should comply with notice and attribution requirements of any third-party open source components that will be included with Software. This includes drafting a file containing the licenses and copyright notices of the third-party software and, if applicable, making available source code or making a written offer for a request of source code.

b. Remove any third-party proprietary code.

c. If the code you are releasing has dependencies on third-party code, you should be prepared to provide this information to your developer community.

8. **Developer or User Community Messaging.** Company should prepare notices to inform potential developer or user community members of the release. Also consider press releases and trade show announcements.

9. **Source Code Headers.** Company should include proper comments in the Software, consistent with its engineering practice, indicating the License terms. See examples below.

10. **Project Managers and Committers.** Decide who will be the primary maintainer of the project. This can be someone within your company or someone in the community. Ensure that the Company has either allocated sufficient resources to run and support the project or selected another party that is willing to do so. For those who will contribute from your company, clarify whether those activities will be on behalf of the Company or at the individual's discretion, and settle related IP ownership via an employee invention assignment agreement other otherwise. The company's exit process for departing employees should also be updated to address collection of any account information related to the open source project, such as source code repository and website passwords, and reminders of any ongoing obligations over ownership of the project (both of course code and of leadership or managerial positions).

11. **Foundation Setup.** Where the project will be run by a separate entity, draft a document describing the terms on which your company is providing the code to the project. (This can be the same as the contribution agreement described below, or it can be a special agreement for your company.)

12. **Export.** Ensure the software does not contain regulated functionality, such as strong encryption, that would be inconsistent with an open source code release. US law provides certain exceptions to export restrictions for open source software. Please ask if you would like to discuss this further.

13. **Hosting.** Decide where the project will be hosted, i.e., on the company's own servers, on a third-party open source repository such as github.com

or sourceforge.net, or as part of an established open source foundation such as Apache. Repositories and existing projects may have requirements ranging from limitations on the kind of allowed licenses to IP licensing commitments.

14. **Third-Party Contribution Agreement.** This can take place after release. Develop a contribution agreement to govern how the project will manage contributions from the community. Require contributors to assign all rights to their contributions or require the contributors to grant a license. This may include decisions about the breadth of patent licenses to be granted, and it may turn on the open source license you have planned to use. This activity can be deferred until you receive third-party contributions.

Appendix D
Exhibit 1

# Examples of Source Code Headers for Code Release

The proper license notices will depend on the license you select. The examples below are for Apache 2.0 and GPL 2, the most commonly used licenses. They are examples only—instructions for preparing such notices are in the text of the license. The underlined portions should be adjusted to suit the facts. You should include a copyright notice (such as Copyright 2015 ABC, Inc.) in each file, in the comments at the head of the file. You may, if you wish, include the short license notice below in each file, but most engineers do not prefer this due to the length it adds to the file. In the download package, you should include the entire text of the license in a text file called "license.txt." The short-form notice should also be used in each directory or folder of the download package.

### Apache 2.0 Example

Copyright 2015 ABC, Inc.

Licensed under the Apache License, Version 2.0 (the "License"); you may not use this file except in compliance with the License. You may obtain a copy of the License at **www.apache.org/licenses/LICENSE-2.0/**.

Unless required by applicable law or agreed to in writing, software distributed under the License is distributed on an "AS IS" BASIS, WITHOUT WARRANTIES OR CONDITIONS OF ANY KIND, either express or implied. See the License for the specific language governing permissions and limitations under the License.

### GPL 2 Example

Foobar Interactive Button Utility
Copyright 2015 ABC, Inc.

This program is free software; you can redistribute it and/or modify it under the terms of the GNU General Public License as published by the Free Software Foundation; *either version 2 of the License, or (at your option) any later version.*

This program is distributed in the hope that it will be useful, but WITHOUT ANY WARRANTY; without even the implied warranty of MERCHANTABILITY or FITNESS FOR A PARTICULAR PURPOSE. See the GNU General Public License for more details.

You should have received a copy of the GNU General Public License along with this program; if not, write to the Free Software Foundation, Inc., 51 Franklin Street, Fifth Floor, Boston, MA 02110-1301, USA.

Appendix E

# Checklist for Contributing Code to an Open Source Project

These are the recommended steps to take for contributions of code by Company to an open source project (the "Project"). This policy is for use with contributions to Projects run by third parties. Release of entire projects by Company under open source licenses should be handled under a separate policy.

I. **Determine Contribution Terms.** The Project will either have a separate contribution license agreement or accept contributions only under the outbound license that governs the Project or a compatible license. (The applicable contribution license or outbound license is referred to in this checklist as the "License.") So, for instance, the Linux kernel does not use a contribution agreement and requires all contributions to be released under GPL 2, or a compatible license like BSD. Apache Foundation projects all require contributions to be made under the Apache Contribution License, individual or corporate forms. Some Projects also require assignments of rights in the contributed code, but this is less common; if you are required to assign your rights, you should conduct an ad hoc analysis of the copyrights you will no longer own, ensure that you have a broad license back to use your contributions, and conduct an assessment of the assignment on your patent rights. The remainder of this checklist assumes you will be contributing under a nonexclusive license.

2. **Variations in CLAs.** Many projects use the Apache CLA or a close variant of it. That license is here: **www.apache.org/licenses/cla-corporate. txt.** Other common variations include the following:

   a.  License or assignment

   b.  Any restrictions on re-licensing (e.g., only under an OSI-approved license)

3. **Committing the Enterprise.** Many contributions agreements (such as the Apache CLA) set a default set of contribution terms for all materials sent to the project by employees of Company and its affiliates. Ensure that you have all of the following:

   a. Authority to make commitments for Company's affiliates, as appropriate

   b. Designated a point of contact for managing contributions.

   c. Implemented business processes to avoid inadvertent contributions

4. **Contributing via Employees.** Some companies prefer to arrange for their employees to contribute directly to open source projects. This strategy requires additional thought and implementing documents; please call if you have questions. You should avoid employees purporting to make personal contributions of Company code via individual CLAs.

5. **Confirm Ownership of Code.** Confirm that Company owns all the code that it intends to contribute, or otherwise has sufficient rights in it (such as an unrestricted, perpetual, irrevocable license). Making contributions of third-party code is not recommended; if the code is freely available from the third party, that third party should contribute or the Project should seek the code itself; if the code is not freely available from the third party, there may be diligence issues with making the contribution. Company may wish to engage a code scanner to scan the code prior to contribution, to identify third-party code, but code scanners usually only look for open source code, and the highest risk will be accidental inclusion of third-party proprietary code.

6. **IP Review—Code.** Ensure that a business decision has been made at a management level that release of the code under the License is consistent with Company's business objectives. Keep in mind that enforcement of copyright in code licensed under open source licenses can be difficult and expensive and might involve unsettled areas of law. Also keep in mind that open source licenses do not restrict the field of use, and thus any competitors of Company will have the right to use the code for any purpose; if the License is permissive, that will include use in competing proprietary products.

   a. Ensure the code does not contain any trade secret information that the company may not want to release to the public (including in comments or headers). Avoid the exposure of non-public APIs.

b.    Ensure that the source code comments do not contain employee names or personally identifying information, product code names, roadmaps, future product descriptions, or disparaging comments.

c.    As a best-practice policy, remove any unused or obsolete code from the code.

7.    **IP Review—Patents.** This is the most important IP review aspect for your company. Be sure the code does not practice inventions that you intend to protect via patents. Although release of the open source code will not necessarily eliminate your effective patent interests in the code, it may substantially reduce your ability to procure or enforce the patents, even outside the scope of open source use. Releasing code that practices an invention for which you have not yet filed a patent application may be considered public disclosure of that invention. Public disclosure of an unpatented invention precludes the filing of a patent application in many foreign jurisdictions and begins the one-year period after which the filing of a patent application is precluded in the United States. Be sure that the code does not practice inventions that you have claimed in any pending, unpublished patent applications. Please contact us if you wish to discuss this.

8.    Confirm that there are no known patent claims threatened or likely to be threatened against the code. You may not wish to conduct a deep review, but a basic understanding is a good idea. Code that is likely to be subject to patent claims is not generally a good candidate for contribution to an open source project.

9.    **License Terms.** You should be clear and transparent about licensing terms for the contribution.

a.    Different Projects have different policies about retention of Company's copyright or licensing notices on contributed code. You should know these policies before making the contribution. For instance, will your copyright notice (Copyright 2015 ABC Co.) be retained? Should your contribution contain a licensing notice in the header?

b.    Consider any other proprietary notices (such as patent or trademark notices or disclaimers) that are appropriate. Please contact us if you have questions.

10. **Source Code Headers.** Company should include proper comments in the code, consistent with its engineering practice, and where necessary or appropriate as described in Section 8, indicating the License terms.

11. **Export.** Ensure the code does not contain regulated functionality, such as strong encryption, that would be inconsistent with an open source code release. US law provides certain exceptions to export restrictions for open source software. Please ask if you would like to discuss this further.

Appendix F

# Examples of Open Source Trademark Policies

## *Foundations*

Mozilla
www.mozilla.org/foundation/trademarks/policy.html
Plain language, transparent.

Android
developer.android.com/distribute/googleplay/promote/brand.html
Plain language, but not tailored to the open source project.

Eclipse
www.eclipse.org/legal/logo_guidelines.php
Plain language, good length.

Apache
www.apache.org/foundation/licence-FAQ.html#Marks
Very brief.

Open Networking Foundation
www.opennetworking.org/images/stories/downloads/about/onf-operating
-documents/trademark-policies/onf-member-trademark-terms-and-
conditions.pdf
More formal standards setting approach.

## *Commercial Products*

Zimbra
www.zimbra.com/partners/trademark_branding_faq.html
FAQ, plain language.

Alfresco
www.alfresco.com/legal/licensing/Alfresco_Trademark_Policy.doc
A bit more formal, but good detail.

Digium
www.digium.com/en/company/view-policy.php?id=Trademark-Policy
More formal.

MySQL
www.mysql.com/about/legal/trademark.html
Now incorporates Oracle terms.

Red Hat
www.redhat.com/f/pdf/corp/RH-3573_284204_TM_Gd.pdf
Extensive trademark usage guide.

SugarCRM
www.sugarcrm.com/crm/trademark-information.html
Extensive.

## And for counterpoint:

Linux
www.linuxmark.org/faq.php, www.isc.tamu.edu/~lewing/linux/
How not to manage a brand.

# Glossary and Index

**Apache Foundation** is an organization that promotes open source projects, including the Apache Web Server. It is the author of the **Apache License**.

**API** (application program interface) is the programmatic interface for software consisting of the type and name of variables that form the input or output of a routine. In object-oriented programming, it can be a class definition.

A **build script** is a set of automated instructions to a build program. A set of objects or other program elements are combined into a whole executable program via a build process. (For low-level languages, this includes linking.)

**BusyBox** is a set of UNIX utilities that is in all of the major Linux distros. BusyBox is licensed under GPL and has been the subject of most open source enforcement in the courts. BusyBox was originally written by Bruce Perens, but the enforcement actions were taken by later authors.

A **compiler** is a program that translates source code into executable code objects.

A **concurrent versioning system (CVS)** is a software tool for controlling versions of software during development. Some CVS tools, like GIT, allow for collaborative development ..................................................................................... *88*

**Contribution agreements** or **contribution licenses** are inbound grants of rights to open source projects, which then usually relicense the contributed material under an open source license or under a dual license. They are usually licenses but sometimes assignments of rights

**Copyleft** describes a license with so-called viral or sharealike terms, sometimes called a "free software" license. It includes GPL, LGPL, MPL, and CDDL, among others. Variations include strong copyleft (usually used to describe GPL only), weak copyleft (used to describe the corporate-style licenses like MPL, Eclipse, CDDL, and often LGPL), and ultra-strong copyleft (usually used for Affero GPL) ........................................................................ *iv, v, 3–4, 8*

**Defensive termination** is a clause in a patent license that terminates the license grant if the licensee engages in certain actions, usually including bringing patent claims against the licensor or challenging enforceable patents. In open source licensing, the trigger is usually limited to bringing a patent claim accusing the licensed software.

**Derivative works** are modifications of copyrightable works of authorship, containing sufficient originality to consist of a protectable work of authorship.

Derivative works are often confused with infringing works, which include not only derivative works but also works that contain unprotectable, trivial variations of the original. *Derivative work* is a term primarily used in US copyright law, and it is defined in 17 USC 101........................... *8, 67, Chapter 8*

**Distribution** (or **redistribution**) is the trigger for compliance conditions in most open source licenses. It is one of the enumerated rights of copyright in US copyright law 17 USC 106. ............................................... *8, Chapter 6*

**Dual licensing** is a business model in which the licensor offers to license a product via an open source license (usually GPL) or a proprietary license. ......................................... *45, 56, 134, 180, 183, 248*

**Free software** is software that meets the Free Software Definition per **www.gnu. org/philosophy/free-sw.html**. It is roughly the same as copyleft but sometimes only refers to GPL software. ....................................... *ii–vi, 3–8, 39*

**FSF** (Free Software Foundation) is an advocacy organization for free software. It is the steward of the GNU project and the GPL family of licenses. ........................................ *19, 76, 184, 213, 220, 223, 227*

**GITHUB** See *Concurrent versioning system.*

**GPL** (GNU General Public License) is the original copyleft license, stewarded by the FSF. Its latest version is version 3, but version 2 is more common. **www.gnu.org/copyleft/gpl.html** .............................................. *v, 7*

**JavaScript** is a scripting language that runs code delivered by a server within a client-side browser; it should not be confused with Java, a web-oriented programming language that was written by Sun Microsystems. JavaScript is one of the often-neglected acts of distribution in SAAS systems................. *13-15, 86, 159*

**LGPL** (GNU Lesser General Public License) is a variation of GPL that enables use of the licensed code as a library for proprietary licenses. Its latest version is version 3, but version 2.1 is more common. **www.gnu.org/copyleft/lgpl.html**

**Liberty or death** is the nickname for one of the provisions of GPL 2, from Section 7: "If, as a consequence of a court judgment or allegation of patent infringement ... conditions are imposed on you ... that contradict the conditions of this License, they do not excuse you from the conditions of this License. If you cannot distribute so as to satisfy simultaneously your obligations under this License and any other pertinent obligations, then as a consequence you may not distribute the Program at all."
................................................................................. *37, 57, 170*

A **license steward** is an organization or person who is responsible for updating an open source license and issuing new versions of it.
.................................................................*36, 125, 227, 267, 287*

**Linking** is the process by which a compiler combines object code files to make a single executable program. **Dynamic linking** is a way of linking objects that executes certain objects only as needed at run time. **Static linking** is a way of linking objects that causes all linked objects to load at program boot time and persist in memory even when the object is not being used. Linking is a means of building programs that is used primarily for low-level languages like C.
................................................................................. *13, 21–27*

**Linus Torvalds** is the original author of the Linux kernel. Torvalds later worked as a technology entrepreneur. He is sponsored by the Linux Foundation to work on improving Linux, and he currently holds the highest-level committer access to the project. ........................................................... *v, 5–6*

**Linux** is a free software operating system, originally created to meet the specification for UNIX, particularly for microcomputer processors. It is sometimes called "GNU/Linux."....................................*i–vi, 3–5, 10, 17, 18–19, 26*

**Mozilla Foundation** is an organization that stewards the Firefox Browser, as well as other software promoting free web access. It also is the licensed steward for the **Mozilla Public License. www.mozilla.org**

**Open source** describes any license that fits the Open Source Definition. Open Source licenses include both permissive and copyleft licenses. The term *open source* was promoted by technologists in the 1990s to broaden the scope and appeal of open source software as compared to free software ... *Preface, Chapter 1*

**Open Source Initiative (OSI)** is an organization dedicated to promoting open source software. **www.opensource.org** .......................... *4, 6, 7, 31, 47, 309, 314*

**Permissive** describes so-called nonviral licenses like BSD, MIT, Apache, and their many variations ................................................. *4, 31–32, 35–36, 40–42*

**Proprietary** describes a license, such as an end user license, that grants restricted rights that usually do not include the right to receive, modify, or redistribute source code. This term is in ubiquitous usage, but I consider it misleading.

**UNIX** is an operating system developed by AT&T Bell Laboratories for "small" systems. It was licensed under permissive licensing terms and then converted to proprietary terms, causing a forking of the system into many incompatible "flavors." Linux was written as a free software alternative to UNIX; Linux met the interface standards for UNIX but was licensed under GPL ............................................................ *ii–v, 17, 19, 113–115, 174, 221*

**Versioning of software** See *Concurrent versioning system.*

**Versioning of licenses** means the release of successive versions of licenses by the license steward, often with the option of the licensor to select a single version, or a version and any subsequent version, released by the steward ............................................................ *36–37, 124–126, 147*

**WTF license** refers to a self-styled "very permissive" license, the "Do What the Fuck You Want to Public License." The FAQ at **www.wtfpl.net/faq** is entertaining reading............................................................ *44, 294*

# Case Index

An attorney in private practice, Heather Meeker is a 20-year veteran of Silicon Valley who specializes in intellectual property transactions for technology clients in a range of industries including software, communications, educational testing, computer equipment, and medical devices. She has extensive experience in open source licensing strategies and in intellectual property and technology matters related to mergers and acquisitions.

Ms. Meeker served as an adjunct professor of law at Hastings College of the Law and University of California Berkeley School of Law, teaching seminars on technology licensing. A member of the American Law Institute (ALI), she has served as an adviser to ALI projects, Principles of the Law of Software Contracts (2010) and Restatement of the Law, Copyright (ongoing). She has also served as counsel for the Mozilla Foundation and other open source organizations.

Ms. Meeker graduated from Yale with a BA in economics and earned her JD from Boalt Hall School of Law, where she served as editor in chief of the *Berkeley Technology Law Review*. Prior to law school, she worked as a software engineer.

29316937R20193

Made in the USA
San Bernardino, CA
19 January 2016